TAX POLICY, WOMEN AND THE LAW

UK and Comparative Perspectives

Tax policy frequently targets the choices that women face in many aspects of their lives. Decisions regarding working away from home, having children, marrying, registering a partnership or cohabiting with a partner all entail tax consequences. The end of the twentieth century saw progress in women's legal and social equality, but many governments began to increase their reliance on the tax system as a means of influencing the choices that women make.

The juxtaposition of this instrumentalist deployment of tax with persisting economic inequality for women is the starting point for this book. Employing a range of theoretical approaches, and grounding its investigations in sociological theory and cultural philosophy, it provides the foundation for a comparative, contextual consideration of the issues that arise at the intersection of women, tax policy and the law.

ANN MUMFORD is a senior lecturer in law in the Department of Law, Queen Mary, University of London.

CAMBRIDGE TAX LAW SERIES

Tax law is a growing area of interest, as it is included as a subdivision in many areas of study and is a key consideration in business needs throughout the world. Books in the Cambridge Tax Law series expose and shed light on the theories underpinning taxation systems, so that the questions to be asked when addressing an issue become clear. Written by leading scholars and illustrated by case law and legislation, they form an important resource for information on tax law while avoiding the minutiae of day-to-day detail addressed by practitioner books.

The books will be of interest for those studying law, business, economics, accounting and finance courses in the UK, but also in mainland Europe, the USA and ex-Commonwealth countries with a similar taxation system to the UK.

Series Editor

Professor John Tiley, Queens' College, Director of the Centre for Tax Law.

Well known internationally in both academic and practitioner circles, Professor Tiley brings to the series his wealth of experience in tax law study, practice and writing. He was made a CBE in 2003 for services to tax law.

TAX POLICY, WOMEN AND THE LAW

UK and Comparative Perspectives

ANN MUMFORD

CAMBRIDGE
UNIVERSITY PRESS

CAMBRIDGE
UNIVERSITY PRESS

University Printing House, Cambridge CB2 8BS, United Kingdom

One Liberty Plaza, 20th Floor, New York, NY 10006, USA

477 Williamstown Road, Port Melbourne, VIC 3207, Australia

314-321, 3rd Floor, Plot 3, Splendor Forum, Jasola District Centre, New Delhi - 110025, India

103 Penang Road, #05-06/07, Visioncrest Commercial, Singapore 238467

Cambridge University Press is part of the University of Cambridge.

It furthers the University's mission by disseminating knowledge in the pursuit of education, learning and research at the highest international levels of excellence.

www.cambridge.org
Information on this title: www.cambridge.org/9780521878036

First published 2010

A catalogue record for this publication is available from the British Library

Library of Congress Cataloging in Publication data
Mumford, Ann.
Tax policy, women and the law : UK and comparative perspectives / Ann Mumford.
p. cm. – (Cambridge tax law series)
Includes bibliographical references and index.
ISBN 978-0-521-87803-6 (hardback)
1. Women – Taxation. 2. Women – Taxation – Law and legislation – Great Britain.
3. Women – Economic conditions. 4. Women – Great Britain – Economic conditions.
5. Poor women. 6. Fiscal policy – Social aspects. I. Title.
HQ1381.M86 2010
336.20082 – dc22 2010033074

ISBN 978-0-521-87803-6 Hardback

CONTENTS

ACKNOWLEDGEMENTS

A wide range of generous colleagues have assisted with this book. In some instances, feedback was so specific (and the contribution so original and important) that I have thanked colleagues in footnotes for drawing arguments and literature to my attention.

Chapter 6 benefited in particular from the kind guidance of two colleagues. Enormous thanks are due to Nick Wikeley, who spent a tremendous amount of time and effort on this chapter. The literature he introduced me to in his insightful comments helped this tax legal academic to bridge the family law gap. Additionally, one of the many pleasures of teaching at the University of London is that I have had the opportunity to meet and to correspond with Anne Redston of King's College London. Her very generous feedback on this chapter helped me to improve the quality of the tax analysis included; and, additionally, to ensure that my engagement with her important research lives up to the high quality of the original.

Many thanks also must be offered to my colleagues at Queen Mary; in particular, to Lizzie Barmes, Malgosia Fitzmaurice, Eric Heinze, Kate Malleson and David Schiff, all of whom generously read and commented on specific chapters. A note of gratitude is owed as well to Kenneth Armstrong, for encouraging my interest in the interaction between new institutionalist theory, tax policy and women.

Chapters from this book have been presented at the 2009 Conference for Law, Culture and the Humanities, at a round table generously chaired by Roger Berkowitz; the tax section of the 2009 meeting of the Law and Society Association, organised by Neil Buchanan; and, at stimulating staff seminars at Queen Mary. Many thanks for the very helpful feedback received at these events. I also had the opportunity to discuss the subject of this book with the participants at a workshop held at the International Institute for the Sociology of Law, in Oñati, Spain. Thanks to all participants at this excellent event, which, by a lucky coincidence, occurred towards the end of this project, and where I was able to meet, for the first time, writers I had spent several years reading.

Additionally, I have been the fortunate recipient of discussions about this topic, generally, with Marjorie Kornhauser.

The anonymous reader for Cambridge University Press offered detailed and insightful advice, which greatly improved the final text. Many thanks for this, and also to Professor John Tiley, and to the editors at Cambridge University Press.

Finally, this project has benefited from the support of my enormously encouraging and accommodating family. Much gratitude to Peter Alldridge, for reading and improving countless drafts, and for much more. This book is dedicated to our children, Fred and Nellie.

The author stopped collecting material for inclusion on 30 June 2009.

This text uses the term 'the Revenue', as opposed to the 'Inland Revenue' or 'HMRC (HM Revenue & Customs)', as it is now known, for the sake of consistency.

London *Ann Mumford*
31 October 2009

TABLE OF AUTHORITIES

Cases

Statutes

1

Introduction

Scope and methodology

The taxation system cannot solve the problem of women's economic inequality. There is a view that to deploy tax law for any instrumental purpose somehow detracts from its purity and causes it to function less well as a system of tax law. The project of this book is to argue, within the constraints of the first observation, that the second observation is not correct and that the tax system should be deployed to militate against economic discrimination against women.

This book hopes to reflect its topic, and to locate itself at the intersection of ideas, disciplines and scholarship. A wide range of sources is considered. Writers who have challenged and formed traditional economic thought are consulted. For example, Karl Polanyi's writings are investigated, to discern whether his advocacy of a cultural approach to economics holds promise for the subject of women and tax. Additionally, Schumpeter's efforts to inform economic theories with sociological perspectives structure several of this book's investigations into the fiscal state. Their projects, in particular, are important because of the nature of the interaction between women and tax law. The problem of women's economic inequality is universal, and cannot be solved by tax law, in any state, or through any tax-based international agreement. There is no solution in fiscal legislation which, on its own, will help women who live in poverty to find a route to a life with more resources. Tax law will not redress the problems caused by the uncomfortable relationship between work in the paid marketplace, and unpaid labour. Simply, tax law is not a capable forum for redressing gender equality.

There are also strong arguments that tax law should not be used in this way. Tax law funds the engines of governments, and provides resources for some of the most important functions that states provide. Burdening tax law with socio-economic problems that society has not proved able to resolve in other ways can lead to complexity – and simplicity is not something for which tax law, globally, is renowned. Tax law should be structured so as to collect taxes fairly and efficiently; and not so as to contain debate for ways of redressing difficult economic problems.

Yet tax law very frequently provides the forum for efforts by governments to deal with the basic, intransigent fact of women's poverty. The value of these efforts in many ways lies in the discussion that they enable. While some aspects of tax law in some countries may serve to redistribute more money to more women – and while the importance of this should not be underestimated in this introduction to the book – the fact of women's poverty persists as a global problem. Women are poor everywhere, but it does not follow that all economies are the same.

Additionally, although feminism, and feminist legal theory, are not homogeneous,[1] a generalised trend away from consideration of women and money has been identified in recent years.[2] What could be described as the feminist materialist project[3] fostered a wide and vibrant literature, concerned with many aspects of women's lives; and, in particular, with their economic well-being. While the 'cultural focus' has enormously enriched legal scholarship, a cost of this development is a lack of engagement with explicitly economic law; and, in particular, with UK tax law. The purpose of this book is to argue for the development of a specifically feminist, materialist analysis of UK tax law and policy. This project is undertaken with the hope that a feminist, materialist analysis of tax policy, women and UK law, also may serve to reinvigorate the 'tax project' of fiscal sociology.[4]

The project is explicitly comparative in focus, as is the feminist scholarship with which it will engage. This text builds upon a generation

1 See discussion in Marjorie E. Kornhauser, 'Through the Looking Glass with Alice and Larry: The Nature of Scholarship', *North Carolina Law Review*, 76 (1998), 1609, at 1616–19.

2 In 1997, Judith Butler observed that 'the cultural focus of leftist politics has abandoned the materialist project of Marxism ...' ('Merely Cultural', *Social Text*, 52–3 (1997), 265–77).

3 Among this vast literature, see, in particular: Christine Delphy and Diana Leonard, 'A Materialist Feminism Is Possible', *Feminist Review*, 4 (1980), 79–105; Jill Dolan, 'In Defense of the Discourse: Materialist Feminism, Postmodernism, Poststructuralism ... and Theory', *Drama Review*, 33 (1989), 58–71; R. Hennessy, 'Materialist Feminism and the Politics of Discourse', in R. Hennessy and C. Ingraham, *Materialist Feminism: A Reader in Class, Difference, and Women's Lives* (New York: Routledge, 1997); S. Jackson, 'Why a Materialist Feminism Is (Still) Possible – And Necessary', *Women's Studies International Forum*, 24 (2001), 283–93; L. Vogel, *Woman Questions: Essays for a Materialist Feminism* (London: Routledge, 1995).

4 On this point, see generally E. J. McCaffery, 'Where's the Sex in Fiscal Sociology? Taxation and Gender in Comparative Perspective', University of Southern California Law and Economics Working Paper Series, July 2008, Working Paper 70.

of endeavours in this field,[5] all demonstrating that paying attention to women and tax law is important and necessary. Every aspect of a tax system has the potential to affect women. A text which analyses every aspect of the tax system, and attendant case law, and then attempts to forge a bridge back to a theory of women, tax and the law may risk finding that the bridge is unable to bear the weight of the analyses. Thus, it is necessary in this introduction to set out the thesis, so as to explain the emphases which follow.

(Implicit) bias

The selection of this topic – fiscal policy, women and the law – itself may suggest an allegation of bias. The thesis of this text does not seek to identify examples of explicit bias in the UK tax system, and to compare these examples with practices in other countries. Questions of 'explicit bias' – addressing, for example, whether an income tax system permits independent taxation – can be easier to address than questions of 'implicit bias', which necessarily involve subjective judgements about appropriate economic behaviour.[6]

Although analyses of questions of implicit bias may be difficult, within tax law in particular, the potential of their engagement is particularly rich. A consideration of gender budgeting is illustrative in this context, as it presents a sturdy point from which to begin construction of the thesis. The fact of gender budgeting establishes that there is a presumption of gender bias in fiscal budgetary processes. It starts the discussion.

The link between gender budgeting and the tax system lies in the significance of the budget itself. There is an initial, obvious link, in that if taxes were not collected, then it would be difficult to finance a budget. The significance of a budget, however, as Schumpeter has established,[7] extends beyond this. It is a blueprint for the aims and ambitions of the nation state. As such, the source of funding for the budget cannot be diminished in importance. Gender budgeting, of course, is something in which Schumpeter would have been enormously interested. If governments have established gender budgeting to account for discrepancies in

5 By writers too numerous to mention in this introduction – a purpose of this book is to provide a resource for consideration of this increasingly wide literature.

6 J. G. Stotsky, 'How Tax Systems Treat Men and Women Differently' (Finance and Development 1997) (at: www.worldbank.org/fandd/english/pdfs/0397/070397.pdf).

7 John L. Campbell, 'The State and Fiscal Sociology', *Annual Review of Sociology*, 19 (1993), 163–85, at 163.

spending according to gender, then it is possible that these discrepancies extend to the tax system. Schumpeter convincingly argued that the budget is not just about spending money; it is also about choosing a way in which an economy might be organised.[8] He also suggested that it is possible for a society to choose the economy it wants. This is an important starting point for the thesis of this book.

A point of investigation for the thesis of this book is the body of socio-legal literature dealing with implicit gender bias in the tax system. Literature dealing with the gendered status of law is also relevant. The literature derives from a range of countries, although focuses on the UK in particular. As indicated by this book's title, comparative perspectives are presented through relational analyses. Different jurisdictions are considered not to determine which affords greater equity, but to analyse tax and gender in different contexts, in relation to divergent cultures, legal systems and market structures. The literature and legal structures of the US are considered perhaps most frequently, largely due to the emergence of the interesting and challenging critical tax movement there, although a range of other jurisdictions are addressed as well. The objective of these relational analyses is to forge a link between the issue of implicit bias, and theories as to the resulting status of women in the market economy. At this point in the analysis, the raw subject of tax law will be relevant. As Stretton explained, '[t]he law is a powerful determinant of status in any society'. It is in this sense an important tool, and, indeed, '[f]eminist historians and campaigners for women's rights have therefore looked to legal codes and legal commentaries to learn the history of inequality between the sexes, and to consider directions for future reform'.[9] The consideration of modern law, however, of law in action, can present a more difficult challenge.

Thesis

To illustrate this point, it is useful to return to the question of implicit bias. Historical legal provisions may present obvious explicit bias, when

8 See Joseph A. Schumpeter, 'English Economists and the State-Managed Economy', *Journal of Political Economy*, 57 (1949), 371–82; C. J. Whalen *et al.*, 'Post-Keynesian Institutionalism and the Anxious Society: Assessing the Evolution and Impact of Alternative Institutional Structures', in Sandra S. Batie and Nicholas Mercuro (eds.), *Alternative Economic Structures: Evolution and Impact* (London: Routledge, 2008), at pp. 273–99.

9 T. Stretton, *Women Waging Law in Elizabethan England* (Cambridge University Press, 1998), p. 1.

viewed from the perspective of modern values. The presence of examples of explicit bias in these historical backward glances also may be identified more easily. But with modern, explicit bias, the possibility exists that outright discrimination is either an anomaly (an unintended clash within a system of precisely drafted rules), or a choice. If it is a choice – and if it is a wrong choice, or an unfair choice – then an appropriate response would be to engage the political process to change the law. In the latter instance, this text could serve the purpose of political manifesto. If it is to perform that function, however, a wider view of facets of the UK tax system may not be necessary. A targeted demonstration of how one aspect of the tax system does not 'work' may suffice.

That targeted demonstration nonetheless would have to confront the fact that the unfair outcome at one point was a choice, from among other options. Choices within a system of competing goals, as Alstott famously examined, are not always straightforward.[10] It does not necessarily follow, as Alstott explained, that it is impossible to 'design tax law changes in ways that are most likely to achieve feminist goals',[11] but it may be the case that, at one point, to achieve one good thing, something else will be sacrificed.[12]

The thesis of this book in some ways starts with a problem. At various points, research will be presented which addresses the disproportionate poverty of women, and the difficulties that women face in the market economy. The thesis, however, does not identify the role of tax systems in remedying the problem. Women are more likely to be poor, and the tax system is part of the problem. It is at this point that the relevance of the question of status may become most evident. To begin with one, perhaps obvious, question: do 'feminist goals' inevitably lead to contradictory choices? If yes, then that inevitability may be linked to disagreement as to what constitutes a feminist goal, or a goal that benefits women. This directly impacts upon the status of women within, among other aspects of society, the economy. Their figurative and symbolic positions

10 A. L. Alstott, 'Tax Policy and Feminism: Competing Goals and Institutional Choices', *Columbia Law Review*, 96 (1996), 2001–82, at 2003.

11 *Ibid.*

12 F. Bennett presented an excellent example of this when arguing that 'independent taxation can sometimes be seen as the major obstacle to a targeted, integrated tax and benefits system' ('Policy Implications of Tax Credits', www.genet.ac.uk/workpapers/GeNet2005p8.pdf, at 20). Both independent taxation and an integrated tax and benefits system are, to engage Alstott, 'likely to achieve feminist goals'. Yet, as Bennett has emphasised, to achieve one, the other may be sacrificed. A section of this book is dedicated to the subject of independent taxation, and the extent to which it has changed the UK tax system since its implementation in 1990.

are unclear. It will be difficult to identify which provisions of tax law exactly benefit women. Thus, a project to advance the thesis of this book will involve engagement with socio-legal literature addressing the status of women within the economy; or, put differently, the gendered nature of the economic structure.

One approach to this project would be to suggest that the status of women within the economy is best analysed by addressing the question of money. If women disproportionately live in poverty, for example, then their status is clear, and it is patently not a good one. Put differently, it should not be difficult to identify exactly which provisions of tax law benefit women: rather, it is necessary to choose those laws which give women, as an interest group, the most money. Sometimes a government initiative which is clearly about redistribution, however, such as benefits, may be difficult to administer effectively in the face of what Alstott would describe as a competing goal (independent taxation). This book will move beyond specific aspects of the law at several points, and consider the question of its administration. Bureaucracy is never a side issue in tax law.[13]

Social science literature, dealing in particular with the 'new institutionalist' turn in governance, may be particularly relevant to an analysis of (implicit) bias, and resultant status of women in connection to fiscal legislation. Ultimately, and among other objectives, the 'new institutionalism' deals with the interaction of aspirations and legal culture.[14] The 'new institutionalist' literature in recent years has been developed in the context of European legal integration.[15] It has been particularly relevant in the identification of what could be described as the emergence of new legal forms from legislative efforts to integrate the European common market. This book will engage with new institutionalist literature within

13 Robin Williamson, Technical Director of the Low Incomes Tax Reform Group, illustrated this when he observed: '[e]xactly 20 years after the discriminatory treatment of women in the tax system was ended by the advent of independent taxation, it will be re-introduced as a by-product of Brownian complexity' ('Winners and Losers among Low-income Taxpayers', *Tax Journal*, 867 (2007), 19–20, at 20). Williamson was responding to changes introduced in the 2007 Budget, which included measures targeting some forms of tax avoidance believed (by the government) to be engaged in by married couples.

14 P. A. Hall and R. C. R. Taylor warn that the 'new institutionalism' 'does not constitute a unified body of thought. Institutional analysis of corporate tax law is not new' ('Political Science and the Three New Institutionalisms', in Karol Soltan *et al.* (eds.), *Institutions and Social Order* (Dearborn, MI: University of Michigan Press, 1998), at p. 15).

15 See, e.g., M. A. Pollack, 'The New Institutionalism and EC Governance: The Promise and Limits of Institutional Analysis', *Governance*, 9 (1996), 429–58; J. Bulmer Simon, 'The Governance of the European Union: A New Institutionalist Approach', *Journal of Public Policy*, 13(4) (1993), 351–80.

this context, but it will also consider what the new (and perhaps the old) institutionalism might offer the question of goals, or perhaps what might in this context be described as aspirations, within UK tax legal culture.[16]

Bradbury and Williams described the sociology of aspirations as the new, 'accessible classlessness',[17] thus coining an alternative title for the restructuring of some legislation in the New Labour era. This restructuring is a pervasive focus in this book. The changes introduced in the past twelve years to tax and benefits law and administration[18] have produced a wide range of socio-legal literature in response, and this book will engage with those aspects of the literature that address tax law specifically. A particular topic to be addressed will include the question of taxation of the household unit.

Most political parties endeavour to be viewed as supportive of the family unit. Given that tax is one of the most important tools that a government has for affecting the economy, it is to be expected that the tax system would be used by a government to promote the impression that it does indeed support the family. The family is however an uncertain locus for promotion of feminist objectives.[19] There is a literature suggesting, in some cases, measures short of – in other cases, measures achieving – the reorganisation of the family unit in the cause of feminism. This book will address to some extent the latter category, but it will mostly engage

16 In particular, the literature engaging with the 'sociology of aspirations' largely has considered, empirically, the factors influencing the educational aspirations of students (and some of the consequences of this.) See, among others: D. F. Alwin and L. B. Otto, 'High School Context Effects on Aspirations', *Sociology of Education*, 50(4) (1977) 259; W. H. Sewell and V. P. Shah, 'Social Class, Parental Encouragement, and Educational Aspirations', *American Journal of Sociology*, 73(5) (1968), 559–72. A new focus for theoretical sociology, emerging in the past few years, has targeted the 'sociology of aspirations' in the context of assessment of the New Labour philosophical project. A 'sociology of aspirations' was developed in consideration of New Labour efforts to target racism in football. S. Bradbury and J. Williams, 'New Labour, Racism and "New" Football in England', *Patterns of Prejudice*, 40(1) (2006), 61–82, at fn. 29. This book aims to extend this theoretical project to the question of fiscal legislation.

17 Bradbury and Williams, 'New Labour', at 61–82, fn. 29.

18 J. Lewis refers to research suggesting that '[o]ver the past century, married women and single women without children have come to rely rather more on earnings and rather less on male kin, while women with children and without men have been able to rely increasingly on earnings and state benefits' ('The "Problem" of Lone Motherhood in Comparative Perspective', in J. Clasen (ed.), *Comparative Social Policy: Concepts, Theories, and Methods*, London: Blackwell, 1999, at p. 189).

19 As Ralph S. Rice wrote in 1969, '[i]t would be very simple if we could believe that however irrational the tax structure, and however irregular and unrelated its parts, all shortcomings may be remedied if we can only establish the proper objectives of taxation and conform the structure to the ideal' ('Tax Reform and Tax Incentives', *Law and Contemporary Problems*, 34 (1969), 782–804, at 784).

with the former. Most of the strains of the socio-legal literature (fiscal sociology, new institutionalist, and others) with which this book will engage could be described as fiscal justice within the family unit.

Tax, policy and the relevance of institutions

Fiscal, sociological literature has been selected as a context for this book because it provides a context within which to assess the difficult question of formulation of tax policy. What exactly is tax policy? There are different ways in which this question might be addressed. Tax policy, for example, could be identified as the goals which tax legislation is structured to achieve. Given that Boyd and Young have warned that, '[w]hen it comes to tax policy decisions, feminists still have little influence',[20] it might thus be assumed that what is necessary is for women to identify feminist goals, and then to lobby for legislation which supports them.

Yet, as this introduction already has acknowledged, there are competing goals.[21] In the face of this, it will be necessary for institutions to make choices,[22] and it is at this point that the relevance of the new institutionalist vein of sociological theory[23] becomes clear. The new institutionalism, among other things, addresses the nature of the relationship between institutions, law and culture.[24] It also presumes a fluidity of definition of the idea of the institution, and enables the comparative perspective approached in this book. It also speaks directly to the question of how goals within institutions are identified and pursued.

Young observed that it is the 'invisibility of the inequalities' suffered by women through tax law that is most troubling,[25] and it is with this aspect of the nature of implicit bias that this book hopes to engage. For example, to what extent does taxation of the family unit support a market

20 S. B. Boyd and C. F. L. Young, 'Feminism, Law, and Public Policy: Family Feuds and Taxing Times', *Osgoode Hall Law Journal*, 42(4) (2004), 545–82, at 580. They were writing about Canada, although this statement appears to this author to be universal in application.

21 Alstott discussion, above n. 10. 22 *Ibid.*

23 This will be discussed throughout this book. Important sources will include: Peter Walgenbach and Anne Tempel, 'Global Standardization of Organizational Forms and Management Practices? What New Institutionalism and the Business-systems Approach Can Learn from Each Other', *Journal of Management Studies*, 44(1) (2007), 1–24; J. Blom-Hansen, 'A "New Institutional" Perspective on Policy Networks', *Public Administration*, 75(4) (1997), 669–93.

24 Victoria Khan suggests that 'the modern tradition of institutional sociology ... sees the law as value-free' ('Rhetoric and the Law', *Diacritics*, 19(2) (1989), 21–34, at 25). The 'new institutionalism', however, does not.

25 C. F. L. Young, '(In) Visible Inequalities: Women, Tax and Poverty', *Ottawa Law Review*, 27(1) (1995), 99–127, at 127.

economy which largely undervalues (if it values at all) unpaid labour?[26] This particular question will be approached from a number of perspectives, and will include consideration of the burgeoning critical tax theory literature. Critical tax theory began as a challenge to the suggestion that tax law is, effectively, neutral.[27] Writers within this tradition advanced the suggestion that tax law contributes to and sustains societal inequities from a number of perspectives, including heteronormativity, racial bias *and* gender. Critical tax theorists drew heavily upon the (already developed) body of outsider legal scholarship to demonstrate this. This book's analysis of unpaid labour will be located within this theoretical perspective, and, thus, will not consider only whether valuing unpaid labour will lead to greater tax relief for women. Indeed, the book will acknowledge that, initially, it may not.

Then what is the value of such an argument, if not ultimately to lessen the amount of tax that many women will have to pay? Lower taxes for women are not the agenda of this book, although enhanced economic equality is. Indeed, structuring a text in pursuit of lower taxes for women (who are able to pay them) would not necessarily make sense. Among other things, lower taxes for some women might mean fewer funds with which the government could assist those living in poverty (and more women and children live in poverty than men). Critical tax scholarship engaging with racial bias moved beyond these questions. Such work, for example, has not pursued lower taxes for minority ethnic groups in the US (which might mean less funding for government assistance programmes), but has sought to demonstrate that the structure of the US tax code is not neutral, and in some cases perpetuates bias.[28] This book's analysis of taxation of the family unit, and the role of unpaid labour within this, will proceed along similar lines.

A difficult question with which this book will engage is whether what could be described (given this book's approach) as *implicit* gender equity is more achievable for women if they are taxed within the family unit,

26 Consider this quote from by Deborah L. Rhode, about Margaret Mead: 'As Margaret Mead once noted, in some villages men fish and women weave, and in other villages women fish and men weave, but in either case the work performed by women is valued less' ('The "No-Problem" Problem: Feminist Challenges and Cultural Change', *Yale Law Journal*, 100 (1991), 1731–93, at 1754).

27 See introduction to Cambridge University Press Critical Tax Theory text by Infanti (at: http://papers.ssrn.com/sol3/papers.cfm?abstract_id=1333799).

28 See, among others: M. Uy, 'Tax and Race: The Impact on Asian Americans', *Asian American Law Journal*, 11 (May 2004), 117, at 129–38; A. G Abreu, 'Tax Counts: Bringing Money-Law to LatCrit', *Denver University Law Review*, 78 (2000), 575–93.

or independently. This is not the same question as whether independent taxation of married women's income should be permitted. On this point, the book is unambiguous – the introduction in the UK of independent taxation for women was an important achievement. Rather, this book will describe and synthesise what MacDonald called '[f]eminist analysis' which has emphasised 'the need for more nuanced alternatives to the lone individual versus the nuclear family as the unit for policy analysis'.[29] Indeed there is literature suggesting that it is possible that gender equity may be achieved within either model; in particular, from the perspective of 'individuals ... in relation' to tax.[30]

Nelson and England have written of 'individuals in relation' to others, and pursued the question, '[w]hat fresh ways of thinking about love and work do we need?'.[31] They continue: '[w]e take as uncontroversial among feminists that we need to move away from the dualistic view that women, love, altruism, and the family are, as a group, radically separate and opposite from men, self-interested rationality, work, and market exchange'[32] – and so does the thesis of this book. Implicit inequities along lines of gender at the basis of the tax system benefit neither women nor men. Additionally, this book will at various points emphasise difficulties that a provision of UK tax policy experienced because it was assumed that its provisions would benefit all women. The difficult question, Nelson (and England) continued, is how to respond to the clashes that occur when the private sphere is combined with the market, or 'what to put in place'.[33]

Tax policy and the law present an excellent example of what has been put in place. It can be examined to determine what has worked and what can work better. An analysis of 'individuals in relation' to tax law raises the question of the topic of study itself. Conaghan wrote in a 2000 issue of the *Journal of Law and Society* that '[i]ndeed few areas of law, no matter how musty or arcane, have remained immune from the feminist legal challenge'.[34] It is not surprising that, in the footnote

29 M. MacDonald, 'Gender and Social Security Policy: Pitfalls and Possibilities', *Feminist Economics*, 4 (1998), 1–25, at 4.

30 MacDonald explains that 'Julie Nelson, discussing this issue, calls for tax/benefit structures that recognize "individuals in relation"' (*ibid.*, 4.).

31 J. A. Nelson and P. England, 'Feminist Philosophies of Love and Work', *Hypatia*, 17(2) (2002), 1–18, at 1.

32 *Ibid.* 33 *Ibid.*

34 Joanne Conaghan, 'Reassessing the Feminist Theoretical Project in Law', *Journal of Law and Society*, 27 (2000), 351–85, at 352.

which followed, a reference to an article by Judith Grbich[35] makes it clear that tax law is included in the category of 'musty and arcane'. This, as Monroe would have lamented, is the fault of the legislation itself.[36] Enormously detailed and frequently difficult to understand, it may appear extraordinarily optimistic to suggest that such multiplicity could produce any clear evidence of intent, whether or not of bias, implicit or otherwise. Tax law attracts scholars hoping to make some sense of it all.

Traditional tax scholarship has a clear motivation: helping the taxpayer – regardless of gender, race or sexual orientation. The assistance may be offered without reference to perceived bias in the system, simply because the problem is too immediate.[37] The combination of the complexity of tax law, with the aim of avoiding essentialism in the analysis of tax law, can hinder understanding of the importance of this subject for women.[38] This importance extends beyond women, to a wider society, and it is within this sense that the thesis of this book places the project within the fields of critical tax scholarship[39] and feminist tax law.

Taxes affect every aspect of women's economic lives.[40] The sections of this book dealing both with theories of a gendered progressivity, and with the idea of an embedded economy, aim particularly to demonstrate

35 Judith Grbich, 'Taxation Narratives of Economic Gain: Reading Bodies Transgressively', *Feminist Legal Studies*, 5(2) (1997), 131–68.

36 H. H. Monroe, *Intolerable Inquisition? Reflections on the Law of Tax* (London: Stevens, published under the auspices of the Hamlyn Trust, 1981).

37 Conaghan, by contrast, 'argue[s] strongly for the recognition and realization of feminism's normative and transformative aspirations' ('Reassessing', at 351). She suggested that the 'drift' between political and academic feminism should be challenged (*ibid.*).

38 Additionally, Conaghan warns that efforts to avoid essentialist arguments in academic feminism have produced a tendency to move away from 'women centred' approaches ('Reassessing').

39 A. C. Infanti has issued a call to reconsider the label of critical tax law, thus rendering such self-categorisations ('A Tax Crit Identity Crisis? Or Tax Expenditure Analysis, Deconstruction, and the Rethinking of a Collective Identity', *Whittier Law Review*, 26 (2005), 707) less easy. Infanti suggests, among other things, that perhaps it is time for the 'tax crits', who may have considered themselves to operate at the margins of mainstream tax theory, to recognise that they have joined the mainstream. Although the coexistence of different approaches has been no more comfortable in tax law than in other legal disciplines, Infanti reminds us that '[t]he existence of different groups of scholars can surely be acknowledged without privileging one group over the other' Infanti (n. 11, at p. 707) provides an excellent summary of participants in the self-reflective 'critical tax theory' movement. This is an important reminder, and it will inform the spirit of enquiry in this book. Among other things, this book hopes to demonstrate that legal theorists interested in women cannot afford to overlook tax.

40 A phrase made famous by E. J. McCaffery: '[t]axes are central to all aspects of women's economic lives' ('Women and Taxes', at: www.ncpa.org/pub/st/st250/st250.pdf).

this. These (and other) sections will not, however, stop at the boundary of tax law. Tax law impacts upon all aspects of (not just) economic life – thus, as Alstott argued over ten years ago, 'any effort to use tax policy to implement feminist goals can usefully look beyond taxation to consider the possibilities for coordinating tax law change with reforms in other legal regimes'.[41] Thus, this book will engage with wider aspects of law, and broader, sociological theories of structuring fiscal, gender equity,[42] acknowledging that many of the principles which benefit women through feminism have the potential of aiding a wider humanity.[43] Yet although tax reform promises to help, essentially, everybody, this book proceeds from the basis that the position of women in the tax system is particularly precarious.[44] This book aims to demonstrate that tax law has contributed to a gendered socio-economy, in an institutionalist sense. The demonstration is effected, however, with a variety of different tools, including institutional sociological theory, theories of corporate social responsibility, and, of course, feminist philosophy.

41 Alstott, 'Tax Policy', p. 2081.

42 E. Amenta *et al.* concluded research with the observation that 'scholars would do well not to treat ... social policy as so exceptional as to require separate images, explanations, and approaches' ('US Social Policy in Comparative and Historical Perspective: Concepts, Images, Arguments, and Research Strategies', *Annual Review of Sociology*, 27 (2001), 213–34).

43 An illustration of this approach was provided by G. A. Cohen's analysis (in 1997) of the classic feminist call to action: 'the personal is political', which he suggests has a wider potential, although it is a specifically feminist call ('Where the Action Is: On the Site of Distributive Justice', *Philosophy and Public Affairs*, 26 (1997), 3–30, at 3–4). Cohen wrote that 'the idea itself ... is a feminist idea. Notice however that in briefly explaining the idea that I shall defend, I have not mentioned relations between men and women in particular, or the issue of sexism. We can distinguish between the substance and the form of the feminist critique of standard ideas about justice, and it is the form of it which is of prime concern to me here, even though I also endorse its substance' (*ibid.*).

44 McCaffery thus sets out the challenge: 'One, the tax system outs women on the margin. Two, the margin is a very rocky place to be. Three, economic theory and a commitment to ideals such as equal concern and respect for all citizens – buttressed by a measure of educated or enlightened common sense – suggest that women on the margin should be taxed *less* by the fiscal system. Four, the large distortions of the tax system interact with labor markets to create severe gender discrimination ...' (*Taxing Women* (Chicago, IL and London: University of Chicago Press, 1997), p. 90). This book aims to be more than a transplantation of McCaffery's approach from the US to the UK, although it acknowledges an obvious debt to McCaffery's project.

2

What is tax policy?

> Anyone who has studied a foreign language knows the difficulty of speaking words when she is not grounded in the culture that shapes them. This problem also arises in one's native language for children who frequently know words but take them literally, for example, giving the house a coat of paint.[1]

It is not easy to define what is meant by the term 'tax policy'. For the purposes of this book, tax policy is broadly defined, and addresses engagement with some forms of policy choices evident in fiscal legislation. A form of traditional 'tax policy' analysis, largely developed in the US literature, involves consideration of tax expenditures.[2] They have been defined as 'revenue losses arising from provisions of the federal tax laws that allow a special exclusion, exemption or deduction from gross income or that provide a special credit, a preferential rate of tax or a deferral of tax liability'.[3] The reason why what is effectively tax relief has been characterised in this way is that a government, rather than simply giving money to a citizen, instead has elected to use the tax system to provide this economic support. Thus, the distinction is that '[t]hese special provisions are not necessary to implement the income tax structure itself but are instead government expenditures made through the tax system, hence the name "tax expenditures"'.[4]

Traditionally tax policy involves consideration of choices about revenue collection and spending. A 'good' tax policy is often described as one that

1 Kornhauser, 'Through the Looking Glass', at 1614, n. 17.

2 The phrase 'tax expenditures' was first coined by Stanley Surrey. Edward R. Kantowicz, 'The Limits of Incrementalism: Carter's Efforts at Tax Reform', *Journal of Policy Analysis and Management*, 4 (1985), 217–33, at 219.

3 Tracey A. Kaye, 'Show Me the Money: Congressional Limitations on State Tax Sovereignty', *Harvard Journal on Legislation*, 35 (1998), 149–88, at 178, fn. 203.

4 *Ibid.*

is equitable, efficient (or neutral) and simple.[5] There is significant debate about the influence of these competing aims upon legislative decision making.

The impact of tax policy upon women might appear at first glance to be a domestic topic. The intersection of tax policy and gender is not immune, however, from what might be described as the pressures of internationalisation. Indeed, as Ring argues, '[t]he central challenge in international tax is navigating the relationship between an individual country's tax system and the rest of the world – a question of how nations should balance competing demands of revenue, domestic policy, retaliation, and global goals'.[6] An important factor in this navigation is pace, as '[t]he question grows more pressing as the pace of intersections among tax regimes escalates'.[7]

The growing internationalisation of tax law has coincided with an increasing reliance upon tax as a vehicle for social policy. Deploying the tax system in this way may hide potentially controversial social policies, and thus have a certain attractiveness for politicians, but it also can be very unpopular with tax scholars. The reason for this is that '[t]he prevailing opinion among academic tax lawyers ... and tax economists is that the tax system is a poor vehicle for social policy'.[8] And yet the proliferation of tax expenditures is not surprising. The complexities of tax law can provide many layers of subterfuge for the politician keen to provide financial support believed to be necessary, and known to be unpopular.

Tax expenditures can provide a form of direct action, without the political cost. The impact, or cost, of tax expenditures is, as Shurtz suggests, that '[e]xisting tax policy taken as a whole is inarticulable and theoretically incoherent, and thus, in effect, an obstacle to effective tax reform'.[9] Tax expenditures, however, also are inherently practical; and, potentially,

5 Adam Smith often is the starting point for this. See, among a vast literature: E. G. West, 'Adam Smith's Public Economics: A Re-evaluation', *Canadian Journal of Economics/Revue canadienne d'économique*, 10(1) (1977), 1–18.

6 Diane M. Ring, 'One Nation among Many: Policy Implications of Cross-border Tax Arbitrage', *Boston College Law Review*, 44 (2002), 79–175, at 79.

7 *Ibid.*

8 Unpopular they may be, but academics frequently find tax expenditures a rich source of material for analysis, as 'virtually all industrialized countries make use of tax expenditures as a substitute for government spending programs otherwise known as direct expenditures' (Tracey A. Kaye, 'Sheltering Social Policy in the Tax Code: The Low-income Housing Credit', *Villanova Law Review*, 38 (1993), 871–931, at 873).

9 Nancy E. Shurtz, 'A Critical View of Traditional Tax Policy Theory: A Pragmatic Alternative', *Villanova Law Review*, 31 (1986), 1665.

faster than other forms of social policy.[10] They are pragmatic.[11] They are prescriptive, however, and not normative.[12]

What is tax policy for women?

In the development of a normative, explicitly gendered, tax policy for women, goals would have to be articulated carefully. Measurable indices of progress would be necessary;[13] although a truly normative approach, with a clearly defined, ideal goal would have to extend beyond empiricism. Indeed, a tax policy that is normative, clear and focused upon gender equality could embrace a form of pragmatism that moves beyond empirical results, and certainly beyond the problems associated with otherwise pragmatic tax expenditures. If the goals for women from tax were clear, questions even concerning essentialism would be less problematic.

The sociological literature engaging with tax policy, from this sort of pragmatic perspective – i.e., what is a normative tax policy for women, or what is wanted from tax on behalf of gender economic equality – is limited.[14] Studies considering the interaction of tax policy and women typically address, by way of example, the differing responses of women (as compared to men) to tax compliance.[15] These studies tend to conclude

10 This is found throughout the legislative process. As I. K. Naumann observed, '[i]t is harder to mobilize support for complex policy reforms than for single issues such as the right to abortion' ('Child Care and Feminism in West Germany and Sweden in the 1960s and 1970s', *Journal of European Social Policy*, 15 (2005), 47–63, at 49).

11 Shurtz's argument that '[t]o develop a tax policy useful in the development of a tax system, the theoretical approach to taxation must be abandoned and a pragmatic approach must be adopted ... ' is compelling ('Critical View').

12 Shurtz insists that '[i]t should ... be apparent that if there is to be a truly normative income tax policy, it is only going to be achieved by taking a different approach from that which has been pursued in the past' (*ibid.*).

13 Shurtz insists that 'a pragmatic approach must be adopted employing as its primary guiding principle the efficient collection of revenue and employing empirical data to measure whether these revenue goals are being met' (*ibid.*, at 1666).

14 In 1998, R. M. Alvarez and E. J. McCaffery called for more 'research ... to gain a better understanding of how tax issues are being raised and discussed by political leaders and elites. How are these leaders and politicians framing tax issues? Do they evoke different frames for men and women? Is this at least partially the source of gender differences in opinions about taxation? Can political elites and candidates produce 'gender gaps' in opinions about tax policy?' ('Gender and Tax', 91–113, California Institute of Technology 1998, at www.hss.caltech.edu/SSPapers/wp1046.pdf, at 22).

15 For example, in terms of attitude, women apparently disapprove least of evasion of VAT: Marta Orviska and John Hudson, 'Tax Evasion, Civic Duty and the Law Abiding Citizen',

that women are likely to place taxation relatively low on their list of priorities or concerns.[16] Such research has been used to inform and structure studies of tax evasion, particularly involving husbands and wives evading taxes together.[17] The 'differing responses' literature also considers the impact of persuasion (both forceful and friendly) upon the tendency of women to comply with tax rules.[18] The goal of this sort of research is to determine whether a gendered, 'tax morality' exists, and if tax laws should be structured accordingly;[19] and, additionally, if knowledge or comprehension of tax rules is connected to this sense of 'tax morality'.[20] The

European Journal of Political Economy, 19 (2003), 83–102, at 94. Disapproval tends to increase with age (*ibid.*, at 96).

16 A MORI poll conducted in 2000 concluded that '[i]n terms of priorities, women were more likely to seek assurances about education, health and *pensions*, but less concerned about Europe or taxes' (J. Lovenduski, 'Women and Politics: Minority Representation or Critical Mass?' *Parliamentary Affairs*, 54 (2001), 743–58, at 753, emphasis added). The question of education, health pensions, taxes and equality, however, are inextricably linked. To choose one example, the question of pensions: in *National Pensions Office* v. *Jonkman*, the European Court of Justice (ECJ) received on referral from the Belgian Higher Labour Court a case involving air stewardesses who received a significantly lower pension on retirement than air stewards. The ECJ held that Article 4(1) of Directive 79/7 prohibited any discrimination whatsoever on ground of sex, in particular in relation to the scope of the schemes and the conditions of access, the obligation to contribute and the calculation of contributions and the calculation of benefits. Thus, Belgium was required to revise its national legislation, and to bring it into line with the policy behind the directive. *National Pensions Office* v. *Jonkman*, C-232/06 [2007] 3 CMLR 25. On the interactive nature of gender, retirement and pensions, see D. K. Smith, 'Superannuating the Second Sex: Law, Privatisation and Retirement Income', *Modern Law Review*, 64 (2001), 519–42.

17 Silvia Fedeli and Francesco Forte found that although, if a husband and wife evade taxes together, criminal law will punish both, this issue can be complicated if crime is considered within an economic context, especially if a crime is the product of a 'chain of exchanges' (see 'Joint Income-tax and VAT-chain Evasion', *European Journal of Political Economy*, 15 (1999), 391–415, generally, and at 392–3 in particular).

18 In a fascinating study, J. Chung and V. U. Trivedi found that 'while friendly persuasion in the form of generating and reading reasons supporting compliance has a slightly positive impact on women's tax ethics it in fact has a slightly negative impact on men's tax ethics' ('The Effect of Friendly Persuasion and Gender on Tax Compliance Behavior', *Journal of Business Ethics*, 47 (2003), 133–45, at 143). Women tend to be poorer than men, and yet they are also more fearful of breaking the law (Orviska and Hudson, 'Tax Evasion', at 92–3). This means that women tend to participate in less tax avoidance than men (*ibid.*, at 96). One study has suggested that women in the US are less likely to engage in tax evasion because of their tendency to view this activity within a context of moral censure (Orviska and Hudson, 'Tax Evasion').

19 They provide a number of possible explanations for this, including the possibility that 'tax compliance is a moral action, and moral actions are susceptible to social desirability bias' (Chung and Trivedi, 'Effect of Friendly Persuasion').

20 For example, a study by Lars Fallan reported 'a relationship between specific tax knowledge and improved tax ethics among male business students' ('Gender, Exposure to Tax

literature on gender and poverty, and the role government should assume in attempts to alleviate the problems of women in the economy, is considerably more extensive.[21] Indeed, feminist analyses of the socio-economy often start with poverty, and it is a sombre place to begin. Poverty is not something that is inflicted on women through tax systems. It is more embedded than that.[22]

The tax system contributes to the 'bleak'[23] fact of women's poverty, but it need not necessarily follow that tax law should be used as a tool of redress. Such an approach could be described as prescriptive, or instrumentalist. When, by way of example, the usefulness of tax in decreasing the number of women who live below the poverty line, however, is considered, it is also undeniably attractive.

Poverty, and women, are classic, globalised topics. As the 'feminisation of poverty' is a global problem, the issue can serve as a starting point for comparative legal analyses. Whether or not domestic tax law targets the problem of women's poverty, the interaction of tax law, women and poverty may commence what are perhaps now described as comparative, legal discussions. The idea of 'tax policy for women' involves an evolving field, which touches upon issues of compliance, morality and poverty, but does not necessarily invoke any clear definition or prescription. And

Knowledge, and Attitudes Towards Taxation; An Experimental Approach', *Journal of Business Ethics*, 18(2) (1999), 173–84, at 182–3). See also discussion of the literature in this area by J. Hasseldine and P. A. Hite, 'Framing, Gender and Tax Compliance', *Journal of Economic Psychology*, 24 (2003), 517–33, at s. 2.3.

21 A famous example of this was the 2008 OECD report into work and the family, which presented the following illustration: in the Netherlands, out of all Dutch women in the workforce, two-thirds are employed in part-time jobs. OECD, *Increasing Working Hours: Helping Reconcile Work and Family* (Geneva: OECD Economic Surveys, January 2008), pp. 109–33, at p. 109. The OECD's report drew a strong correlation between the prevalence of women in part-time jobs and Dutch policies for taxing second earners, and the availability of childcare (*ibid.*). There is also research into the impact of tax policy upon the decision to have children. In the US, for example '[M]arried couples with a high [personal tax exemption] tend to shorten the length of the second and third birth intervals. Furthermore, the hazard rate increases until four years after the preceding birth and then decreases in the case of the third birth, although this is not so for the second birth' (J.-T. Huang, 'The Personal Tax Exemption and Married Women's Birth Spacing in the United States', *Public Finance Review*, 36(6) (2008), 728–74, at 728).

22 As McCaffery explained, 'the feminization of poverty is a passive, descriptive and negative phenomenon. Passive, in that it is something inflicted on women. Descriptive, in that it is simply true, a stark fact of our collective social life. Negative, in that it is bleak and unfortunate ... ' ('Last Words (?): Towards a Feminization of Wealth', *Southern California Review of Law and Women's Studies*, (1996–7), 605–27, at 606).

23 *Ibid.*

yet it is similarly challenging to grapple with the idea of comparative tax policy, without the factor of gender. It is as difficult to compare tax policies around the world as it is to compare law generally.

The challenges of comparative law have been developed into a rich literature, which, among other contributions, has considered the way in which this subject has been taught. Observations from this literature are helpful to the project of this book, and will be referred to throughout; and, in particular, when the interaction of international tax law and gender is considered. For example, Mattei has argued that comparative law is a distinctive topic and a distinctive discipline; and, 'because of its subject matter, comparative law is different from any other discipline taught in law schools'.[24] He refers to the raw materials of comparative law for illustration. 'It does not deal', Mattei explains, 'with a body of law as, for example, civil procedure or labor law'.[25] It is almost wholly theory, or 'a method, or a variety of methods, used to compare different bodies of law'.[26] Comparative law thus stands alone, and '[i]n this perspective, it is not difficult to see the difference between comparative law and international law or between comparative law and foreign law'.[27]

The position of comparative tax policy is not dissimilar. Some arguments within the literature have striven to highlight what is described as the elimination of comparative law under the guise of internationalisation. This is evident through consideration of some of the restructuring of legal analysis. The comparative law section is increasingly replaced with the comparative law 'element'.[28] Domestic law analyses have been reduced to a component of an internationalised, or globalised, analysis. A problem in this approach is that 'otherness' can be reinforced if only small parts of a foreign system are discussed.

The difficulties with the 'old' approaches to comparative law are well established. Some of the tensions include the allegation that '[c]omparative lawyers are in ... dialogue with critics who charge that they have not sufficiently purged themselves of aspirations to the universal or the will to power'.[29] This is a strong criticism, and it is accompanied by the allegation that comparative lawyers 'have therefore not really

24 Ugo Mattei, 'Some Realism about Comparativism: Comparative Law Teaching in the Hegemonic Jurisdiction', *American Journal of Comparative Law*, 50 (2002), 87–99, at 87.

25 *Ibid.* 26 Mattei, 'Some Realism about Comparativism'. 27 *Ibid.*

28 Nora V. Demleitner, 'A Response to Mathias Reimann: More, More, More But Real Comparative Law', *Tulane European and Civil Law Forum*, 11 (1996), 73–83, at 73–4.

29 David Kennedy, 'New Approaches to Comparative Law: Comparativism and International Governance', *Utah Law Review*, 2 (1997), 545–637, at 560.

understood the other, have unwittingly privileged either their own or the other legal culture, have been tainted by the anti-intellectual temptation to place "doing business with" above "understanding", and so on'.[30]

Comparative lawyers hoping to avoid such criticisms may shirk from the task: '[w]ell, let's try harder, study more rigorously, listen more carefully, suppress our egos more fully'.[31] Given this context, Kennedy argues, '[w]e should not be surprised to find comparative law preoccupied with an exaggerated image of its own marginality to governance, compensating in various ways, edging up to the political or pragmatic, while preserving the viability of its project of erudition and understanding'.[32] The reluctance stems from the fact that, as a project, comparative law is an invasive political enterprise with considerable practical impact.[33] This was particularly evident in the 1990s when, with the dramatic changes in South Africa, Germany and the former communist countries, comparative law underwent a reinvention as governance, in particular, with respect to societies that were 'in transition'. Comparative law underwent several changes during this period; and, perhaps, this book is being written in what could be described as the post-1990s period, in the aftermath of the pragmatic, 'in transition' phase of comparative law.

The 'transitional' project in the 1990s led to the emergence of what Frankenberg has identified as four key features of comparative legal discourse during this era.[34] First, critical theory and method assumed a 'marginal role'.[35] Second, 'the comparatists' coped with 'ambivalence toward being marginalized from mainstream legal study'.[36] Third, Frankenberg identifies 'the dominant mode of academic comparative work – 'strategic comparison' for the sake of "cognitive control"'.[37] Finally, 'legocentrism', or 'the paradoxical overestimation of law', ruled supreme. Frankenberg presents several examples of the political, comparative lawyer

30 Tensions along these lines were found at the base of the criticisms of the harmful tax competition project, discussed in Kennedy, 'New Approaches'.

31 *Ibid.*, at 561. 32 Kennedy, 'New Approaches'.

33 This field has been developed, in particular by David Nelken and Roger Cotterrell. See, among others: D. Nelken, 'Disclosing/Invoking Legal Culture: An Introduction', *Social and Legal Studies*, 4 (1995), 435–52; D. Nelken, 'Comparing Legal Cultures', in A. Sarat (ed.), *The Blackwell Companion to Law and Society* (Oxford: Blackwell, 2004); Cotterrell, *Law, Culture And Society: Legal Ideas in the Mirror of Social Theory* (Aldershot: Ashgate, 2006); Cotterrell, 'Seeking Similarity, Appreciating Difference: Comparative Law and Communities', in E. Örücü and A. Harding (eds.), vol. 4, *Comparative Law in the Twenty-First Century* (The Hague: Kluwer, 2002).

34 Gunter Frankenberg, 'Stranger than Paradise: Identity and Politics in Comparative Law', *Utah Law Review*, 2 (1997), 259–74, at 260.

35 *Ibid.* 36 Frankenberg, 'Stranger than Paradise'. 37 *Ibid.*

at work, noting that '[t]heir vocabulary, goals, methods, and discursive practices betray a strong bias for the home law'.[38] This will be evident most clearly in their classifications: '[t]he classical comparativist will frequently invoke "evolution" and "history" or "ideal law" and "humanism," while the better-solution comparatist will refer to "interdependence" and "functions" without renouncing "humanism"'.[39]

Issues of tax, law and gender may find a receptive forum within some of the 'new' approaches to comparative law. This scholarship endeavours 'to bring ... critical traditions together by showing how the internal contradictions and pragmatic limitations of international law are connected to its cultural exclusions'.[40] What is particularly relevant to the question of tax and gender is the demonstration of 'how both the identity of the culturally excluded and the modes of its possible representation are marked by the contradictions and pragmatic failings of the discourse from which it seeks recompense or engagement'.[41] Even some of the previously described modern issues for tax treaties – including categorisation of income, qualification conflicts, and interpretation – might be reconsidered within the context of this scholarship.

The evolution of the 'new' approach to comparative law may be linked, theoretically, with recent work on the difference model. Two examples of this are found in the work of, among others, Young and Menkel-Meadow. Young concluded research for the Canadian government by suggesting that '[i]n order to take into account the full impact of a tax measure on women, certain questions should be addressed as part of the tax policy-making process'.[42] These questions may be used to formulate a clear structure for comparative analyses of women, tax policy and the law, and so are repeated here in full. Young asks, would a suggested tax subsidy favour high-income taxpayers more than low-income taxpayers because the latter receive less of the subsidy than the former?[43] Additionally, would the tax subsidy be offered to individuals who do not pay tax?[44] In terms of accessibility, is a tax subsidy more available to those who work in the paid workforce on a full-time basis, rather than those who work part time or only in the home?[45]

Entitlement to tax subsidies is also an important part of the analysis. Thus, as Young asked, will interruptions in work in the paid workforce

38 *Ibid.* 39 *Ibid.* 40 Kennedy, 'New Approaches', 562. 41 *Ibid.*

42 C. F. L. Young, *Women, Tax and Social Programs: The Gendered Impact of Funding Social Programs through the Tax System* (Ottawa: Status of Women Canada, 2000), p. 69.

43 Young, *Women, Tax and Social Programs.* 44 *Ibid.* 45 *Ibid.*

adversely impact upon women's entitlement to the tax subsidy?[46] Will the proposed tax measure act to discourage women's participation in the paid workforce?[47] Does access to the tax subsidy rely upon the private market or the private family playing a role in its delivery?[48] Does the tax measure contribute to the undervaluation of women's labour in the home?[49] Is the subsidy only available to those in heterosexual relationships?[50] Where the tax subsidy is in respect of an individual who is economically dependent on another, is it delivered to the economically dominant person in the relationship?[51] Does the tax measure undermine the autonomy of women? 'If the answer to any of the above questions is yes', Young writes, 'could the subsidy be reconfigured to avoid the negative impact on women or should it be delivered in another manner, such as by way of a direct grant?'[52]

These questions present challenges to tax subsidies that might otherwise be portrayed as helpful to women. The questions operate from the presumption of difference. Menkel-Meadow has addressed the question of difference from two (comparative) perspectives, in work considering the differences between the US and the UK's approach to gender equality in the legal profession.[53] She notes that women lawyers in the UK address the issue from a 'difference model', and make claims (for example, for childcare) on the basis of accommodation.[54] The US legal profession, however, attempts to create an environment which will 'not penalize' women if they, for example, take a career break to raise children.[55] Menkel-Meadow advocates thinking which extends beyond these categories, asking, by way of example, why law firms should not provide on-site childcare rather than relying on workers to make individual arrangements.[56]

Steinmo suggested that the basic question, 'why do different democracies pursue different public policies?' is 'one of the broadest and most complex issues faced by students of comparative politics'.[57] Menkel-Meadow's work demonstrates the complexity of this difference. In the above

46 *Ibid.* 47 *Ibid.* 48 *Ibid.* 49 *Ibid.* 50 *Ibid.* 51 *Ibid.* 52 *Ibid.*

53 C. Menkel-Meadow, 'Exploring a Research Agenda of the Feminization of the Legal Profession: Theories of Gender and Social Change', *Law and Social Inquiry*, 14 (1989), 289–319, at 309.

54 Menkel-Meadow, 'Exploring a Research Agenda'. 55 *Ibid.*

56 *Ibid.* It is useful to remember that other forms of law, beyond tax, are useful to the cause of gender equity. For example, research by Ginn *et al.* suggests that 'employee-friendly and women-friendly legislation could ameliorate persistent gender gaps in earnings and the long-term impact of family caring on pension income' (*Women, Work, and Pensions*, Philadelphia, PA: Temple University Press, 2001, p. 10).

57 S. Steinmo, 'Political Institutions and Tax Policy in the United States, Sweden, and Britain', *World Politics: A Quarterly Journal of International Relations*, 41(4) (1989), 500–35, at 500.

example, she does not privilege either the difference model or the 'no penalty' model, but suggests an alternative response. The response in this example turns away from the employee/woman, and towards the responsibilities of the employer. This approach is filled with potential, not least because it declines to problematise the presence of women in the workplace. The question is not whether the problem is caused by women's difference; or that it is important not to penalise women for their difference from men – but, rather, what are the obligations of employers to their employees.

The question of a much broader obligation, between the citizen and the state, in particular in the arena of tax and budgeting, will be explored in the next chapter. In that chapter, the gender-budgeting movement will be analysed. This movement is premised upon the existence of global, tax policy of economic gender equality. The techniques used to advance this policy, however, are very much of the twenty-first century. Thus, the next chapter will explore auditing, process, and, intriguingly, from the perspective of gender, a truly pragmatic strategy.

3

Tax policy in action

Gender budgeting[1]

Tax as an embedded institution

There is a new legal requirement upon the UK Treasury, and, at the moment, we are still figuring out what it means. It is called gender budgeting, and it is an obligation imposed upon every budget presented by a Chancellor, and passed by Parliament. The obligation is imposed by the European Union (EU) Gender Directive,[2] and has been in effect from the 2008 Budget. The Directive, 'implementing the principle of equal treatment[3] between men and women in the access to and supply of goods and services',[4] requires an accounting by government, to explain the impact of its expenditure upon gender equality.[5]

The Budget is important,[6] as it involves a regular statement of intent from a government to society, and a renewing reflection from society as

1 This chapter was presented at the workshop Crafting Effective Interventions in Pursuit of Equality and Diversity, organised by the Centre for Research in Equality and Diversity, School of Business and Management, and the School of Law, at Queen Mary. Many thanks to all of the participants at this excellent workshop for their valuable feedback.

2 Gender Directive (Council Directive 2004/113/EC).

3 In *Molinari et al.* v. *Agenzia delle Entrate*, the issue of whether tax advantages granted at different ages according to gender violated Council Directive 79/7/EEC on the progression of equal treatment of men and women in social security was referred for a preliminary ruling. The ECJ held that the provision of equal treatment for men and women was not applicable to tax law. *Molinari et al.* v. *Agenzia delle Entrate*, Joined Cases C-128/07 to C-131/07. But see the 2005 *Vergani* case, where the ECJ addressed Italian legislation which provided different tax treatment of severance payments according to age and gender. The ECJ held that this difference was contrary to Articles 2(1) and 5(1) of Directive 76/207, and could not be justified. Case C-207/04, [2006] 1 CMLR 5.

4 Directive 76/207.

5 S. Walby, 'Gender Mainstreaming: Productive Tensions in Theory and Practice', *Social Politics: International Studies in Gender, State and Society*, 12 (2005), 321–43, at 321–2. See also explanation provided by the Women's Budget Group (at: www.wbg.org.uk/GBA_What.htm).

6 Mary Condon and Lisa Philipps describe the production of an annual budget as 'a signature function of nation-state governments' ('Transnational Market Governance and Economic Citizenship: New Frontiers for Feminist Legal Theory', *Thomas Jefferson Law Review*,

to the pact it has formed with government. This chapter will consider the interaction between tax and women, as evidenced through the budgetary process. Additionally, the potential impact of the gender-budgeting movement upon the formulation of tax policy will be addressed. The chapter will proceed from the starting point that the global spread of gender budgeting is in many ways a positive development. Surprisingly, empirical research into, for example, responses based upon gender towards aspects of tax systems is almost non-existent.[7] The objective appears to be to require a government to explain itself, in the event of intentional or accidental discriminatory expenditure along the lines of gender – and, to let in the light of day on budgetary processes that perhaps for too long had occurred in the shadows of rote process, or unthinking repetition.[8] Women, particularly those with children, frequently are the target of tax instrumentalism (otherwise described as 'budgetary nudging')[9] with programmes such as tax credits, or childcare vouchers[10] – but, are they sufficiently frequently also the beneficiaries of investment? The aspiration of gender budgeting is to find this out. Gender budgeting has been defined by the European Commission as:

> an application of gender mainstreaming in the budgetary process. It means a gender-based assessment of budgets, incorporating a gender perspective in at all levels of the budgetary process and *restructuring revenues and expenditures in order to promote gender equality.*[11]

28 (2005), 105–50, at 139). In this, they are fiscal sociologists, and echo Schumpeter. This is discussed in A. Mumford, 'Towards a Fiscal Sociology of Tax Credits and the Fathers' Rights Movement', *Social and Legal Studies*, 17(2) (2008), 217–35.

7 Alvarez and McCaffery, 'Gender and Tax', in S. Tolleson-Rinehart and J. J. Josephson (eds.), *Gender and American Politics: Women, Men, and the Political Process* (Armonk, NY: M. E. Sharpe, 2000), at p. 91.

8 J. True, 'Mainstreaming Gender in Global Public Policy', *International Feminist Journal of Politics*, 5 (2003), 368–96, at 368–9.

9 For an analysis of tax instrumentalism and contemporary political philosophy, see K. A. Kordana and D. H. Tabachnik's response to Murphy and Nagel's, *The Myth of Ownership* (New York, NY: Oxford University Press, 2002), in 'Tax and the Philosopher's Stone', *Virginia Law Review*, 89 (2003), 647–8.

10 See generally: R. Blundell and C. Meghir, 'Active Labour Market Policy vs Employment Tax Credits: Lessons from Recent UK Reforms', Institute for Labour Market Policy Evaluation Working Paper No. 1 (2002); R. Blundell *et al.*, 'The Labour Market Impact of the Working Families' Tax Credit', *Fiscal Studies*, 21 (2000), 75–104; S. Himmelweit, 'Making Visible the Hidden Economy: The Case for Gender-impact Analysis of Economic Policy' *Feminist Economics*, 8 (2002), 49–70.

11 Gender budgeting page on the EUROPA website (at: http://ec.europa.eu/employment_social/gender_equality/gender_mainstreaming/budgeting/budgeting_en.html (emphasis added)).

Gender mainstreaming is a bureaucratic tool that has grown in popularity over several years, and which owes its success largely to the lobbying efforts of 'non-state actors', such as the United Nations (UN).[12] The value of the tool is presumed to be an intensification of public interest in the function and value of the Budget. At the least, a government's budget is a 'statement of its priorities'.[13] As Schumpeter famously argued that a budget provides the clearest insight into the sinews that bind the nation state,[14] the incorporation of gender budgeting into the UK's fiscal legislative process has been awaited eagerly.[15] The hope is that gender budgeting should not only push gender equality forward, but also perhaps provide unexpected insight into the status of gender within the market.[16] Many of the questions have not been asked before, so curiosity is high. As this chapter will discuss, gender budgeting has been in place in many countries around the world for several years, and has come to be viewed as an important socio-political tool by activist groups.[17] While the UK government faced different challenges than those faced, for example, in India[18] or Sierra Leone,[19] the relative success[20] of gender budgeting internationally has established a strong anticipation in the UK of a productive and meaningful process.

12 Jacqui True and Michael Mintrom, 'Transnational Networks and Policy Diffusion: The Case of Gender Mainstreaming', *International Studies Quarterly*, 45 (2001), 27–57, at 28.

13 M. Marks Rubin and J. R. Bartle, 'Integrating Gender into Government Budgets: A New Perspective', *Public Administration Review*, 65 (2005), 259–72, at 259.

14 J. A. Schumpeter, *Capitalism, Socialism and Democracy* (London: Routledge, 1994), p. 180.

15 See: S. Himmelweit, 'The Experience of the UK Women's Budget Group' (posted online at: www.e-quality.nl, at 15–16); K. Rake, 'Gender Budgets. The Experience of the UK's Women's Budget Group', in paper prepared for the conference Gender Balance – Equal Finance 2002.

16 Simone Walby, 'Gender and the New Economy: Regulation or Deregulation?', presented to ESRC seminar Work, Life and Time in the New Economy, LSE, October 2002.

17 This point is made in N. Kardam and Selma Acuner, 'National Women's Machineries: Structures and Spaces', in S. Rai, *Mainstreaming Gender, Democratizing The State?: Institutional Mechanisms for the Advancement of Women* (Manchester University Press, 2003), pp. 108–11. See also the discussion of the uses of gender budgeting for '[p]olicy-makers and civil society groups' (at: www.wbg.org.uk/GBA.htm).

18 *Hindu News Update Service* (20 May 2008) (at: www.hindu.com/thehindu/holnus/002200805201822.htm).

19 *The New Citizen*, Tolongbo, Sierra Leone (20 May 2008) (posted online at: www.christiantrede.com).

20 Gender budgeting is discussed as a 'success' in South Africa, Tanzania and Uganda, in a report submitted to the UN Development Programme, 'Policy Dialogue on Legislative Development' (posted online at: www.undp.org/).

Barnett and Grown suggest that there is a renewed interest in using tax to redistribute resources in a way that promotes gender equality, particularly with two goals in mind.[21] First, tax policy might assist women in developing countries.[22] Second, tax policy might assist governments in their otherwise not effective enough efforts to reach 'the very poor'.[23] The outcome of the gender-budgeting process will have implications far beyond the amount of public funding that is invested in what might be described as women's projects, or women's activities. Tax law, the Budget's ultimate product, is often instrumentalist at its core.[24] Tax legislation need not only have as its objective the collection of sufficient funds to run government and fulfil important social functions. It also often aims to influence and change the behaviour of taxpayers – indeed, revenue collection can be a secondary objective.[25] For women in particular, given the myriad of tax legislation aimed at influencing their behaviour as parents, caretakers and paid and unpaid market participants, tax law often addresses their actions, and attempts to influence their choices.[26] For example, frequently, tax law attempts to convince women, especially those with children, to enter the paid marketplace. This influence is exerted in a way that indicates that such decisions are inherently very difficult, because caring for one's own child takes place outside of the paid marketplace, and, therefore, a parent must choose between the two. Perhaps the marketplace values child caring as too important, or special, to be included by it, and, thus, the market organises itself[27] around child caring, rather as one might sidestep a rock on a path.

This chapter will argue the importance of Polanyi's observation that markets need not be structured in such a way that the satisfaction of what might be described as fundamental needs (for example, homemaking and

21 K. Barnett and C. Grown, *Gender Impacts of Government Revenue Collection: The Case of Taxation* (London: Commonwealth Secretariat, 2004), p. 50.

22 Barnett and Grown, *Gender Impacts*. 23 *Ibid.*

24 Sol Picciotto, 'Constructing Compliance: Game Playing, Tax Law, and the Regulatory State', *Law and Policy*, 29 (2007), 11–30, at 12–13.

25 Or they can coincide. Hausman and Ruud observed that, in the US (as in the UK) '[t]axes in labor supply raise the largest proportion of federal tax revenue'. Thus, it can make sense to factor for different objectives. J. Hausman and P. Ruud, 'Family Labor Supply with Taxes', *American Economic Review*, 74 (1984), 242–8, at 242.

26 See C. F. L. Young, *Women, Tax and Social Programs: The Gendered Impact of Funding Social Programs Through the Tax System* (Ottawa: Status of Women Canada, 2000).

27 This happens with other forms of law as well. A. Schwartz and R. E. Scott explain that 'contract law contains a number of mandatory rules that apply in the absence of an externality or market failure' ('Contract Theory and the Limits of Contract Law', *Yale Law Journal*, 113 (2003), 541–620, at 617, emphasis added).

raising children) is a central organising factor.[28] The necessity of satisfying these needs has been used to justify gender economic inequality, but, simply, it is possible to organise a market differently. It would be a mistake to focus solely on the market as an object of change, when the institutions which support the market wield so much power over its activities. The modern market is not what Polanyi would have described as self-regulating, but, rather, relies on the support of various social institutions for its form. Neither the market nor the institutions are necessarily more powerful than the other, and, indeed, the institutions become deeply intertwined with the market. Polanyi's analysis of the 'double movement', whereby measures to protect labour and other resources grow alongside a rapidly expanding capitalist economy, reveals that measures intended to regulate the market often become subsumed with it.[29] They are not enough.

Ultimately, Polanyi promised that it is possible to plan for an economy that promotes gender equality. Given that markets are 'embedded', as Polanyi would describe them, in social institutions, this leaves societies with a significant amount of power. In essence, it is possible to plan for the market that society decides it wants. The objective of this chapter is to consider how this might be achieved. It will begin by providing a background to the gender-budgeting movement, and address its relationship with international tax law, regulatory theory, and theories of globalisation. The chapter then will introduce Polanyi's concept of the 'embedded market', and argue that understanding Polanyi's concept of 'embeddedness' can help a society to plan for the market it wants – which, ultimately, is the goal of gender budgeting. The analysis then will return to gender budgeting as a legal process, and suggest that it is part of what Polanyi might have described as a 'double movement', on several fronts. The final section will consider the objectives of gender budgeting, and address why simply identifying them (never mind achieving them) is quite possibly the most difficult question. Polanyi's importance to this analysis derives from the fact that his book, *The Great Transformation*, changed economic thought in the twentieth century.[30] His explanation of the ways in which

28 This is the basis of much of his work, perhaps the most famous example of which is Polanyi, *Great Transformation.*

29 Joel M. Ngugi, 'Forgetting Lochner in the Journey from Plan to Market: The Framing Effect of the Market Rhetoric in Market-oriented Reforms', *Buffalo Law Review*, 56 (2007), 1–97, at 51, citing Polanyi, *Great Transformation*, at p. 76.

30 See generally: J. Beckert, 'The Great Transformation of Embeddedness: Karl Polanyi and the New Economic Sociology' (ms, at: www.mpifg.de/pu/mpifg_dp/dp07–1.pdf);

economies are embedded in cultures and societies challenged assumptions about what is 'natural' in economies, and subverted the assumption that societies are victims to machinations of the market. In short, he suggested that it might be possible to choose, and to craft, the economy we want. Thus, his work is vital to an analysis of women, tax and the law.

The gender-budgeting movement: the 'new' old

By 2002 gender budgeting – the process of producing disaggregated analysis of the impact of spending allocation in national budgetary processes, so as to identify impact along lines of gender – was described as having been incorporated into the budgeting processes of more than forty countries globally.[31] Gender budgeting embraces a variety of different forms and formats. In short, it 'provides a range of methodologies for analysis of expenditure and revenue streams by gender, enabling policy makers, analysts and governments to understand any differential impacts on men and women of policy decisions'.[32] A benefit of gender budgeting is that it should move the discourse of gender, money and the state from the fringe of political analysis, to the centre. Calls to tax housework, in contrast,[33] are unlikely to move to the mainstream. Yet evidence that more money has been spent on sport provision for boys than girls, by way of example, might provide powerful political capital to a Member of Parliament (MP) attempting to achieve public funding for a sport that perhaps is not very popular, but is favoured by women. Whereas previously an MP in opposition to the plan might have been able to respond that a comparatively unpopular sport did not deserve more funding than, for example, football, this MP will now have to face the cold, hard fact of, perhaps, a significant discrepancy in sports funding for women. Gender budgeting should invigorate the discourse of gender in politics, and provide politicians working towards gender equality with powerful tools. In this

F. Block, 'Karl Polanyi and the Writing of *The Great Transformation*', *Theory and Society*, 32 (2003), 275–306; Jean-Michel Servet, 'L'institution monétaire de la société selon Karl Polanyi', *Revue économique*, 44 (1993), 1127–49; John Lie, 'Embedding Polanyi's Market Society', *Sociological Perspectives*, 34 (1991), 219–35.

31 R. Sharp, 'Budgeting for Equality: The Australian Experience', *Feminist Economics*, 8 (2002), 25–47, at 25.

32 HM Treasury/DTI, 'Gender Analysis of Expenditure Project (Final Report)', July 2004 (at: www.womenandequalityunit.gov.uk/research/gender_analysis.pdf, at p. 5).

33 The leading article in this area is N. C. Staudt, 'Taxing Housework', *Georgetown Law Journal*, 84 (1995), 1571–1647.

example, gender might not initially have been the focus of debate; but, after gender budgeting, the debate *is* gender.

Gender budgeting skirts the edges of a policy that might actually be quite subversive, despite its apparently benign place within the standard 'equality principle' European constitutional discourse.[34] From the 'benign' perspective, the 'let us check whether any unintentional underinvestment for women has occurred' objective of gender budgeting is uncontroversial. Additionally, any policy that appears to address the overrepresentation of women (and, by extension, their children) below the poverty line is equally uncontroversial – and, as gender budgeting is patently about money and government investment, it would appear by definition to do so. As Watson suggested (in the Australian context), 'women gain most from a strategy which aims at influencing the economic mainstream in the areas of wages, tax, budgetary policy, social welfare, employment and industry policy'.[35] Gender budgeting explicitly addresses tax, the Budget and social welfare, and would indirectly influence government support for industry, and thus as a policy qualifies as one of those initiatives from which women are likely to benefit.

Although it is not likely to be a strong part of the public discussion of gender budgeting, the probable questions that will be raised by such a policy reveal the possibility for debates that could, potentially, prove subversive to mainstream institutions. Consider, for example, the observation that the 'equality principle' is a mainstay of European constitutionalism.[36] Why, then, is gender budgeting needed, if equality on the basis of gender and other factors is an 'accepted' part of European (and UK) constitutional governance? The reasons, perhaps, may not be addressed, but even their allusion may move the discourse of gender equality to different levels.

This is a possibility, but it is only that, and in this way gender budgeting has been criticised as being too timid.[37] It is only an accounting, and not a demand for fundamental change.[38] This is not to imply that some form

34 See generally Jo Shaw, 'Process and Constitutional Discourse in the European Union', *Journal of Law and Society*, 27 (2000), 4–37.

35 S. Watson, *Playing the State: Australian Feminist Interventions* (Melbourne: Verso, 1990), p. 134.

36 Jo Shaw, 'The European Union and Gender Mainstreaming: Constitutionally Embedded or Comprehensively Marginalised?', *Feminist Legal Studies*, 10 (2002), 213–26, at 218.

37 See generally, Sally Baden and Anne Marie Goetz, 'Who Needs [Sex] When You Can Have [Gender]? Conflicting Discourses on Gender at Beijing', *Feminist Review*, 56 (1997), 3–25.

38 The UK entered this discussion relatively late, compared to other nations. It is largely thanks to the lobbying efforts of the Women's Budget Group (WBG) that gender

of economic accounting for gender has not occurred in the UK until this point, and, indeed, equality impact assessments could be described as a forerunner of gender budgeting.[39] Squires has explained that gender impact assessments extend beyond gender in the UK, and 'are clearly being applied across many of the equality strands'.[40] This comes with the warning however that 'the technocratic complexities of attempting to conduct impact assessments in relation not only to gender, but also to race, religion, sexuality, disability and age are enormous'.[41] This chapter will not criticise such an expansion, but, indeed, will suggest that it is possible to organise the market that society decides it wants, from a number of different perspectives.

Objectives of gender budgeting

At this point, the question of the objectives of gender budgeting arises. What should it involve? To begin with, the impact of disaggregated budgetary expenditure upon women[42] is likely to enable clear, policy-based articulation of the importance of gender equality. Additionally, gender budgeting may hold governments accountable for pre-existing commitments to human rights agendas, such as those promulgated by the Convention on the Elimination of all Forms of Discrimination against Women (CEDAW).[43] If every Budget is in the control of the government of the moment, treaty obligations signed by predecessors may not be under such control. If a government is fixed with pre-existing commitments, one possible route is of course to ignore them, but this is less easy with a process like gender budgeting in place.

budgeting has stayed on the agenda in the UK, even before EU legislation. It is difficult to underestimate the importance of the WBG, especially if one considers, by way of example, that Australia published the first 'gender sensitive budget' in 1984. Helen Leadbetter, 'Gender Budgeting' (at: www.dfid.gov.uk/aboutdfid/organisation/pfma/pfma-gender-budget.pdf).

39 J. Squires, 'Equality and diversity: a new equality framework for Britain?', unpublished paper presented at School of Public Policy, University College, London University, December 2003 (at: www.bath.ac.uk/esml/Library/pdf-files/squires.pdf, at 28).

40 *Ibid.* 41 Squires, 'Equality and diversity'.

42 Walby, 'Gender Mainstreaming', at 333.

43 Bakker observed that 'gender budget analysis is increasingly recognized as an important way to hold governments accountable for their commitments to human rights and gender equality as they connect these commitments to the distribution, use, and generation of public resources' (I. C. Bakker and Alternatives Canadian Centre for Policy, 'Gender Budget Initiatives: Why They Matter in Canada', Technical Paper 1, Canadian Centre for Policy Alternatives, 2006, at 1).

Political strategy will play an important part in the success of gender budgeting. Gender economic inequality has always existed; thus, how will its redress be 'sold'? Further, how will the political obstacles presented by the inevitable upheaval accompanying social and economic change? With gender budgeting, the government has responsibility for redressing gender economic inequality, but it does not necessarily possess all of the necessary power to do so. A starting point of Polanyi's analyses is that the institutions which support a market stretch far beyond government and its agencies, and include, essentially, all of wider society. It is a difficult problem, but the process and aura of expertise surrounding gender budgeting may assist.[44] Indeed, the appearance of a 'number exercise' may be politically useful.

The number exercise, even if initially, political uncontroversial,[45] will assist governmental accountability, and will track the progress of policy goals. Economic governance will increase in transparency.[46] When the impact of spending initiatives are analysed post-Budget, change will be sought for forthcoming Budgets.[47] That a disproportionate impact will be identified is inevitable, as even if domestic, national budgets start from a premise of fiscal neutrality and dispassionate revenue allocation, the combination of women's disproportionate share of unpaid work, inferior levels of pay to men and reduced political voice all result in inequity.[48]

Gender budgeting is in essence a 'stepped up' version of a process that has been occurring in the UK Treasury, to differing degrees, since

44 Walby has explained that 'the representation of the intervention as one that is based on expertise may itself be a political strategy' ('Gender Mainstreaming', at 333).

45 As a 2002 report by the World Bank stated, '[g]ender equality is an issue of development effectiveness, not just a matter of political correctness or kindness to women' ('Gender Equality as Smart Economics', January 2002, posted at: http://web.worldbank.org, at 1).

46 The significance is that '[g]ender budgeting helps to monitor the achievement of policy goals and to hold governments accountable in this regard. By tracking how money is spent, gender budgeting helps to increase accountability and transparency and, thus, good economic governance in a country' ((OECD) Department for International Development, 'Evaluation of DFID's Policy and Practice in Support of Gender Equality and Women's Empowerment', August 2006) (at: www.oecd.org/dataoecd/52/38/37390142.pdf, at slide 5). D. Budlender has written that two of the main benefits of gender budgeting are 'increased transparency' and 'accountability' ('The Political Economy of Women's Budgets in the South', *World Development*, 28 (2000), 1365–78, at 1377).

47 Yet '[g]ender budgeting initiatives traditionally analyse budgets ex-post and then use that analysis to advocate for change in the subsequent budget' (OECD, 'Evaluation', p. 34). Perhaps most importantly, they are also a 'tool for change' (Budlender, 'Political Economy', at 1376).

48 Ruth Pearson, 'Feminist Responses to Economic Globalisation: Some Examples of Past and Future Practice', *Gender and Development*, 11 (2003), 25–34, at 32.

1998.[49] In 2004, aware of the impending impact of the EU Gender Directive, and the work that had been performed by the UN in this area over the years, the Treasury structured a 'Gender Analysis of Expenditure' pilot project.[50] This project was conducted in close consultation with the Women's Budget Group (WBG), which by 2004 had become the prime means of engagement with gender budgeting by the Treasury.[51] Perhaps because of this – and according to a report presented at the Regional Symposium on Mainstreaming Gender into Economic Policies – the Women's Budget Group focuses on presenting efficiency arguments[52] to the Treasury (what might be described as the Treasury's language), but has not abandoned the goals of fairness or equality.[53]

Thus, from 'efficiency arguments', to political acceptance – one of the conclusions of the 2004 Pilot Project was that 'in order to conduct gender analysis in future, there needs to be a clear buy-in from key stakeholders across government and a significant improvement in gender disaggregated data'.[54] 'Numbers exercises' and efficiency arguments may delay political resistance, but not indefinitely.[55] The resistance will be external, as gender budgeting will be positive – the Budget will be 'broken down', and its impact upon men, women, boys and girls quantified[56] – and will not involve a search for obstructions. Such a search, in any case, would be

49 HM Treasury/DTI, 'Gender Analysis', at 3. 50 *Ibid.*

51 S. Himmelweit, 'The Experience of the UK Women's Budget Group' (2000). Contribution to the International Workshop on Gender Auditing of Government Budgets, 15–16, at slide 3.

52 Addressing this argument, Garrett argued that '[t]he efficiency view focuses solely on one aspect of the globalization–redistribution nexus – the economic costs of large and progressive public economies. This neglects the assertion made by a long line of scholars – [starting with] Polanyi ... that there are also clear political incentives to expand welfare effort in response to internationalization' (G. Garrett and D. Mitchell, 'Globalization, Government Spending and Taxation in the OECD', *European Journal of Political Research*, 39 (2001), 145–77, at 151).

53 E. Villagomez, 'Gender Responsive Budgets: Issues, Good Practices and Policy Options', at the conference Regional Symposium on Mainstreaming Gender into Economic Policies (NNUU Comisión Económica para Europa, 2004), at 11.

54 HM Treasury/DTI, 'Gender Analysis', at 3.

55 Julia Adams and Ann Shola Orloff, 'Defending Modernity? High Politics, Feminist Anti-modernism, and the Place of Gender', *Politics and Gender*, 1(1) (2005), 166–82, at 175.

56 'Gender budget initiatives break down the government's budget in order to see how it responds to the differentiated needs of and impacts on women, men, girls and boys. Their main purpose is to examine whether public expenditures are allocated in an equitable way and hence promote gender equality' (Helena Hofbauer Balmori, 'Gender and Budgets', Bridge: Development – Gender, posted online at: www.bridge.ids.ac.uk).

unlikely to prove fruitful.[57] Rather, gender budgeting will involve a search for the norms that underpin budgetary processes, and determine their outcomes,[58] and a determination of whether goals that are already in place might be achieved more efficiently, and with greater accountability.[59]

Relationship between gender budgeting and gender mainstreaming

Gender mainstreaming is a precursor to gender budgeting, and may be described as one of the barriers established to check the power of the market. Its aim was to encourage the consideration of gender equality as an instinctive, or 'mainstreamed' check, yet the achievement of these objectives does carry the possibility of disturbing the market, or the 'rational economic man' upon which the market is structured. This can be positive, and feminist economic literature has emphasised that the rational economic man is capable of being replaced by alternative models – and, indeed, that even the capitalist market economy may be organised differently.[60] There is an element of reorganisation, and restructuring, already incorporated into the objectives of gender budgeting, as envisaged within the EU.

Interestingly, True and Mintrom observed that '[t]he recent rise of gender mainstreaming across states has been paralleled by the emergence over the past decade or so of feminist approaches to international relations'.[61]

57 For example, as L. Barmes and S. Ashtiany have acknowledged, '[t]here are so many factors that may inappropriately impede a person's career progression that it would be absurd to address each of these structurally' ('The Diversity Approach to Achieving Equality: Potential and Pitfalls', *Industrial Law Journal*, 32 (2003), 274–96, at 279).

58 'Every budget reform has a normative emphasis that seeks to reorient the budget process and perhaps tilt budget outcomes in favour of those norms' (Rubin and Bartle, 'Integrating Gender', at 269).

59 Thus, '[t]he normative value of the current emphasis on performance budgeting seeks to reorient the budget process toward greater efficiency and accountability in attaining program goals' (*ibid.*).

60 L. Beneria, 'Globalization, Gender, and the Davos Man', in Mutari and Figart (eds.), *Women and the Economy: A Reader* (New York: M. E. Sharpe, 2003), p. 318. See also: S. Duncan and R. Edwards, 'Lone Mothers and Paid Work – Rational Economic Man or Gendered Moral Rationalities?', *Feminist Economics*, 3 (1997), 29–61; G. J. Hewitson, *Feminist Economics: Interrogating the Masculinity of Rational Economic Man* (Cheltenham: Edward Elgar, 1999).

61 True and Mintrom, 'Transnational Networks and Policy Diffusion: The Case of Gender Mainstreaming', *International Studies Quarterly*, 45(1) (2001), 27–57.

Indeed, mainstreaming has been a described as part of an 'international gender agenda'.[62]

This agenda is based on three principles:

> (i) the realization that unequal power relations is at the core of gender relations; (ii) the re-examination of all social, political, and economic structures as well as development policies from the point of view of gender differentials; and (iii) the recognition that achieving gender equality between women and men requires 'transformative change'.[63]

This 'international, gender agenda' may have found its way to EU government, but whether it has achieved tangible change, or restructuring, is unclear. Explaining that the EU 'is not a state in any conventional sense',[64] although it acts like one, Shaw has argued the worth of determining whether gender mainstreaming can become 'constitutionally embedded' in European law.[65] She wrote (in 2002) that while an 'equality principle' exists in EU constitutional law which is 'deeply embedded',[66] 'the embedding of mainstreaming in the constitutional politics of the EU has some way yet to go'.[67] The reason for this is that while the EU White Paper on gender mainstreaming 'is quick to deal with "powers"', it is nonetheless 'slow to face head on the question of "power"'.[68] Shaw writes that '[t]o follow the gender mainstreaming project to its logical conclusion is to raise some fundamental questions about who decides who gets what, where and how'.[69]

Shaw is not utilising 'embeddedness' in a Polanyian context, but as a representation of whether a concept has been legally embraced. Put differently, does gender mainstreaming (and will gender budgeting) involve a true accounting, or is it a paper exercise? On this question, whereas gender mainstreaming has been susceptible to criticisms that it is a paper exercise,[70] gender budgeting may be portrayed as a positive development from what was started by gender mainstreaming, and a move beyond mere auditing. Indeed Fredman and Spencer have applauded the fact that gender mainstreaming is proactive (as compared to reactive redress for discrimination via litigation), yet have criticised the inherent voluntariness of its structure in the EU.[71] They also question whether a process which

62 Yakin Erturk, 'Considering the Role of Men in Gender Agenda Setting: Conceptual and Policy Issues', *Feminist Review*, 78(1) (2004), 3–21, at 3.

63 *Ibid.*, at 6. 64 Shaw, 'European Union', at 214. 65 *Ibid.*, at 216. 66 *Ibid.*, at 218.

67 *Ibid.*, at 226. 68 Shaw, 'European Union'. 69 *Ibid.* 70 *Ibid.*

71 Sandra Fredman and Sarah Spencer, 'Beyond Discrimination: It's Time for Enforceable Duties on Public Bodies to Promote Equality Outcomes', *European Human Rights Law Review*, 6 (2006), 598–606, at 598–9.

does not have a stronger, mandatory foundation can ever achieve a truly fundamental restructuring. Gender budgeting, as a process, is mandatory, and this indeed is an important step forward, and also builds upon other distinct accomplishments of gender mainstreaming. For example, one of the advantages of gender mainstreaming is that it develops the concepts of inequality beyond specific instances of interaction, to wider questions of how the markets and society relate.[72] Gender mainstreaming thus set the stage for the integrated approach to addressing gender within the budgetary process. It also raises the possibility that clashes will occur (and this is potentially quite useful to the cause of restructuring) between expectations that now were 'mainstreamed', and processes or institutions that perhaps had cloaked themselves in illusions of gender neutrality. To explain with an example, Liebert predicted a potential 'collision' between gender mainstreaming and the 'male breadwinner model' which underpins, in particular, the tax system in Germany.[73]

A further difference is that gender mainstreaming is an essentially European idea, whereas gender budgeting aims to become part of domestic processes in individual Member States. Indeed, Beveridge explained that the crucial difference between gender mainstreaming and gender budgeting is that the latter encompasses both national and local authority budgets.[74] Gender mainstreaming, by way of contrast, is more focused on the Community's budget.[75] Beveridge says this is very 'significant', because it signals an evolution in the Commission's approach to equality. Whereas before it viewed its role as one of an 'instigator', with gender budgeting it is moving to a model of 'facilitator/evaluator'.[76]

Gender mainstreaming was adopted as the official policy for the promotion of gender equality in the EU and its Member States in the Amsterdam Treaty (1997).[77] New Member States are required to devise a gender-mainstreaming approach as a precondition of EU membership.[78] There

72 Ulrike Liebert, 'Europeanising Gender Mainstreaming: Constraints and Opportunities in the Multilevel Euro-polity', *Feminist Legal Studies*, 10 (2002), 241–256, at 250.

73 Liebert, 'Europeanising Gender'.

74 Fiona Beveridge, 'Building against the Past: The Impact of Mainstreaming on EU Gender Law and Policy', *European Law Review*, 32 (2007), 193–212, at 194.

75 Beveridge, 'Building against the Past'. 76 *Ibid.*

77 T. Rees, 'Reflections on the Uneven Development of Gender Mainstreaming in Europe', *International Feminist Journal of Politics*, 7 (2005), 555–74, at 555, citing the Treaty of Amsterdam, Amending the Treaty on European Union, the Treaties Establishing the European Communities and Certain Related Acts, 1997 OJ (C 340) (hereinafter Amsterdam Treaty), incorporated into the Treaty Establishing the European Community, 7 February 1992, OJ (C 224) 1 (1992) [1992] 1 CMLR 573 (1992), Art. 141(4).

78 Rees, 'Reflections'.

is significant uncertainty as to what gender mainstreaming entails, and the processes that have been developed are 'uneven'.[79] Rees suggests that three principles form the foundation of gender mainstreaming in Europe – 'treating the individual as a whole person; democracy; and justice, fairness and equity'.[80] Rees argues that there are only a small number of instances in which 'gender equality is the main policy goal (agenda setting)'.[81] Rather, gender mainstreaming is used to advance other policies.[82]

The institutions and economies under consideration do not have limits provided by national borders, whether national, European or international, although gender budgeting as a structural process seems to presume that these borders exist. Thus, the Commission's facilitator ambitions, while significant from the perspective of law and enforcement, also potentially makes everything much more complicated. As part of a global movement, gender budgeting is part of a shift from pursuing global order goals with purely political means or by way of armed force, to a focus on economic order, or a strong reliance on the benefits of global trade.

From gender mainstreaming, to global governance (through tax)

A global economic order, in part achieved through tax, has been on the agenda of organisations like the International Monetary Fund (IMF) and the Organisation for Economic Co-operation and Development (OECD) for at least ten years.[83] The targeted countries have objected that the only way that they are able to compete with wealthier and more powerful countries is by offering tax incentives, and have complained that the project is likely to deprive them of the only foreign investment that they have.[84] The OECD has countered that the only true response to global

79 *Ibid.* 80 *Ibid.* This is discussed throughout this article by Rees.

81 *Ibid.* 82 *Ibid.*

83 Of particular relevance to this analysis is the OECD's Harmful Tax Competition project, which was designed ultimately to assist countries who have objected strongly to it. For a discussion of the early experiences of this initiative, see C. M. Radaelli, 'Harmful Tax Competition in the EU: Policy Narratives and Advocacy Coalitions', *Journal of Common Market Studies*, 37 (1999), 661–82. The HTC project aims to 'name and shame' countries who run harmful tax regimes, or tax havens, and to in this sense threaten isolation from global trading and investment opportunities until a structured tax regime is put into place. R. Sanders, 'The Future of Financial Services in the Caribbean' (2002) (at: www.itio.org/documents/Speech-RonaldSanders.pdf, at 1). R. M. Alba, 'Offshore Centres of Latin America and the Caribbean: The Need for a Level Playing Field in the Search for Integrity' (2003) (at: www.freedomandprosperity.org/alba.pdf, at 11).

84 J. C. Sharman, 'Norms, Coercion and Contracting in the Struggle against "Harmful" Tax Competition', *Australian Journal of International Affairs*, 60 (2006), 143–69, at 143–5.

poverty is global trade: if we are all trading with each other, then resources will be spread more equitably.[85] The most significant threat to global trade is tax havens, as, if the proliferation of tax havens continues, the stronger and wealthier countries will simply forbid their traders to invest offshore.[86] This would harm poorer countries, because wealth would stagnate within these countries.[87]

Such developments may be viewed as part of the long and lingering death of the revenue rule,[88] or the principle of international law that dictates that there is no more domestic area of law than taxation. Under the revenue rule, tax law is ultimately only the business of each individual country: only each country may determine its own tax structure, and certainly a country could not be expected to enforce another country's taxes. With the proliferation of double taxation treaties (under models provided by the OECD, the UN and the US), multilateral trade agreements, mutual agreement procedures (MAP) and codes of practice in the EU, among many other initiatives around the world, at the least, it may be observed that countries now help in the enforcement of other countries' taxes, and take an interest in the tax structures.

International organisations charged in some way with tasks of global governance take an interest in taxation, and in the relationship between taxation and poverty. As more women than men live in poverty, the extension of such movements to projects involving women is natural; and, indeed, the OECD has been a strong supporter of gender budgeting.[89] Similarly, as the countries targeted by the HTC project objected to the

85 As discussed throughout R. T. Kudrle, 'The OECD's Harmful Tax Competition Initiative and the Tax Havens: From Bombshell to Damp Squib', *Global Economy Journal*, 8 (2008), 1.

86 Although many of these arguments changed to an anti-terrorism focus, after 11 September 2001. See R. Biswas, *International Tax Competition: Globalisation and Fiscal Sovereignty* (London: Commonwealth Secretariat, 2002), p. 25.

87 See generally M. Littlewood, 'Tax Competition: Harmful To Whom?', *Michigan Journal of International Law*, 26 (2004), 411–87. To stave off this threat, the HTC project aims to stymie this form of ultimately unfair competition. Tax incentives may be one of the only ways in which poorer countries feel they can compete, the argument runs, but this does not make it fair. As discussed in J. G. Salinas, 'The OECD Tax Competition Initiative: A Critique of Its Merits in the Global Marketplace', *Houston Journal of International Law*, 25 (2003), 531–61. The HTC project will be discussed at several points in this book.

88 See generally B. A. Silver, 'Modernizing the Revenue Rule: The Enforcement of Foreign Tax Judgments', *Georgia Journal of International and Comparative Law*, 22 (1992), 609–33, discussing the modern status of the principle that tax law is innately domestic, and no state should have to force foreign tax law.

89 See 'Economics and Finance, Budget Impact Assessments (Gender Budgeting)' (at: www.oecd.org/dataoecd/3/27/1896544.pdf).

way in which the issue was framed by the 'global schoolyard bully'[90] OECD,[91] so women have been taking an interest in how they may be framed by gender budgeting. Although it must be emphasised that gender budgeting is a domestic requirement, and demands dialogue between a government and its taxpayers, with no extension of that dialogue to an international audience, the very existence of that domestic dialogue is the product of a global movement. It is thus important that Runyan has asked: 'how is global governance, in its current stunted form of economic regime building, "framing" women in ways that can undermine feminist struggles?'[92]

Framing

The 'framing' is likely to be cloaked in the aim of the pursuit of 'neutral' tax initiatives. As Budlender *et al.*, explain:

> [f]ew government revenue raising activities are designed on the basis of gender. Indeed many countries have been replacing measures that were regarded as discriminatory with gender-neutral approaches.[93]

The replacement has been occurring as a result of a collection of international initiatives[94] addressing gender and the economy. Indeed, gender budgeting is part of a number of UN initiatives dedicated to gender equality, including the CEDAW, the Beijing Platform of Action, and the Millennium Development Goals.[95] The pace has increased particularly in the last fifteen years, as '[a]fter the Beijing Conference on the status of women in 1995, the impetus to use transnational pressure to implement

90 A. Townsend, Jr., 'Global Schoolyard Bully: The Organisation for Economic Co-Operation and Development's Coercive Efforts to Control Tax Competition', *Fordham International Law Journal*, 25 (2001), 215, at 251–8.

91 See M. Webb, 'Defining the Boundaries of Legitimate State Practice: Norms, Transnational Actors and the OECD's Project on Harmful Tax Competition 1', *Review of International Political Economy*, 11 (2004), 787–827.

92 A. S. Runyan, 'Women in the Neoliberal Frame', in Mary K. Meyer and Elisabeth Prügl (eds.), *Gender Politics in Global Governance* (Lanham, MD: Rowman & Littlefield, 1999).

93 D. Budlender, *et al.*, *How to Do a Gender-sensitive Budget Analysis: Contemporary Research and Practice*, Gender Responsive Budget Initiatives (London: Commonwealth Secretariat, 2002), p. 5.

94 The United Nations' Beijing Platform for Action specifically recommended the integration of gendered perspectives into the budgeting process (Budlender, *et al.*, *How to Do a Gender-sensitive Budget*, at 26).

95 Bakker and Canadian Centre for Policy, 'Gender Budget Initiatives', p. 1.

domestic policy reform through common strategic mechanisms, such as gender budgeting, spread around the world'.[96]

CEDAW contains the requirement that there should be 'incentives in the field of social security and tax incentives in order to promote hiring for indefinite periods and job stability'.[97] Additionally, CEDAW provides for '[g]rants allocated to non-governmental organizations both by the Institute [for Women's Issues] and using the income tax collected [to] provide ... for ... programmes for immigrant victims of trafficking in women'.[98] These are clear movements beyond auditing – do we have a problem? – to an acknowledgement that problems exist (in job security for women, and in trafficking and exploitation), and that funding is appropriate. That gender budgeting has been paired with this investment indicates a suspicion of more deeply rooted, or less obvious, difficulties; i.e., a suspicion that problems will be detected, but it will be appropriate to require individual states to fund the solutions themselves.

Will these difficulties really be found to be that deeply rooted, however, or difficult to detect? Indeed, is it possible that gender budgeting will provoke an unnecessary delay in addressing such problems, and that its very auditing requirements will only be effected by wasting resources which will be needed later? A double-handed approach of contemporaneous investment and inquiry is clearly needed, and indeed: 'the Commission has highlighted the need to redress gender inequalities as an integral part of the Community's development policy. To do so, it promotes a twin track approach for women's empowerment and mainstreaming gender equality.'[99]

One element of the 'framing' of women that may be evident at this point is a suggestion that women's economic equality, while desirable, is perhaps uniquely difficult to achieve (perhaps even for reasons that are 'hidden', and will only become evident after the establishment of 'special' auditing procedures). An alternative explanation is that the causes of gender economic inequality are not necessarily hidden, or difficult to detect, but are deep rooted, and ultimately the excuses for their existence

96 Tetyana Pudrovska and Myra Marx Ferree, 'Global Activism in "Virtual Space": The European Women's Lobby in the Network of Transnational Women's NGOs on the Web', *Social Politics*, 11 (2004), 117–43, at 122.

97 CEDAW, p. 17, s. 2.1, 'Legislation on Employment'.

98 CEDAW, p. 37, Art. 6, 'Elimination of the Exploitation of Women'.

99 OECD, 'European Community (2007), DAC Peer Review: Main Findings and Recommendations', 2007) (at: www.oecd.org/document/0/0,3343,en_2649_34603_38897408_1_1_1_1,00.html).

are easier to service than the calls for change.[100] Gender budgeting could be about removing these excuses, and making it less easy to maintain the status quo, and ignore calls for change. If this is the case, then a heavy-handed approach would be appropriate (if one is not going to act directly, then an indirect approach should at least be overwhelming), and evidence of what might be described as a heavy-handed approach does exist. For example, Lombardo explains that '[g]ender budgeting has been introduced in the guidelines of the European Structural Funds 2002–2006, together with a review of the gender dimensions of the tax/benefit systems in EU countries'.[101]

Additional evidence includes a public hearing which was held on gender budgeting in the European Parliament on 23 January 2003.[102] This hearing included reports on gender-budgeting projects that already existed at that point in both the Spanish Basque country and in Genoa, and concluded that the evidence from these regions was sufficiently positive that it justified an extension of gender budgeting throughout the EU. Thus, in July 2003, the European Parliament passed a resolution on gender budgeting, requiring that, among other things, 'Member States ... monitor and analyse the impacts of macroeconomic and economic reform policies on women and men, and the development of strategies, mechanisms and corrective measures to address gender imbalances in key areas, with the aim of creating a broader economic and social framework in which gender budgeting could be positively implemented'.[103] This language is very wide-reaching, and indicates the hope that gender budgeting would be incorporated into every level of government within Member States.

The European Parliament also produced a report on gender budgeting, which called, in particular, for:

100 Direct challenge of discrimination against women through tax and spending systems, even if the discrimination could be described as unintentional, has been occurring in the courts for a number of years now. The case of *Vergani*, for example, held that Italian law which discriminates against women in terms of the taxation of pension payments was forbidden by European law. *Vergani* v. *Agenzia delle Entrate Ufficio di Arona* (C207/04) [2006] All ER (EC) 813; [2005] ECR I-7453; [2006] 1 CMLR 5; [2006] CEC 96.

101 Emanuela Lombardo, 'Integrating or Setting the Agenda? Gender Mainstreaming in the European Constitution-Making Process', *Social Politics*, 12 (2005), 412–32, at 421–2.

102 'Gender Budgeting – The Gender Perspective in the Public Budgets', 23 January 2003, Public Hearing, Brussels, Chairperson, Anna Karamanou (at: www.europarl.europa.eu/hearings/20030123/femm/programme_en.pdf).

103 European Parliament Resolution on Gender Budgeting – Building Public Budgets from a Gender Perspective (2002/2198(INI)) (2003), at para. 12 (posted online at: www.europarl.europa.eu).

> an analysis of the impact of public expenditure measures on time use (the aim is to consider the implications of budgetary policies for unpaid work, social reproduction activities, domestic work, family and community care, etc., in respect of which 'time budgets' must be drawn up making it possible to assess the real living conditions of individuals and families in order to determine adequate measures in terms of resources and services to be made available through budgetary policies).[104]

This is very ambitious language, as it involves calls for integration of the paid and unpaid economy. Women far outnumber men in the latter, and this is a clear cause of economic inequality.[105] The establishment of 'time budgets' at the least will achieve public acknowledgement of the fact that, although men on the whole earn more than women, it is not because women do not work. Rather, women labour, far more extensively than men, in the unpaid economy.

From framing, to the framework: gender budgeting in the EU, and how we got from there to here

The unpaid economy could be described as a collection of some of the institutions upon which, under Polanyi's analysis, the market depends for its existence and form. The EU has attempted to quantify these institutions, in an (equally ambitious) 'Roadmap for equality between women and men'.[106] Beveridge predicted the potential role of gender budgeting in 'roadmapping' initiatives:

> [i]n the Roadmap initiatives such as gender budgeting are aimed as much at national and local authorities as at the Community's own budget. This is a significant development, given the vital role which Member States play in the implementation of Commission initiatives. This new focus on Member State behaviour is accompanied by a gradual evolution in the role of the Commission from instigator to facilitator/evaluator.[107]

That the budgeting process has been targeted as the forum within which the Commission will begin this evolution is not accidental. Neither is the use of an auditing procedure as part of process which involves the

104 (16 June 2003) 'Report on Gender Budgeting on Gender Budgeting – Building Public Budgets from a Gender Perspective' (A5–0214/2003), European Parliament Session Document, at 17 (posted online at: www.europarl.europa.eu).

105 Discussed throughout J. C. Gornick, 'Gender Equality in the Labour Market: Women's Employment and Earnings', *Gender and Welfare State Regimes*, (1999), 210–42.

106 See description on the EUROPA website (at: http://ec.europa.eu/employment_social/esf/news/article_6917_en.htm).

107 Beveridge, 'Building against the Past'.

Commission redefining the way in which it chooses to exercise its power. One historical precedent for this involves the introduction of the Eurostat agency, which provided a monitoring function of Member States for entry into the European Monetary Union, and created a significant amount of power at an EU level through the auditing process – power that extended to influencing the domestic budgetary processes of Member States.[108]

Eurostat may have involved a *redefinition* of the Commission's power, but it also involved an *empowerment* of the Commission. The situation is likely to be different with gender budgeting, as the auditing function is delegated to each Member State. It is clear that '[l]ocal and regional authorities should use the gender-budgeting technique when drawing up draft budgets for sports facilities and planning sports provision'.[109] The European Parliament has supported the Commission at each stage of the gender-budgeting process; and, indeed, could even be described as the instigator. In fact the EU Parliament issued a reprimand to the Commission in 2003, for not moving the process along more quickly.[110] The reprimand was acknowledged, and things moved quite quickly in the next five years. By 2006, gender budgeting was carried along on the flow of the emerging Roadmap. The Roadmap, released in March 2006, operates on a wide scale.[111] It covers the 2006–10 period, and is designed to influence all 'internal and external' policies of the

108 J. D. Savage, *Making the EMU: The Politics of Budgetary Surveillance and the Enforcement of Maastricht* (Oxford University Press, 2005), pp. 5–8.

109 Opinion of the Committee of the Regions on 'Equal opportunities and sport', OJ C 305, 15/12/2007, at p. 53, para. 20.

110 '[European Parliament] [r]eiterates its request to the Commission made in its resolution of 3 July 2003 on gender budgeting and regrets that the discharge report does not give it the possibility to assess the impact of the budget from a gender perspective; regrets the lack of budgetary data concerning funding allocated to the promotion of gender equality in the context of different budget lines'. Resolution of the European Parliament with comments forming an integral part of the decision on the discharge for implementation of the European Union general budget for the financial year 2004, Section III – Commission, OJ L 340, Celex No. 506BP1206(01), 06/12/2006, at p. 5.

111 'The roadmap outlines six priority areas for EU action on gender equality: equal economic independence for women and men, an area in which the SF [Structural Funds] are contributing to achieving the Lisbon employment targets; reconciliation of work and private life; equal representation in decision-making in politics, economics and science and technology; eradication of gender-based violence and trafficking; eliminating gender stereotypes in society; and promotion of gender equality in external and development objectives. The roadmap is designed to improve governance by exploring the possibilities to develop gender budgeting at EU level, particularly in the Structural Funds within the possibilities of shared management for the new period' (Commission staff working document – Annex to the Report from the Commission – 18th Annual Report on Implementation of the Structural Funds (2006), EU: SEC (2007) 1456, Celex No. 507SC1456).

Commission.[112] The driving force behind the Roadmap is what could be described as the success of gender mainstreaming.[113]

From the trend of global governance through tax, to the trend of gender-focused initiatives in the EU, gender budgeting might be described as a convergence. Indeed, gender budgeting has been referred to as part of a 'trend' in which 'administrations ... treat gender mainstreaming in an "à la carte" fashion'.[114] Also included in this 'trend', with gender budgeting, are the production of gender disaggregated statistics, and the use of gender impact assessment methods.[115] Yet, above all, '[g]ender budgeting aims to produce a budget in which gender has been "mainstreamed" by analyzing public expenditure and methods of raising public revenue from a gender perspective and identifying the implications for women as compared to men'.[116] Once these implications have been identified, doing something about them will be the next big step.

The search for embeddedness: gender budgeting as an auditing process

Gender budgeting has been criticised as a repackaging of political feminism in a perhaps more palatable and manageable way – at worst, as a way of neutralising claims by women that perhaps had been put forth in a political arena for thirty or forty years, and had become increasingly difficult to ignore. Walby in particular has warned that gender budgeting 'involves the reinvention, restructuring, and rebranding of a key part of feminism in the contemporary era'.[117] She acknowledges, however, that it is also something new – a new way of pursuing political goals, and providing ammunition to debates that, again, had been occurring for a

112 *Ibid.*

113 This is a success which was predicted, with reservations, by C. McCrudden, who wrote in 1998: '[m]ainstreaming is an idea whose time has come, but whose meaning is uncertain and subject to varying interpretations' ('Mainstreaming Equality in the Governance of Northern Ireland', *Fordham International Law Journal*, 22 (1998), 1696–1775, at 1698–9).

114 Mary Daly, 'Gender Mainstreaming in Theory and Practice', *Social Politics*, 12 (2005), 433–50, at 436.

115 Daly, 'Gender Mainstreaming'.

116 Lombardo, 'Integrating or Setting', at 422. D. Budlender explains that '[e]xpenditure analysis ... covers three aspects – gender-specific expenditures; expenditures which promote gender equity within the public service; and all other mainstream expenditures' ('The South African Women's Budget Initiative', 24–6 March 1999, at http://iggi.unesco.or.kr/web/iggi_docs/02/952310746.pdf, at 5).

117 Walby, 'Gender Mainstreaming', at 321. Indeed the entire process of gender mainstreaming has been criticised as an attempt to 'buy off once committed activists' (Baden and Goetz, 'Who Needs [Sex]', at 6, describing a Philippines-based pamphlet protesting against the issue of gender mainstreaming as advanced at the 1995 Beijing conference).

long time.[118] As such, '[i]t is both a new form of gendered political and policy practice and a new gendered strategy for theory development'.[119]

Gender budgeting represents a hard-won victory for lobbying networks. Internationally, the battle for gender budgeting is not complete. It has yet to be adopted in the US, and activists are working to change this.[120] It is important not to dismiss gender budgeting as a palliative offered, without potential for more, from governments that are not disinterested. It is equally important, however, not to allow the fact that gender budgeting is a hard-won, political victory to function as protection against further inquiry. Inquiry, after all, is within the nature of the initiative itself.

It is not clear what kinds of 'accountability' are endorsed with gender budgeting.[121] The perceived audience also is unclear: who, for the purposes of gender budgeting, constitutes the 'public'?[122] Are the statistics being produced by gender budgeting intended to provide tools for politicians, or for a wider audience? Additionally, even the most sympathetic politician to the cause of gender equality may find that statistics are not a powerful enough tool to effect real change. Finally, accountability processes only result in information of real value when the participants are sufficiently impartial. Can a politician ever become truly impartial, given the practical necessity of operating within the political process?

Gender budgeting assumes its place within a host of auditing initiatives that have been introduced throughout the EU – perhaps most relevantly, including environmental audit.[123] This would appear to present a classic, and parallel, example of a process within which a government could have produced information with the purpose of dispelling further inquiry and

118 The political history of tax credits in the UK is discussed in A. Mumford, 'Marketing Working Mothers: Contextualizing Earned Income Tax Credits within Feminist Cultural Theory', *Journal of Social Welfare and Family Law*, 23 (2001), 411–26.

119 Walby, 'Gender Mainstreaming'.

120 Indeed, writing of the US, R. Copelon has argued starkly that '[g]ender-mainstreaming, gender analysis, and gender budgeting would make a difference if adopted as domestic policy' ('International Human Rights Dimensions of Intimate Violence: Another Strand in the Dialectic of Feminist Lawmaking', *American University Journal of Gender, Social Policy and the Law*, 11 (2003), 865–76, at 874.

121 Condon and Philipps in particular have stressed that '[i]t is important to interrogate the new standards to determine how the "public" is conceived for this purpose and what forms of accountability are being promoted' ('Transnational Market Governance', at 139).

122 *Ibid.*

123 See M. Power, 'Auditing and Environmental Expertise: Between Protest and Professionalisation', *Accounting, Auditing and Accountability Journal*, 4 (1991), 30–42.

criticism, and little more. Even if an auditing process (such as gender budgeting, even if it is seldom described as such) is structured along these lines, it does not necessarily follow that the process will be completely without value.

For example, Power has explained that the process of environmental audit may be viewed simply as a form of protest.[124] Gender budgeting also may have value as acknowledgement from the state that women are entitled to a public response to economic inequality. Interestingly, Power has also suggested that these forms of public audit may be constructed within a classic framework of economic agency.[125] Power's effort to move standard, 1970s agency theory away from the corporation and into the venue of government is striking, but also ripe with potential; for, as he argues, this approach 'throws into sharp relief the dimension of accountability and problematises the processes, such as contracting, which bind "agents" to "principals"'.[126] A standard principle of agency theory is that the way in which inferior or subordinate agents of a business interacts with 'principals' or senior managers will influence greatly the behaviour of the firm.[127] The relations which bind 'agents' to 'principals', or that bind MPs to the Treasury, are open to analysis from a Polanyian perspective. Indeed, the act of and the methods employed within auditing are important – 'the idea of audit is important and provides a reminder that definitions are attempts to fix a practice within a particular set of norms or ideals'.[128] European environmental audit has become a process which is both employed and criticised.[129] Gender budgeting may not fully address gender economic inequality, but that does not mean that it will not produce outcomes of value.[130]

124 *Ibid.* 125 *Ibid.* 126 *Ibid.*, at 39.

127 Agency theory, as developed in the 1970s, analysed the variety of ways in which agents, linked by contractual arrangements with a firm, seek to influence the firm's behaviour. See generally, K. M. Eisenhardt, 'Agency Theory: An Assessment and Review', *Academy of Management Review*, 14(1) (1989), 57–74.

128 M. Power, *The Audit Society: Rituals of Verification* (Oxford University Press, 1997), at p. 5.

129 See, among others: K. Clement, 'Environmental Auditing for Industry: A European Perspective', *European Environment*, 1(3) (1991), 1–4; A. Jordan and A. Lenschow, '"Greening" the European Union: What Can Be Learned from the "Leaders" of EU Environmental Policy?', *European Environment*, 10 (2000), 109–20; J. Franke, 'Political Evolution of EMAS: Perspectives from the EU, National Governments and Industrial Groups', *European Environment*, 5 (1995), 155–9.

130 The point is that, although criticised, environmental audit, in the context described, has been valuable.

The objectives of environmental audit involve identifying the perhaps unintended impact of all activities of government upon the environment. Gender budgeting is both more limited in scope, because it only considers expenditure on social programmes through the Budget, and, yet, in a way, more ambitious, because of its target of inquiry. This pact does not involve a homogeneous society any more than it involves a homogeneous government, speaking with only one voice. Indeed gender budgeting is predicated on the assumption of dissent in politics. The role of the market activist, and the concomitant concern about how much market regulation could, or should, encourage those in pursuit of profit to refocus on the pursuit of gender equality instead is another Polanyian concern.[131] The analytical separation of the market economy from other institutions reveals a much more complicated question than a choice between profit, or gender equity. Indeed, jobs themselves may be gendered, and '[a] woman who accepts a "male" job arguably creates a disutility, in terms of her identity, since this is not "what woman commonly do," if one assumes the "traditional" identity of women to be preferable'.[132]

Which institutions, then, within or without the market, should be analysed? The Budget is not targeted at any gender, specifically, nor will it be after gender budgeting.[133] As an objective of gender budgeting is the promotion of an understanding, or a 'cognizance' of gender relations,[134] the process itself would appear to admit that it can be difficult to identify which aspects of society are 'gendered'. Given that a plausible answer might include '*all* aspects', other forms, perhaps a proliferation of auditing processes will need to accompany gender budgeting.[135] Proponents of gender budgeting thus concede that more questions need to be asked, beyond the (nonetheless powerful) forum of the Budget itself, and a Polanyian analysis would need to consider all of these attendant processes

131 Jon Gunnar Bernburg stresses that 'Polanyi is convinced that modern economic motives, realized in profit-seeking individuals, are the creation of the decoupling of the market economy from other social institutions' ('Anomie, Social Change and Crime: A Theoretical Examination of Institutional-Anomie Theory', *British Journal of Criminology*, 42 (2002), 729–39, at 734).

132 Patrik Aspers *et al.*, 'An Economic Sociological Look at Economics' (March 2008) 9 *Economic Sociology: European Electronic Newsletter*, at 10.

133 Sharp, 'Budgeting for Equality', at 25.

134 Budlender *et al.*, *How to Do a Gender-sensitive Budget*, s. 2, p. 1.

135 As M. Sawer writes, '[i]deally it is combined with other forms of gender audit integrated into routine auditing processes' ('Women's Ministries: An Australian Perspective', *Feminist Review*, 63 (1999), 91–4, at 93).

before clear next steps for planning a non-gendered economy could be mooted.

Gender budgeting represents a search for embeddedness, through a reliance on auditing processes. The institution of gender budgeting throughout the EU is in many ways a success of the process of gender mainstreaming.[136] One of the achievements of gender mainstreaming is that gender budgeting involves 'how (not whether)' gender equality should be taken into account in the budgeting process.[137] Gender, thus, has gone mainstream. Gender budgeting also reflects another achievement of gender mainstreaming, that gender economic disparity is taken as a given – there is no expectation that gender budgeting will reveal that more money has been spent on women than men. This is an important starting point: the acknowledgement that men both earn more money than women, and have more money spent on them.

At a basic level, gender mainstreaming involved a successful amendment of ongoing social discourse, in that gender is no longer discussed separately from the economy. The embeddedness of which Polanyi spoke has been acknowledged. Additionally, although gender budgeting is 'limited' to the Budget, and will depend upon other forms of audit, the analysis of budget that is recommended is expansive – a scope which also owes a debt both to gender mainstreaming, and to the examples presented by approaches that have been adopted in other countries.[138]

Obviously everything for which the Budget pays is fair game for gender-budgeting analysis. The extent of analysis is limited by the connection of the subject to the Budget – childcare, for example, demands significant consideration of issues within the unpaid market, or the private sphere, but these issues are not necessarily within the scope of gender budgeting. How, thus, is it possible to address a subject like childcare only within the confines of the paid economy? Himmelweit,[139] a leading figure in the UK

136 J. Rubery *et al.*, 'Gender Equality Still on the European Agenda – But for How Long?', *Industrial Relations Journal*, 24 (2003), 477–97, at 480.

137 Walby, 'Gender Mainstreaming', at 332.

138 For example it has been explained that, in Australia, gender budgeting involves the consideration of many different aspects of government and finance: '[w]omen's wages, employment, education and training, aged income support, childcare, and the gendered aspects of taxation and poverty traps arising out of interaction of the tax-benefit systems were major areas of public debate during the implementation of the Australian gender budgets' (Sharp, 'Budgeting for Equality', at 35).

139 Prof. Susan Himmelweit, Professor of Economics (Open University), a former chair of the WBG.

gender-budgeting movement, identified four, main objectives of gender budgeting:

> (1) Develop analysis and lead debate on the gender implications of economic policy; (2) Expand understanding among policy makers and opinion formers of the gender implications of economic policy and give policy advice; (3) Promote gender mainstreaming in economic policy making and presentation; and (4) Monitor progress to hold government accountable for the gender effects of its policies.[140]

The first principle could perhaps be characterised as a hope, such that if information about disparate gender impacts is publicised, then it is likely that public debate will follow. It also challenges the traditional internal–external distinction within auditing discourse.[141] An internal audit is intended to inform only management, who perhaps might wish for privacy concerning information that might be damaging to it. The process of gender budgeting is similar to internal audit, in that the government in effect is auditing itself, but it is auditing itself for external consumption.[142] This impacts upon the relationship between government and taxpayer, and perhaps casts both in different roles. Certainly, it may no longer be accurate to describe taxpayers as consumers, or as 'the regulated', in this relationship. In one sense the taxpayer has been elevated to the level of agent.

In another sense, however, while the taxpayer will be given potentially useful information about, for example, childcare, this information is given within a relationship which has very different levels of power, and in a remarkably fluid way – all, of course, depending upon perspective. If the perspective includes a single mother living in poverty, then the difference in power between her and the government is dramatically uneven. While an increase in government expenditure in, for example, childcare might improve her position, it is difficult to imagine how information about gender impact expenditure analysis, and even the resulting debate, will assist (although it is interesting to note that this woman is likely to be

140 Himmelweit, 'Experience of the UK WBG', at slide 4.

141 See discussion of this in K. Hollingsworth *et al.*, 'Audit, Accountability and Independence: The Role of the Audit Commission', *Legal Studies*, 18 (1998), 78–99.

142 M. J. Graetz argued that a progressive consumption tax presented a way of preserving the benefits of progressivity, while avoiding the difficulties of taxing income ('Implementing a Progressive Consumption Tax', *Harvard Law Review*, 92 (1979), 1575–1659). In Graetz's hypothesis, the group of taxpayers most likely to suffer were the elderly, although he suggests remedies for this (*ibid.*, at 1657).

the subject of a great deal of discussion within both the analysis and the debate).[143]

Himmelweit's third and fourth principles, the promotion of gender mainstreaming and the monitoring of government, have led to successes in other countries, especially when combined with parallel strategies. Thus, Denmark, for example, has examined gender budgeting as part of specific poverty reduction strategies in Tanzania, Bolivia, Vietnam and Mozambique.[144] Gender budgeting holds specific promise in the arena of poverty reduction, generally. Certainly, women, and their children, comprise the largest segment of the UK population to live in poverty, and this fact appears inextricably linked with powerlessness.[145]

Gender budgeting aims to redefine the relationship between taxpayer and government, which is perceived differently according to the gender of the taxpayer. Money and power are almost equal in analysis of gender budgeting, and the hope is to give women taxpayers more of both. With money comes power, and thus gender budgeting (as indicated in the third and fourth point, above) concerns itself with direct allocations of both. As a consequence, gender-budgeting analysis tends not to embrace indirect taxes, such as VAT, on the grounds that there 'is no perceived need' to address the impact of such revenue neutral taxes.[146]

143 Nonetheless, as J. Rubery warns, '[i]t remains ... clear that the full implications of a commitment to promoting general equality and gender mainstreaming have not been understood; it is not just a question of allowing women access to the labour market but also a question of changing and indeed transforming the economic and social structures underpinning the labour market system' ('Gender Mainstreaming and Gender Equality in the EU: The Impact of the EU Employment Strategy', *Industrial Relations Journal* 33 (2002), 500–22, at 517). This is where Himmelweit's second objective becomes important, in that policy makers will be less able to describe efforts to assist such women as sufficient, when faced with stark numbers suggesting otherwise.

144 See E. Bell, 'Gender and PRSPs: With Experiences from Tanzania, Bolivia, Viet Nam and Mozambique', in BRIDGE Report (development–gender) (prepared for the Ministry of Foreign Affairs, Denmark, March 2003). [PRSPs stands for Poverty Reduction Strategy Papers.]

145 It is for this reason that Himmelweit has posited that there are four specific arguments in favour of gender analysis: '(1) Men and women [are] in structurally different positions in the economy (a result of existing inequalities)[,] [t]herefore policy affects women and men differently; (2) All policies will be improved and better targeted if their differential effects are known (efficiency); (3) Such knowledge will enable policies to be chosen that lessen rather than exacerbate existing inequalities or if the latter that other policies are put in place to counteract the worsening of inequalities (equity); and (4) Requires knowledge of existing inequalities' ('Experience of the UK WBG', at slide 6).

146 Budlender *et al.*, *How to Do a Gender-sensitive Budget*, at 74.

As Himmelweit[147] provided a driving force behind the enactment of gender budgeting, her explanations of the process, and even her publicity for what can be expected of gender budgeting, are important indicators of the potential place of this practice within the political process, and the economy. The effects of the budgeting process on individuals and families may be quantifiable, but the interaction of 'gender differentials' and economic incentives, 'gender norms', the unpaid economy, and a lifetime perspective of budgeting and gender are enormously ambitious. Great expectations have been placed on this process.

The expectations, however, are not without limitations, not least because this process is set to occur within the complicated arena of the state.[148] But there is reason to be optimistic: there is material with which to work,[149] and there are plans to take the processes forward.[150] Concerns have centred on the experience in Australia, where budgeting has been reported as less than a complete success. Sawer writes that '[i]t became more a public relations exercise than a longitudinal analysis of progress in improving gender equity in design and delivery of mainstream policy and programs'.[151] She is more optimistic about the prospects for success in the UK and Europe, given that 'the weakness [in Australia] caused by lack of parliamentary oversight has been addressed in new overseas versions of gender budgeting'.[152]

147 From Himmelweit's four main objectives of gender budgeting, to her four arguments in favour of gender to, now, her five principles underpinning the gender budgeting process: '(1) Analyse effects on both individuals and families; (2) Understand gender differentials in response to economic incentives; (3) Consider impact on gender norms and roles; (4) Extend analysis to unpaid, caring economy; and (5) Take a lifetime perspective' ('Experience of the UK WBG', at slide 7).

148 As Walby has explained, '[t]he State is a contested arena, with a mix of coherence and contradiction among a set of core institutions and complex linkages to other political and non-political domains' ('Gender Mainstreaming', at 338).

149 Himmelweit presented the outcome of a gender analysis of the working families' tax credit (WFTC) (as it was then called) by way of example. Such an analysis reveals three main problems: '(1) Household means-testing provides disincentive to second earner; (2) Mitigated somewhat by childcare subsidies for those who use paid childcare, but this paid to "main earner"; and (3) Supplement for a full-time earner provides disincentive to sharing paid work and are within couples' ('Experience of the UK WBG', slide 8).

150 Himmelweit suggested that there are four points to address, in order to take gender budgeting forward: '(1) Not necessary to do everything at once; (2) Capacity building takes time; (3) Can focus on particular areas (not necessarily the most obviously gendered ones); and (4) International experience suggests best done as a partnership between government, auditors and outside experts (from NGOs)' ('Experience of the UK WBG', at slide 14).

151 Sawer, 'Women's Ministries', at 93.

152 Sawer, 'Women's Ministries'.

The importance of politics to taxation is often ignored, in a maelstrom of lawyers engaged with rules, economists concerned with efficiency, and scholars of government concerned with administration.[153] 'As a result', Karran has argued, 'there is a tendency to ignore the political determinants of taxation policy'.[154] A political victory of the international gender-budgeting movement is that the welfare of women in different (autonomous) countries becomes more important with the spread of globalisation. The reasons for this are that, first, a veneer of equality and fair treatment makes a country more attractive as a partner in trade, especially if women in one country will object to the treatment of women elsewhere (and attempt to influence trade as a manner of protest). Gender equity can be good business. Second, if treating women unfairly in some way upsets the paid marketplace (by depriving it of the support of unpaid labour), then that country will prove an unstable participant in global trade.

The World Bank report on gender budgeting identified the three categories into which legislatures may fall: first, legislatures which may fashion their own budgets, or accept budgetary proposals, of their own accord (such as the US Congress); second, legislatures which may adopt or decline proposals, but may not devise their own (the majority of legislatures); and, finally, legislatures that cannot substantively amend executive proposals or fashion their own, but may simply accept or decline proposals (the Westminster model: UK, Canada, Australia, and others).[155] In reality there are few constitutional bars on the UK Parliament's capacity to devise its own Budget. The Westminster model is, rather, a matter of political science. What these three categories have in common is the fact that budgeting policies become deep-rooted.

The next step after an initial year of gender budgeting in the UK will involve calls to reform the Budget such that gender equality is promoted, or calls to use the Budget to tackle barriers to gender equality within the market. Some responses will argue that the market is too biased to ever promote gender equality. These arguments also however counter the value of gender budgeting in the first place. Other responses, particularly those that support gender budgeting, will try to find ways to enforce gender equality within the market, or to fashion a materialist feminist theory.

153 T. Karran, 'The Determinants of Taxation in Britain: An Empirical Test', *Journal of Public Policy*, 5 (1985), 365–86, at 366.

154 Karran, 'Determinants'.

155 As identified in Alex Brazier, 'The Fiscal Maze: Parliament, Government and Public Money' (16 March 2007) 60 *Parliamentary Affairs* (*Hansard Society*) 346–55, at 347.

Gender and the embedded economy: a new focus on materialist feminist theory

Materialist feminist theory, as developed in English and French academic journals in earnest in the early1980s, is a bit of a hybrid, seeking to benefit from the strengths of competing schools of feminism.[156] Boyd argued that 'a materialist feminist theory must incorporate the strengths of Marxist feminism and the strengths of postmodernist feminism'.[157] By the end of the twentieth century, materialist feminism had been identified as a growing trend, particularly (and perhaps surprisingly) in the US. This was a remarkable development, as compared, say, with the UK or Canada, given the predominant focus given by materialist feminist theory with economic class structure. Thus, Boyd argued that '[t]he new materialist feminist literature emerging from the United States is particularly interesting given the relative lack of attention to class relations historically in academia in the United States (in contrast to the UK and Canada, where somewhat more attention has been paid to the Marxist tradition) and given general moves everywhere towards "postsocialist" politics'.[158] Materialist feminist theory represents a combining of gender relations with economic relations.[159] A combination of class with gender, and of both with tax and the economy, was never going to be easy. This, however, is exactly what gender budgeting requires. The reasons for this difficulty are, first, that analyses of class and gender are strained – Gottfried writes of the 'unhappy marriage of feminism and Marxism'[160] – and, second, analyses of tax law, in particular, have resisted Marxian perspectives (in no small part due to the views of Marx himself on the relative lack of importance of tax).[161] If arguments promoting gender equality start with

156 For an example of such controversy, see Delphy and Leonard, 'Materialist Feminism'.

157 S. Boyd, 'Family, Law and Sexuality: Feminist Engagements', *Social and Legal Studies*, 8 (1999), 369–90, at 370.

158 *Ibid.*, at 371.

159 Dolan suggested that materialist feminism resulted from an influx of 'British materialism, with its focus on ideology formation in representation' into American feminist theory in the 1980s, which at that point was heavily influenced by cultural studies ('Defense of the Discourse', at 58–9ff.).

160 Heidi Gottfried, 'Beyond Patriarchy? Theorising Gender and Class', *Sociology*, 32 (2000), 451–68, at 451.

161 Marx viewed tax as a necessary evil, or tide over, during the economic revolution, and thus did not write much about tax – a point made by R. Musgrave, 'Theories of Fiscal Crises: An Essay in Fiscal Sociology', in H. J. Aaron and M. J. Boskins (eds.), *The Economics of Taxation* (Washington, DC: Brookings Institution, 1980), pp. 316–90, at p. 361. The significance of this for tax lawyers is discussed in Mumford, 'Towards a Fiscal Sociology'. Marx, additionally, was 'all but silent on the subject of women in his writings'

the premise that the market is the most significant proponent of inequality, then arguments proceed to challenging, or dismantling the market, as opposed to regulating it. For gender budgeting to succeed, regulatory theory must inform theories of gender equality.[162]

The embedded economy and regulatory theory: what next for the market economy?

If the market is the problem, then efforts to combat or modify it also might produce the difficulty that its worst excesses are ignored, or even seized as evidence of its overall lack of fitness – but, ultimately, left unchecked. Both Durkheim and Polanyi 'are concerned with the social consequences of the unchecked market',[163] and it is to Polanyi, in particular, that this chapter will now turn, given the relevance of his work with the embeddedness of economies to questions of gender equality and the market. In particular, this chapter will consider whether Polanyi's thesis of the 'disembedded market economy'[164] explains the difficulty encountered thus far by efforts to incorporate gender equality within markets. As gender budgeting operates on the premise that identifying gender disparities in the budgeting process is the first step towards remedying inequality, this chapter suggests that identifying the assumptions that have obstructed feminist objectives from merging with theories of (class and) market egalitarianism is the next step towards enabling gender budgeting's remarkable and laudable objectives to succeed.

The work of Karl Polanyi is an ideal starting point for investigations of the assumptions that persist within the market economy. One of the founding fathers of twentieth-century economic sociology, Polanyi's work, most famously *The Great Transformation*,[165] studied the history of what he described as the self-regulating market, especially (but not exclusively) as related to the Industrial Revolution.[166] A theme of *The Great Transformation* is that there is a difference between economies which *host* markets, and what might he described as self-regulating markets

(Rae Lesser Blumberg, 'A General Theory of Gender Stratification', *Sociological Theory*, 2 (1984), 23–101, at 33).

162 On the challenges of regulation and tax law, generally, see M. Burton, 'Responsive Regulation and the Uncertainty of Tax Law', *eJournal of Tax Research*, 5 (July 2007), 71–104.

163 Bernburg, 'Anomie', at 733.

164 See discussion throughout Bernburg, 'Anomie' of the concept developed in Polanyi, *Great Transformation*.

165 Polanyi, *Great Transformation*.

166 See *ibid.*, pp. x, 7, 3–40, 76–7ff.

(such as existed in the nineteenth century, and collapsed with the Industrial Revolution).[167] According to Polanyi, markets provide for the sale and trading of goods, and enable social interactions and relationships. Self-regulating markets, however, involve a network of different markets across all of society. Everything that is contributed to the markets is for sale, and (a subtle point) the profit from the sale of these contributions, or inputs, is strictly exchanged for the outputs of the market processes. The exchange is perfect, so the market regulates itself – hence, the self-regulating market, which is an almost perfect market model, and cannot survive. Humanity needs more to survive than market exchange – including, for example social relationships – so humans were always going to interact with each other for reasons *other* than market exchange.[168] Each of these interactions is a potential distraction from the self-regulating market.

An essential theme of Polanyi's work is that it is necessary to challenge suggestions that it is natural for humans to organise trade into markets (and that the by-products of this 'natural' organisation are inevitable). Some things are natural, and others are not. Consider, by way of example, Polanyi's analysis of the question of the division of labour along lines of gender. As he wrote, '[d]ivision of labor, a phenomenon as old as society, springs from differences inherent in the facts of sex, geography, and individual endowment; and the alleged propensity of man to barter, truck and exchange is almost entirely apocryphal'.[169] Division of labour may be a 'natural' occurrence, but not for reasons to do with the market. Indeed, labour can be separated from the market. Humans will divide work according to ability, location or gender, but it does not necessarily follow that the work will include the organised trade or sale of materials or services for profit.

What is the importance of this suggestion? Nicholson suggests that the value of Polanyi's work is that 'while it is true that all societies must satisfy the needs of biology to stay alive, it is only true of modern society that the satisfaction of some of these needs in ever increasing amounts becomes a central motive of action'.[170] What does this mean? The most important reason for what has been described as women's 'sexual'

167 *Ibid.*, ch. VI.

168 See discussion of the self-regulating market throughout *ibid.*, ch. I, 'The Hundred Years' Peace'.

169 *Ibid.*, p. 44.

170 L. Nicholson, 'Feminism and Marx: Integrating Kinship with the Economic', *Praxis International*, 4 (1985), 367–80, at 371.

inequality[171] is their relative economic inequality.[172] Marx's fundamental argument is that it is important for people who were not in power to seek to control the means of economic production,[173] but Polanyi moves a step beyond this,[174] and acknowledges the profound importance of the development of what might be described as the 'rational economic man'.[175]

Economic rationality – defined as the assumption that every human organises behaviour so as to make the most money, collect the most goods – was challenged by Polanyi.[176] Indeed Polanyi's work is in many ways a reaction against Spencer's application of Darwinian survivalist principles to the economic sphere, in that not every human interaction hosted by the market is motivated by profit. Polanyi's work also contributed to the European liberal feminist literature of the 1970s, which suggested that, unlike the tenets of Marxist feminism, gender is more than an economic class. This literature would appear to have strongly informed the late twentieth-century, materialist feminist analyses of class and gender, and also would have promise for the incorporating, blending aims of that genre. If, as Boyd argued, the strengths of Marxist and postmodern feminism should be combined, fuller understanding of the embeddedness of markets could contribute to this process.

The concept of the 'embeddedness of markets' is perhaps the most famous of Polanyi's contributions to economic sociology. In work described as 'prophetic',[177] Polanyi described the embeddedness of the market to other, vital aspects of the human experience, which also, conversely, are responsible for the existence of the market itself.[178] He explained that 'markets for commodities call for highly sophisticated institutional arrangements for their coordination, if their efficiency and self-adjusting property are to be obtained in really existing economies'.[179] The modern market is not self-regulating, but is supported by social relations and institutions (institutions, as understood within a Durkheimian

171 Understood as their relative lack of power, in all aspects of society, as compared to men.

172 Blumberg, 'General Theory', at 25. 173 *Ibid.*

174 Polanyi, *Great Transformation*, p. 151: 'the essential philosophy of Marx centered on the totality of society and the noneconomic nature of man'.

175 Beneria, 'Globalization', at 314. 176 *Ibid.*

177 J. R. Hollingsworth and R. Boyer, *Contemporary Capitalism: The Embeddedness of Institutions* (Cambridge University Press, 1997), at p. 60.

178 See Polanyi, *Great Transformation.*

179 Hollingsworth and Boyer, *Contemporary Capitalism*, at p. 61.

context).[180] 'Support' is too weak a word, in that markets are *embedded* within these networks, interactions and institutions.

This concept revolutionised economic sociology. As Beckert observed:

> [h]ardly any article associated with the new economic sociology fails to mention 'embeddedness' as the core concept indicating a sociological approach to the economy. Few economic sociologists would disagree with the statement 'We are all Polanyians now'.[181]

Although '[e]mbededness is not a pivotal concept in *The Great Transformation*, Polanyi only uses the term twice',[182] nonetheless, the concept itself is fundamental to modern sociology.[183] Also, its promise for analysis of the Budget, as an institution which supports the embedded market economy, is great. Polanyi's concept of 'the embedded economy' is 'often misunderstood', as 'he has been interpreted to be making the argument that before the rise of market society, economies were always embedded in social relations, but with the rise of market societies, the situation is reversed – and the market becomes dominant'.[184] In fact, however, Polanyi 'argues that market liberals wanted to embed society in the autonomous economy, but their project *could not* succeed'.[185]

Why is the goal of merging social institutions, or even objectives for an egalitarian society, with an economy doomed to failure? A driving concept of Polanyi's work was there is a 'need for a planned socialist economy and the rejection of the argument that only a free market system could preserve liberal values'.[186] Operating a process of gender budgeting alongside an unregulated, free market system will not be successful, but planning for an economy which promotes gender equality is possible. It is also necessary, if gender equality is ever to be achieved. As Bernburg writes, 'Polanyi recognizes that the disembedded economy has profound influence on society's culture'.[187] The free market is not designed to promote gender

180 See discussion of this in Ann Mumford, 'Inheritance in Socio-political Context: The Case for Reviving the Sociological Discourse of Inheritance Tax Law', *Journal of Law and Society*, 34 (2007), 567–93.

181 Beckert, 'Transformation of Embeddedness', at 7.

182 Kurtulus Gemici, 'Karl Polanyi and the Antinomies of Embeddedness', *Socio-Economic Review*, 6 (2008), 5–33, at 10.

183 See Block, 'Karl Polanyi', at 275: 'After years of relative obscurity, Karl Polanyi's 1944 book, *The Great Transformation*, is increasingly recognized as one of the major works of twentieth-century social science'.

184 *Ibid.*, at 282. 185 *Ibid.* (emphasis in text).

186 S. C. Humphreys, 'History, Economics, and Anthropology: The Work of Karl Polanyi', *History and Theory*, 8 (1969), 165–212, 172.

187 Bernburg, 'Anomie', at 734.

equality, and thus has the impact of discouraging efforts to achieve it in society.

Planning for the market that society decides that it wants can have enormous benefits, because of the powerful influence that markets exert on social institutions. For example – and this is a point likely to appeal to the tax instrumentalist authors of every budget – markets can even encourage people to be good parents. Polanyi dispelled the assumption that providing, or self-sacrificing, for one's family, is instinctive.[188] Rather, the practice evolved with the establishment of agricultural market economies.[189] It took the form of the 'closed group',[190] and *was not necessarily dependent upon sex* as an organisational factor. Polanyi explained that, '[t]he nature of the institutional nucleus is indifferent; it may be sex as with the patriarchal family, locality as with the village settlement, or political power as with the seigneurial manor'.[191]

Polanyi noted however that in ancient societies gender did appear to determine who travelled with work, and who did not: 'Travelling traders are, with rare exceptions, men'.[192] Women, thus, were staying home with the children. Polanyi studied ancient societies largely to establish that 'modern society is fundamentally different from pre-existing societies in that the economic system is not embedded or regulated by other social institutions'.[193] It may be presumed that the embeddedness of modern economies renders them more difficult to regulate, as it is difficult to extract aspects of the modern economy, thus to study and perhaps to improve them. If women do not benefit from the paid economy, then which aspect of it should be extracted (if it can be) and fixed?

The above question includes, 'if it can be', because few of the factors at play are fixed. As Ngugi explained, '[t]he consequence of this rise of the "social ethos" in the midst of capitalist legal regimes is what Karl Polanyi refers to as the "double movement": the institution and spread of markets coupled with a corresponding "network of measures and policies ... integrated into powerful institutions designed to check the

188 Polanyi wrote that '[t]he individualistic savage collecting food and hunting on his own or for his family has never exited' (*Great Transformation*, p. 53).

189 'Indeed the practice of catering for the needs of one's household becomes a feature of economic life only on a more advanced level of agriculture; however even then it has nothing in common either with the motive of gain or with the institution of markets' (*ibid.*).

190 Polanyi, *Great Transformation*. 191 *Ibid.*, p. 53.

192 K. Polanyi and H. W. Pearson, *The Livelihood of Man* (New York, NY: Academic Press, 1977), at p. 191.

193 Bernburg, 'Anomie', at 733.

action of the market relative to labor, land, and money".'[194] These policies, initially intended as regulators of markets, become subsumed by them – thus, deeply embedded. The next chapter will identify several, existing or past initiatives which were put in place as part of an effort to regulate the market economy in the cause of gender equality, and discuss what happened to them.

Double movements: subsumed, or restructured?

There should be no expectation that gender budgeting will produce any dramatic changes, at least in the immediate context.[195] Gender budgeting is perceived as a long-term process.[196] If gender budgeting is only about producing information now, for later use, then what should those future utilities involve? The prediction is that gender budgeting will embrace a variety of different forms and formats. Gender budgeting should invigorate the discourse of gender in politics, and provide politicians working towards gender equality with powerful tools. After gender budgeting, gender becomes the debate, and this is its success.

This chapter also has argued that, for gender budgeting to succeed, regulatory theory must inform theories of gender equality. Put simply, something will need to be done with the information collected. If, as Power reminded us, '[a]udit is not simply a solution to a technical problem; it also makes possible ways of redesigning the practice of government',[197] then the potential for this information to translate into action is compelling. Despite the success of the implementation of the Gender Directive within the EU, internationally, the battle for gender budgeting is not complete. Yes, gender has 'gone mainstream', and there is reason for optimism. And, yes, obviously everything for which the Budget pays is fair game for gender-budgeting analysis, so the potential for thoughtful progress, in a range of areas, is possible. Targets should be indentified if they are to be achieved, however, and it is within the arena of poverty reduction, generally, that gender budgeting holds specific promise. Overall, however, gender budgeting should invigorate the discourse of gender in politics,

194 Ngugi, 'Forgetting Lochner', at 51, citing Polanyi, *Great Transformation*, at p. 76.

195 F. Raes explains that '[g]ender sensitive budget initiatives are long term processes and should be regarded as tools, not as an end' ('What Can We Expect from Gender Sensitive Budgets? Strategies in Brazil and in Chile in a Comparative Perspective', 2006, at www.eurosur.org/wide/home.htm, at 4).

196 *Ibid.* 197 Power, *Audit Society*, p. 11.

and provide politicians working towards gender equality with powerful tools.

Polanyi's thesis of the 'disembedded market economy' explains the difficulty encountered thus far by efforts to incorporate gender equality within markets. As gender budgeting operates on the premise that identifying gender disparities in the budgeting process is the first step towards remedying inequality, this chapter has proposed that identifying the assumptions that have obstructed feminist objectives from merging with theories of (class and) market egalitarianism is the next step towards enabling gender budgeting's remarkable and laudable objectives to succeed. Self-regulating markets, however, involve a network of different markets across all of society. Operating a process of gender budgeting alongside an unregulated, free market system will not be successful, but planning for an economy which promotes gender equality is possible. It is also necessary, if the cause of gender economic equality is to be advanced.

The next chapter will move away from discussions concerning the obligations of the state, and commence consideration of the potential role of business in analyses of the intersection between women, tax law and policy. Specifically the corporate social responsibility movement has started to engage with tax, and to consider its role within a wider social agenda. The objective of the next chapter is to carry the broader analyses of gender budgeting – dealing with budgets, states and actors – to the specific context of business. The chapter will explain that the corporate social responsibility literature has started to engage with tax; and, indeed, to lay the theoretical framework for consideration of the interaction between tax and economic gender inequality.

4

Corporate social responsibility and the possibility of common aims

The corporate social responsibility movement has been recognised as having particular potential for gender equality.[1] For example, gender equality in the workplace has been integrated with the corporate social responsibility platform, specifically through the gender mainstreaming movement in EU law.[2] There is a growing literature acknowledging the importance of tax law to influencing corporate behaviour, and the significance of this to the corporate social responsibility movement.[3] Is there a place for gender equality in this literature; or, indeed, for the possibility of common aims? This chapter will consider the potential of assimilating the objective of gender equality in the wider economy with corporate social responsibility, through the medium of tax law.

Corporate social responsibility is a wide concept, with an interesting, and long, history.[4] At various points in its history, the corporate social responsibility concept has embraced social performance theory, stakeholder theory, and business ethics theory.[5] At present, corporate social responsibility embraces all of these theories, and more. Stakeholder theory, however, remains an important constant in theories of the connection between corporate activity and wider social objectives.[6] This, perhaps, is the starting point for this chapter. Women are not stakeholders,

1 See, generally, K. Grosser and J. Moon, 'Gender Mainstreaming and Corporate Social Responsibility: Reporting Workplace Issues', *Journal of Business Ethics*, 62 (2005), 327–40.

2 Grosser and Moon, 'Gender Mainstreaming'.

3 This is a relatively new literature, see, for example: Doreen McBarnet, 'Corporate Social Responsibility Beyond Law, Through Law, for Law' (SSRN, 2009); Arne Friese, *et al.*, 'Taxation and Corporate Governance' (SSRN, 2006); Reuven S. Avi-Yonah, 'Corporate Social Responsibility and Strategic Tax Behavior' (SSRN, 2006).

4 Discussed throughout A. B. Carroll, 'Corporate Social Responsibility: Evolution of a Definitional Construct', *Business and Society*, 38(3) (1999), 268–95.

5 *Ibid.*, at 268–9.

6 See R.W. Roberts, 'Determinants of Corporate Social Responsibility Disclosure: An Application of Stakeholder Theory', *Accounting, Organizations and Society*, 17 (1992), 595–612.

in the traditional sense of voices heard in participatory processes,[7] in the economy. Tax law presents a useful forum for exploring this. In particular, it is useful to consider when gender is an issue in tax law, or is problematised, and solutions are offered through tax.[8]

This chapter will begin by describing the conceptual relationship between corporate social responsibility and tax law. This relationship typically is approached in two ways: either by considering whether tax avoidance by businesses can be controlled, or curbed, through a corporate social responsibility agenda; or, alternatively, by consideration of whether tax law could be used in an instrumental way to compel corporations to make choices which benefit a wider society. This chapter will detail both of these choices, and attempt to define the place for gender equality in both. It will begin, however, with corporation tax in the UK, as an example of tax introduced both to address deficiencies in existing taxes, but also with an eye towards wider, social agenda.

Introduction to tax and corporate social responsibility: corporation tax as a starting point

Analysis of the relationship between corporate social responsibility and tax law in the UK starts with corporation tax, perhaps the ultimate exercise of corporate social responsibility. Introduced by a Labour government in 1965,[9] corporation tax is justified, among other reasons, as a payment of sorts for the costs to society of supporting business activities (including limited liability, and other benefits).[10] Corporation tax and capital gains tax were introduced in the same year in the UK, and can be considered

7 I am very grateful to Roger Berkowitz, Director of the Hannah Arendt Center at Bard College, for this starting point. See also A. Cornwall, 'Whose Voices? Whose Choices? Reflections on Gender and Participatory Development', *World Development*, 31 (2003), 1325–42, at 1325: 'Yet Claims to "Full Participation" and "the Participation of All Stakeholders" – familiar from innumerable project documents and descriptions of participatory processes – all too often boil down to situations in which only the voices and versions of the vocal few are raised and heard. Women, many critics argue, are those most likely to lose out, finding themselves and their interests marginalized or overlooked in apparently "participator" processes.'

8 *Ibid.*, at 1326. 9 *Per* Finance Act 1965.

10 See discussion of this history in L. Lazar, 'Finance Act 1965: The Corporation Tax', *Modern Law Review*, 29(1) (1966), 50–3. On the question of the justification for the corporation tax, see J. Mintz, 'The Corporation Tax: A Survey', *Fiscal Studies*, 16 (1995), 23–68, at 24–5.

'in tandem'.[11] The introduction of these two taxes resulted in a remarkable 'overhaul' of the British tax system.[12]

This overhaul had been several years in the making. A line can be drawn from the introduction of capital gains tax in 1965, to the Final Report of the 1955 Royal Commission on the Taxation of Profits and other Income,[13] which declined to provide a definition of either capital or income, offering the 'badges of trade' in a definition's stead.[14] Interestingly, Cretney points out that this Commission also engaged with the issue of independent taxation, and 'had denied that the rule aggregating spouses' incomes ... embodied an "outmoded or unworthy conception of the relations of man in woman in marriage"'.[15] The main problem before the Commission, however, was that, before 1965, strong incentives existed to engage in schemes that produced that 'mythical cow',[16] capital. A definition of income, or a definition of capital, would have provided taxpayers with a rule, weighed down by the limitations of language. Less weighty 'badges', however, are less open to manipulation.

What does this have to do with corporation tax, and, by extension, corporate social responsibility? The answer is context, provided by a new 1960s-era Labour government, sweeping (swinging) into office, primed to institute a new idea of what constitutes fair taxation.[17] Confusing schemes attempting to disguise income as capital, it was hoped, would be less attractive, as both forms of wealth now would be taxed.[18] This was a perfect campaign issue for the Labour Party. Who tends to have capital? Income? Capital gains taxation would redress a system which appeared to

11 For an analysis of the background to the Finance Act 1965, and the (continuing) political impact, see H. Pemberton, 'Taxation and Labour's Modernisation Programme', *Contemporary British History*, 20 (2006), 423–40.

12 *Ibid.*, at 436.

13 See Final Report of the Royal Commission on the Taxation of Profits and Income 1955, Cmnd. 9474.

14 Referring to the Final Report in 1955, J. Tiley suggests that '[i]t is not immediately clear why the British have not thought much about the concept of income' ('Aspects of Schedule A', in J. Tiley (ed.), *Studies in the History of Tax Law* (Oxford: Hart Publishing, 2004), p. 87).

15 Stephen Michael Cretney, *Family Law in the Twentieth Century* (Oxford University Press, 2003), at p. 112: fn.152, citing the Final Report, Cmnd. 9474, at paras. 117–34.

16 Leonard Lazar, 'Finance Act 1965: The Capital Gains Tax', *Modern Law Review*, 29 (1966), 181–4, at 182.

17 See Pemberton, 'Taxation'.

18 M. Gammie describes capital gains tax as an 'unpopular compromise', which would not be needed if a comprehensive income tax functioned well ('Taxing Capital Gains – Thoughts from the UK', *University of New South Wales Law Journal*, 23 (2000), 309–12).

favour the capital of the wealthy over the salaried classes.[19] This context extended to corporation tax. Corporations were viewed as yet another source of wealth, possessing too much control over the timing and nature of their tax obligations. Why not simply tax dividends as income in the hands of shareholders; or, put differently, why was another layer of taxation needed? Corporations wishing to avoid a tax obligation could simply hold onto their dividends.[20] Among other perceived benefits, the timing of corporation tax would not necessarily be within the control of the corporation itself.

Corporation tax (and capital gains tax) were instituted to effect a fairer tax system, primarily through burden shifting. The tax encounters some difficulties in design. For example, given that corporations are legal fictions, who will be paying the taxes? The incidence of corporation tax is notoriously difficult to identify.[21] The tax may be passed to employees, or customers – the point is, that it is not easily measured.[22] It may be presumed that the burden of corporation tax would be passed to that sector of the marketplace with the least control, or the least ability to avoid paying it, and it is at this point that engagement with feminist literature is possible. The 'sweat off a man's brow'[23] is an obvious starting point for the next part of this discussion – adding the link of gender to an analysis of the connection between tax and corporate social responsibility – as the terms are evocative. It is, primarily, a man who is targeted by a personal income tax, which focuses solely on activities performed within the public marketplace. Unpaid labour within the private sphere of the home is ignored.[24] Women comparatively are both underrepresented and underpaid within the labour market, thus their efforts are not included within the tax base. Housework, for example, is both

19 Young's observation that '[i]t is axiomatic that poor women tend not to own capital property that would be taxable upon its disposition' is particularly meaningful. She continues, 'neither do women generally' ('(In) Visible Inequalities', at 108).

20 Of course, employees, by contrast, face a tax obligation at the time that they have earned their salary.

21 See, among others: Lazar, 'Finance Act 1965'; D. F. Bradford and P. Str, 'The Incidence and Allocation Effects of a Tax on Corporate Distributions', (1981) NBER Working Paper.

22 Two classic articles exploring this point are: A. C. Harberger, 'The Incidence of the Corporation Income Tax', *Journal of Political Economy*, 70(3) (1962), 215–40; P. Mieszkowski, 'Tax Incidence Theory: The Effects of Taxes on the Distribution of Income', *Journal of Economic Literature*, 7(4) (1969), 1103–24.

23 B. I. Bittker, 'Dedication: Charles Stuart Lyon – Being an Epitome of His Letters, Marginalia, Graffiti, and Other Fugitive Scribblings', *Tax Law Review*, 37 (1981), 159–92, at 170, presents some of this imagery.

24 But see the discussion of imputed income, in Chapter 8, of this book.

unpaid and untaxed, and yet contributes to a variety of forms of wealth.[25] How is this contribution recognised? Or, put differently, where can the contribution of unpaid labour be 'spotted' within the tax system?

Income is part of the corporation tax formula, which includes an amalgamation of both trading profits and capital gains. It is tempting to suggest that wherever estimations of wealth and its origins are inexact – or, perhaps, are less exact than income – then, perhaps similar to an apparition to whom all creaky floorboards in an old house are attributed, the contribution of unpaid labour has been identified. Wealth has come from somewhere, it is not certain where, thus the phantom of unpaid labour has been recognised. One of the problems with this sort of reasoning is that it relies on the assumption that tax is always connected to one source of money, and that it is only so connected once. Even a brief perusal of the tax system would reveal this to be untrue.[26]

Corporate social responsibility, tax and gender

Corporation tax (and capital gains tax) were instituted with clear social, perhaps redistributive, objectives in the UK. The revenue from corporation tax however is significant, and government programmes which are crucial for the well-being of women and men depend upon the funds collected.[27] In that sense, the very existence of corporation tax can be described as an example of corporate social responsibility. Perhaps governments depend too much on the revenue raised to worry too much about its design, or its impact upon businesses. Such an important source of wealth to states also will be important to women. Compliance with corporation tax – indeed, compliance with tax – can be portrayed as

25 W. N. Espeland and M. L. Stevens write, '[t]hat commensuration has the potential to transform what it measures is demonstrated in the repeated efforts of feminists to value household work in metrics used to quantify paid labor' ('Commensuration as a Social Process', *Annual Review of Sociology*, 24 (1998), 313–43, at 334). Commensuration is defined as 'the transformation of different qualities into a common metric' (*ibid.*, at 314).

26 Similarly, double taxation occurs at several points in the UK (and other tax systems), although is it is acknowledged as one of the basic problems that should be avoided in a tax system. There is a growing literature, however, challenging traditional views of double taxation, particularly on the question of the taxation of corporate dividends. See, for example: R. Morck, 'Why Some Double Taxation Might Make Sense: The Special Case of Inter-corporate Dividends' (2003) NBER Working Paper and 'How to Eliminate Pyramidal Business Groups – The Double Taxation of Inter-corporate Dividends and Other Incisive Uses of Tax Policy', (2004) NBER Working Paper.

27 See J. Creedy and N. Gemmell, 'Corporation Tax Buoyancy and Revenue Elasticity in the UK', *Economic Modelling*, 25 (2008), 24–37.

a woman's issue, and indeed has been described as a key part of the corporate social responsibility movement.

Two writers have addressed the question of tax compliance, generally, within a corporate social responsibility context: McBarnet and Braithwaite. McBarnet has explained that corporate social responsibility 'generally is portrayed as the voluntary adoption by business of "responsible" practices, beyond the demands of law'.[28] She explains that 'since Enron, the corporate social responsibility agenda is widening to include ... tax avoidance'.[29] Her predictions complement important work published relatively recently by Braithwaite, whose text *Markets in Vice, Markets in Virtue*,[30] involves a vast comparative study of taxation in the US and Australia.[31] Braithwaite argues that tax collection agencies need to regulate 'conversational(ly)', 'collaborative(ly)', and in a 'way that people can understand', thus providing necessary support for the 'heavy penalties' that 'promoters of vice' should attract.[32] *Markets in Vice, Markets in Virtue* focuses upon the impact that the provision of aggressive schemes has on the creation of an unregulated and dynamic market. The act of provision is the focus of analysis, and consideration of what can be done to protect the tax system from the effects of these acts is perhaps the driving force of the research.[33] This type of analysis of tax in both a corporate governance, and corporate social responsibility context is growing in influence. Braithwaite's work echoes McBarnet's analysis of the pursuit of KPMG for 'abusive' tax schemes, in which she explains that these 'perfectly legal' schemes might be dismissed as mere exploitation of loopholes, but actually involved degrees of 'hiding'.[34] This is an important distinction, and raises the question of whether corporations can be persuaded to conclude that such behaviour is not worth the risk (an important theme of Braithwaite's book).

28 D. McBarnet, 'After Enron will "Whiter than White Collar Crime" Still Wash?', *British Journal of Criminology*, 46 (2006), 1091–1109, at 1106.

29 *Ibid.* 30 (Oxford University Press, 2005).

31 Braithwaite's demonstration of how a market in tax avoidance effectively could be switched from a market in vice, to a market in virtue, has become a reference point in this literature.

32 Braithwaite, *Markets in Vice*, pp. 208–9.

33 Braithwaite's work with the Australian Tax Office is discussed to particularly illustrative effect, and reveals the drawbacks of punitive, exemplary approaches to enforcement. Taxpayers are alienated, rather than frightened into compliance, by such approaches, and, simply from a resources standpoint, effecting compliance without assistance is difficult. Responsive regulation is revealed as key. Markets in vice can be transformed into markets in virtue, if the markets in aggressive schemes finally are regulated, but in a way which acknowledges and responds to the ways in which they operate.

34 McBarnet, 'After Enron', at 1092.

Tax compliance

International tax avoidance as a forum for gender

Both McBarnet's and Braithwaite's work with tax and corporate social responsibility consider tax avoidance as an international problem. The taxpayers in their analyses have managed to avoid domestic tax laws, but gaps in international tax law are an important part of the success of the taxpayers' schemes to minimise tax obligations. The Beijing Platform, in particular, helped to advance the idea of gender equality as an international issue, which is not out of place in treaties and other aspects of international law.[35] Is there a place for analysis of gender in international tax law?

It is not an easy question. Avery Jones famously observed in 1999, '[t]axpayers have become global; tax authorities have not'.[36] If gender equality is treated as a global issue, it is not clear if the tax treaty system would be able to bear the weight. Interestingly, however, Avery Jones also has queried whether tax authorities would become more global if there were multilateral treaties.[37] A sampling of some of the current issues for tax treaties reveals some of the modern challenges of diversity. These include the problems associated with categorisation of income, qualification conflicts and – one of the most difficult problems – interpretation.[38] Additionally, the OECD has addressed some of the difficulties associated with variations of interpretation of terms in its treaties in different courts around the world with its Commentaries, although the sub-legislative status of the OECD Commentaries has meant that countries are free to disregard their advice.[39] Is there a place in a system formulated around the question of tax administration, for the integration of questions of tax policy?

This question might be approached from the perspective of what constitutes an abuse of the tax treaty system; or, put differently, upon what policy is administration of the international tax treaty system based, such that a violation of it might be described as an abuse of principle? Kingson has explained that the concept of abuse of the tax treaty system itself is based upon a number of assumptions, and among them is '[t]he conclusion that another country is taking advantage of expectations [which] rests, at

35 Division for the Advancement of Women and United Nations, Beijing declaration and platform for action (United Nations Division for the Advancement of Women 1995). See also Baden and Goetz, 'Who Needs [Sex]'.

36 John Avery Jones, 'Are Tax Treaties Necessary?', *Tax Law Review*, 53 (1999), 1–38, at 1. Avery Jones was writing about the administration of international tax law.

37 'Are Tax Treaties Necessary?' 38 *Ibid.* 39 *Ibid.*

bottom, on the premise that those expectations are legitimate'.[40] The concept of legitimate expectations is founded upon the idea of consensus, as '[l]egitimacy derives from commonly accepted principles'.[41] Additionally, the question is very much one of perspective, as '[w]hen another country's actions do not conform to expectations, it is abusing our system only if it should have accepted those expectations as principles'.[42] In this context, the tax treaty system already bears responsibility for the enforcement of certain kinds of tax policy questions.

The purpose of organisations like the OECD is to assist in this process of legitimacy; and, indeed, 'countries use international organisations to confer on some expectations the legitimacy of principles'.[43] This is most evident with the issue of tax competition. In the arena of domestic tax, taxpayers compete with each other. In the arena of international tax law, countries compete. Treaties to some extent act as protection against the excesses of competition. This is apparent in the substance of tax legislation itself, as national 'code provisions identify the competing interests of taxpayers, treaty provisions identify those of countries'.[44]

The process by which treaties are formed involves its own element of competition, and would not appear to present a process which easily could adopt goals of gender equality. It is a highly politicised process, in which each side is encouraged to exaggerate the potential unfairness of its own system, perhaps as a bargaining tool.[45] Kingson explains that, '[i]n a treaty, each country is bargaining away both the current and the potential unfairness of its internal law'.[46] Incentives also exist for countries to exaggerate the degrees of unfairness to be found within their tax systems, as 'any such unfairness strengthens its negotiating position and may exist for that very purpose'.[47]

While the prevention of tax avoidance[48] and evasion is an important motive for entire tax treaty system, the question of stability is an additional

40 Charles I. Kingson, 'The Coherence of International Taxation', *Columbia Law Review*, 81(6) (1981), 1151–1229, at 1155.

41 Kingson, 'Coherence'. 42 *Ibid.* 43 *Ibid.* 44 *Ibid.*, at 1157.

45 See generally C. M. Radaelli, 'Harmful Tax Competition in the EU: Policy Narratives and Advocacy Coalitions', *Journal of Common Market Studies*, 37 (1999), 661–82.

46 Kingson, 'Coherence', at 1158. 47 *Ibid.*, at 1157.

48 Within such an exaggerated context, it is perhaps not surprising that it can be difficult to define the term 'international tax avoidance'. A common understanding has developed, however, and indeed the standard definition was put forward by Sol Picciotto over thirteen years ago, when he suggested that international tax avoidance encompasses 'an institutionalised system of offshore finance, which facilitates not only "legal" tax planning and avoidance but also capital flight from developing countries, illegal tax evasion, and other fraud and money-laundering (in *International Business Taxation* (London:

concern. On this point, there is increasing dissatisfaction in the academic literature with the effectiveness of bilateral treaties in addressing the challenges of international tax law.[49] The suggestion that the system is failing to live up to its objectives has been treated as a serious criticism,[50] and has highlighted the issue of, and the questions surrounding, difference.[51]

The OECD has answered the question of why it is important to target harmful tax competition by setting out a philosophy of global taxation[52] which has potential for the project of integrating gender issues into the fabric of international tax law. This philosophy is based on the premise that cross border trade raises living standards. Trade eliminates poverty, and distributes global resources more equitably. The benefits of globalisation, generally, may be located in the expansion and exponential growth of international trade.[53] Harmful tax competition, the OECD has argued,

Weidenfeld & Nicolson, 1992)). It is in the fight against these sorts of activities that there is a presumed commonality of purpose.

49 The criticisms may be represented by Victor Thuronyi's argument that '[t]he treaty network has become cumbersome and inflexible and, in many instances, has spawned opportunities for tax avoidance' ('International Tax Cooperation and a Multilateral Treaty', *Brooklyn Journal of International Law*, 26 (2001), 1641–81, at 1641.

50 Thuronyi cautions though that improving the system is not a matter of devising the best treaty or fashioning the best legislation. Rather, what is required is political consensus, as '[t]hose experienced in treaty negotiation rightly have pointed out that it would be impossible to achieve such uniformity without substantial political will and harmonization of tax systems' (*ibid.*, at 1642). Thuronyi, however, is not optimistic about this. He writes that '[n]either is forthcoming in the near future' (*ibid.*, at 1643). He suggests that this does not mean that improving the international tax system should not be attempted, because 'it is possible to approach this ideal in a gradual manner' (*ibid.*).

51 Perhaps the most famous, modern example of problematic difference to be addressed by international tax law, upon which what might now be described as a delicate consensus was reached by the OECD, is the now decade-old harmful tax competition project. Harmful tax competition is a product both of history and of globalisation. Where (as has been discussed) formerly domestic questions of tax rates and bases were treated as domestic, the impact of globalisation meant that unregulated tax competition could produce 'distortion in patterns of trade and investment and reduce global welfare' (OECD Report, *The OECD's Project on Harmful Tax Practices: The 2001 Progress Report* (2001), p. 23). By way of explanation, the 1998 Report addressed the problems presented by the possibility of 'free riders'; i.e., those who 'benefit from public spending in home country and yet avoid contributing to its financing' (OECD, 1998, *Harmful Tax Competition: An Emerging Global Issue*, OECD Publications, p. 14). The OECD has produced three reports on harmful tax competition: *Harmful Tax Competition: An Emerging Global Issue* (1998); *Towards Global Tax Co-operation: Progress in Identifying and Eliminating Harmful Tax Practices* (2000); and *The OECD's Project on Harmful Tax Practices: The 2001 Progress Report* (2001).

52 As discussed in the above note.

53 Thus, the Report emphasised that it was important to protect all forms of fair competition for 'real' economic activities. The best way to achieve this would be to ensure the existence

presents a very real and difficult threat to the goods associated with global economic growth. Yet one of the reasons that harmful tax competition is so difficult to combat is that it is very difficult to define. Additionally, the collection of evidence to aid in steps towards a definition of 'harmful' proved enormously challenging to collate.[54] With the Harmful Tax Competition project, however, international tax law has taken steps towards the possibility of global consensus; or, indeed, of a common policy.

If gender equality were to be integrated into international tax, how would this goal be framed, and on what terms? There is not even a global consensus on what constitutes income. Indeed, it is a standard search in tax law, driven by a hope that, if such a definition were achieved, then an 'ideal' tax system might be possible.[55] If income tax is indeed some version of a tax on the sweat off a man's brow, then (presuming a gender neutral interpretation of man) the crucial ingredient is the work which produced the sweat. 'Sweat off a man's brow', as a phrase, is cannily accurate, both in terms of the work which traditionally is valued by a tax system, and those taxpayers who generally benefit from progressive taxation.[56] It is a

of a 'level playing field', as the best forum for fostering continued global economic growth. This is discussed throughout G. Rawlings, 'Taxes and Transnational Treaties: Responsive Regulation and the Reassertion of Offshore Sovereignty', *Law and Policy*, 29(1) (2007), 51–66.

54 OECD 1998 Report, p. 35. Among other factors, the Report recommended reliance upon a 'reputation test', which was a product of earlier work by the OECD, as this had been addressed in the 1998 Report. It was also a controversial point (*ibid.*, p. 6). The types of taxes targeted included what the Report described as 'geographically mobile activities, such as financial and other service activities, including the provision of intangibles'. Income taxes were addressed, under the heading 'general income tax systems, as well as those taxes levied on certain kinds of income' (*ibid.*, p. 7). The Report at that point delayed targeting 'interest on cross-border saving instruments, cross-border interest flows' (OECD 2001 Report, pp. 12–13). The Report also identified several key factors to assist in identifying harmful preferential tax regimes in OECD member and non-member countries. These included the presence of 'no or low effective tax rates' as the obvious starting point of any evaluation. The '"Ring-Fencing" of Regimes', by which a regime is restricted to non-residents and otherwise isolated from the domestic economy, however, was dropped in the 2001 Report. The reliance upon a '[l]ack of transparency' – 'a broad concept that includes, among others, favourable application of laws and regulations, negotiable tax provisions, and a failure to make widely available administrative practices' – however, was preserved (*ibid.*).

55 J. Bossons, 'The Value of a Comprehensive Tax Base as a Tax Reform Goal', *Journal of Law and Economics*, 13 (1970), 327–63, at 363.

56 Yet as L. Friedman emphasises, '[i]t would be hard to argue that divine inspiration or pure reason lay behind income tax law ...' ('Is there a Modern Legal Culture?', *Ratio Juris*, 7(2) (1994), 117–31).

conglomeration of past incentives and current ambitions, fuelled by the legislator's need to draft laws as broadly as possible.

The Haig–Simons definition of income was only ever a starting point in the US, and what followed in tax law did not necessarily follow a predetermined path.[57] In the UK, the situation is not dramatically different. The legislator in the UK is, in truth and in practice, the Revenue, on the grounds of a constitutional trade-off that tends not to receive as much attention as the 'is the court acting too legislatively?' constitutional crises that have defined tax theory (and judicial and legislative angst) over the past thirty years.[58] There is, of course, no definition of 'income' in tax law because of the material that that would provide to tax lawyers, who quickly would ensure that, whatever the definition of income, then certainly their clients would never have any.

As the Haig–Simons definition is so often the starting point in the US, however, so the 'badges of trade' are an important reference point in UK analyses. In a study published when the 1955 Commission was impending and thus still something of a hot topic, Carter wrote of the significance of the diminishing, wealthier class with evocative language, suggesting that, '[l]ike Professor Schumpeter's analogy of the capitalist class, sub-replacement birth rates in the higher economic and social strata make it more like a hotel, always full of people, but with the residents always changing'.[59] Carter suggested that this presented a change from the nineteenth century, as '[u]ntil this century the situation has

57 An important point in this discussion of the Haig–Simons definition was brought to my attention at the Law and Society Conference 2009, by Dennis Ventry. Non-market activities generally are not considered by an accretion tax under the Haig–Simons definition, because (among other reasons) '[t]he hallmark of imputed income is that the economic benefits are both produced and exhausted by the taxpayer outside the marketplace'. Mary Louise Fellows, 'Rocking the Tax Code: A Case Study of Employment-related Child-care Expenditures', *Yale Journal of Law and Feminism*, 10 (1998), 307–95, at 358ff. Fellows' 1998 article presents an excellent analysis of the feminist context for imputed income. In this article, she argues that an 'insubordination' principle should be applied to considerations of imputed income: '[t]he point is not to diminish the importance of the distinction between business and personal or the concept of imputed income. Rather the point is that those concepts can gain more analytical power when they are analyzed within a framework that includes the antisubordination principle' (*ibid.*, at 393).

58 B. Staveley, 'The Quest for the Allowable Loss: Reflections on Lord Hoffmann's Approach to *Ramsay*', *British Tax Review*, 6 (2005), 609–19 and J. Freedman, 'Interpreting Tax Statutes: Tax Avoidance and the Intention of Parliament', *Law Quarterly Review*, 123 (2007), 53–90 provide a review of this era.

59 A. M. Carter, 'Income-tax Allowances and the Family in Great Britain', *Population Studies*, 6 (1953), 218–32, at 227.

been rather the reverse, the law of primogeniture in company with large families providing a steady stream of persons trickling from higher to lower strata'.[60] Taxation would have played a role in reversing this; and, in particular, inheritance taxation would have been implicated.[61] Carter warned against overly romanticising this (then) new, twentieth century trend, arguing instead that '[t]his type of social fluidity was in many ways a beneficial movement, and its reverse in this century is not necessarily an unmixed evil.[62]

Carter was arguing that beneficial social objectives were possible within both economic structures. The task within this context is to identify the economic structure, consider its social consequences, and then pursue socio-economic objectives within that arrangement. Adjustments can be made as necessary, and international taxation is a good example of that. The point is that efficiency, among other economic factors, on its own cannot influence the decision whether or not to pursue a socio-economic objective, such as gender economic equality.

Tax and corporate social responsibility in partnership

There are several questions that need to be asked before it is possible to determine whether, or how, tax should play a role in considerations of corporate social responsibility. The final section of this chapter will pose these questions, and suggest some answers. This section then will conclude with a survey of the literature that suggests the place that gender equality may find within the corporate social responsibility and tax movement.

The first question would ask whether tax has been set up in such a way as to place distinct groups of persons at a disadvantage. An essentialist analysis of this question might consider whether there are distinctly female characteristics which lead to women either being treated unfairly by tax systems, or somehow managing them less effectively than men.[63] A different approach might engage institutionalist thought, and ask whether

60 *Ibid.* 61 Carter, 'Income-tax Allowances'. 62 *Ibid.*, at 227.

63 See, among others: Note, 'The Myth of Context in Politics and Law', *Harvard Law Review*, 110 (1997), 1292–1309; A. P. Harris, 'Race and Essentialism in Feminist Legal Theory', *Stanford Law Review*, 42 (1990), 581–616; and, most famously, the 'debate' between Cornell and Mackinnon on the essentialist question, in Drucilla Cornell, 'Review: Sexual Difference, the Feminine, and Equivalency: A Critique of MacKinnon's "Toward a Feminist Theory of the State"', *Yale Law Journal*, 100 (1991), 2247–75.

the tax system historically has been set up in such a way as to place women at a disadvantage.[64]

An institutionalist approach would consider the extent to which the organisation of political life makes a difference to the taxation of corporations. This consideration would include the role of state obligations, and their ambitions towards the least powerful members of economies. This is a standard social, scientific enquiry, which is not exclusive to institutionalist analysis. Seligman specifically considered whether it is the duty of the state to redress all 'inequalities of fortune', and concluded that it was not.[65] Indeed, he warned that this would be a 'dangerous step'. Although he acknowledged that the idea of progressivity has (what he described as) 'socialistic' origins, he preferred to phrase the question of equity thus: 'when differences of wealth are due to the state's own omissions, compensation should be made therefor'.[66]

Seligman argued that it was important that he frame his arguments so as to target his audience well, and it is at this point that this chapter should emphasise again the significance of difference. Seligman wrote for the US, and he believed that there is '[n]o country so conservative as the US'.[67] Indeed, he suggested that '[t]he danger is not that we shall go too rapidly, but that we shall not go at all'.[68] He was attempting to spur a specific country, with a specific history, to action. He also was of his (early twentieth-century) time, and thus pre-dates the globalised, corporate social responsibility movement. The search for a place for tax and gender in this modern movement confronts a vast literature, some of which (like Seligman) even precedes it. Within the modern literature, corporate social responsibility has addressed issues as diverse as the impact of tax ideology on managers and corporate form.

One aspect of this modern literature involves 'isomorphism',[69] which 'suggests that social action is a product of ideology and conceptions that

64 See, among others: Herman L. Boschken, 'Institutionalism: Intergovernmental Exchange, Administration-centered Behavior, and Policy Outcomes in Urban Agencies', *Journal of Public Administration Research and Theory*, 8 (1998), 585–614; T. Eggertsson, 'The Old Theory of Economic Policy and the New Institutionalism', *World Development*, 25 (1997), 1187–1203; A. Hira and R. Hira, 'The New Institutionalism Contradictory Notions of Change', *American Journal of Economics and Sociology*, 59 (2000), 267–82.

65 Edwin R. A. Seligman, 'The Theory of Progressive Taxation', *Publications of the American Economic Association*, 8 (1893), 52–5, at 52.

66 *Ibid.* 67 *Ibid.*, at 55. 68 Seligman, 'Theory of Progressive Taxation'.

69 Proponents of isomorphism 'argue that the emergence of organizational forms cannot be explained by advantages, such as efficiency, inherent to specific forms; rather, they are explained by their embeddedness in a cultural context'. Mary Zey and Tami Swenson, 'Corporate Tax Laws, Corporate Restructuring, and Subsidiarization of Corporate Form, 1981–1995', *Sociological Quarterly*, 39(4) (1998), 555–81, at 558.

define the reality (culture) of managers and create similarities among organizations as they adopt the prevailing conception of the legitimate corporate form'.[70] So, what does that mean? Essentially, proponents of isomorphism argue that the emergence of organisational forms cannot be explained by advantages, such as efficiency, inherent to specific forms; rather, they are explained by their embeddedness in a cultural context.[71] Put simply, corporate behaviour is both of its time, and of its culture. Corporations do not necessarily act upon society, but with society.

The second question would query the place of tax within the modern corporate social responsibility movement. A possible answer is that this is not a difficult question; and, in fact, tax long has occupied a place within analyses of the responsibility of business to society, but within a slightly older literature. Tax as a corporate responsibility construct may be a relatively new development, as the analysis of Braithwaite and McBarnet's work indicates, but it could also be suggested that an analysis of tax policy within the context of corporate social responsibility is really a branch of the modern law and economics movement; or, perhaps, what has been described as the Chicago school. Considerations of the role of tax law and policy within the context of corporate social responsibility is actually much older than that, and is more accurately described as the 'first great law and economics movement'.[72] What is the difference between the two? The law and economics movement which emerged in the 1970s and 1980s, in many ways led by the influential writings of Judge Posner, has been described (by Hovenkamp) as both strongly pro-market, and anti-statist.[73] The 'first' movement, by contrast, was quite different. This movement was dominated by liberal economists, who in many ways were dubious about the value markets to wider society.[74] This movement, dubbed the 'progressive era', viewed common law in particular as a welfare enhancing device.

During the 'first great law and economics movement' in the early twentieth century, progressivity frequently was defended in economic terms, and other possible defences were dismissed as 'unscientific'.[75] Within

70 *Ibid.*, at 557. 71 Zey and Swenson, 'Corporate Tax Laws'.

72 This is detailed in B. Fried, *The Progressive Assault on Laissez Faire: Robert Hale and the First Law and Economics Movement* (Cambridge, MA: Harvard University Press, 1998).

73 H. Hovenkamp, 'The First Great Law and Economics Movement', *Stanford Law Review*, 42(4) (1989), 993–1058, at 993.

74 Hovenkamp, 'First Great Law'.

75 *Ibid.*, at 1003–4. Hovenkamp described institutionalism as 'one of the most important intellectual achievements of the first great law and economics movement, and, with marginalism, supplied one of the greatest critiques of classical economics' (*ibid.*, at 1013).

this era, '[t]he Progressive Era economist with the greatest explicit influence on judicial policymaking was Edward Robert Anderson Seligman'.[76] Indeed, '[m]ost of Seligman's work was devoted to two issues of tax theory that lay at the heart of Progressive legislative policy: the justification for progressive rather than constant or proportional income taxes, and the shifting and incidence of taxation'.[77]

Critics of the corporate social responsibility movement have argued that, insofar as tax is relevant to such work, it is being employed within an old tradition of using tax as a weapon *against* corporations.[78] This is reminiscent of the link between corporation tax and Marxian analyses, which was an important part of the 'radical sociology of the 1960s'.[79] This branch of sociology presented a serious challenge to institutional sociology at the time.[80] What remains, today, from this era is a reliance on institutional sociology as a tool useful in understanding institutional change, in ways that are perhaps more sophisticated than identifications of inertia and persistence.

Tax law and policy can play an important part in modern, corporate social responsibility analyses. It enables a neo-institutionalist analysis of corporations. Further, it stands at the intersection of the 'old' and the 'new' institutionalism. A good illustration of how corporate behaviour can be changed through tax law is presented by the example of corporate deductions for interest payments, in particular, as presented by the Modigliani–Miller theory of finance.[81] Modigliani and Miller were awarded the Nobel Prize in 1985 for their demonstration of how the favourable tax treatment of debt enables firms to leverage.[82] The reason for this is that tax deductions for corporate interest payments are one of the few benefits to leveraging. Their demonstration of this simple idea formed the basis of modern thinking on capital structure.

76 *Ibid.*, at 1004. 77 *Ibid.*

78 S. L. Wartick and P. L. Cochran explain that '[i]f, through socially responsible acts [e.g. urban investments, philanthropy, or minority purchasing programs], managers reduce the return to stockholders, then they are, in effect, levying taxes on the corporation' ('The Evolution of the Corporate Social Performance Model', *Academy of Management Review*, 10 (1985), 758–69, at 759–60).

79 See I. Sperber, 'Sperber's Fashions in Science', *Social Epistemology*, 6 (1992), 91–105; S. B. Banerjee, 'Corporate Social Responsibility: The Good, the Bad and the Ugly', *Critical Sociology*, 34(1) (2008), 51–79.

80 Hovenkamp, 'First Great Law', at 993–4.

81 See discussion of the importance of this development in sociological theory in K. S. Cook, 'The Power of Sociological Ideas', *Sociological Perspectives*, 34(2) (1991), 115–26, at 119.

82 See R. C. Merton, 'In Honor of Nobel Laureate, Franco Modigliani', *Journal of Economic Perspectives*, 1(2) (1987), 145–55.

It is possible to move from the Modigliani–Miller theory to other possibilities for the place of gender and tax within corporate social responsibility, and it is upon this final point that this chapter will begin to draw to a close. In this concluding analysis, the Tobin tax, in particular, will be presented as an example of corporate social responsibility, and tax, in tandem. But, first, and in a review of the arguments presented, creative compliance emerges as the obvious link between corporation tax and corporate social responsibility. And yet, what questions should we ask to determine whether, or how, wider tax issues – from the wider spectrum of policy, to the narrow issue of rates – should play a role in considerations of corporate social responsibility? Tax and corporate social responsibility have particular potential with respect to discussion of trade and human rights. These are discussions with particular meaning for women. What questions should we ask about the interaction between corporate social responsibility and tax, however, that have relevance for women?

Institutional analysis in action would ask the question, 'why do some countries tax corporations more than others?'. By contrast an economic analysis might consider the fact that tax on profitable investments have fallen throughout the EU, and might endeavour to identify a reason for this.[83] Devereux's work presents an excellent example of this. His study addressed a link between a fall in the cost of income shifting, with downward pressure on rates of taxation.[84] He concluded that international tax competition was increasing capital mobility in what ultimately could be described as a race to the bottom. The result of this was an increase in tax on labour, a key factor in rising levels of unemployment. This is significant, because any shift in taxation from business owners to workers, generally, can be read as a shift of the burden of taxation from men to women.[85]

Such analyses consider the connection between the individual taxpayer and the operation of corporations. Tax avoidance can be an unintended consequence of the law, and corporate tax law traditionally has been analysed in connection with corporate behaviour in a variety of ways. For example, managerialist sociology has demonstrated that organisations have more similarities than differences. New institutionalism, in many ways an amalgamation of managerialism and other approaches in

83 See M. P. Devereux, *et al.*, 'Corporate Income Tax Reforms and International Tax Competition', *Economic Policy*, 17(35) (2002), 449–95.

84 *Ibid.*

85 N. Çeagatay, 'Gender Budgets and Beyond: Feminist Fiscal Policy in the Context of Globalisation', *Gender and Development*, 11 (2003), 15–24, at 17.

sociological theory, represents the emergence of a social theory that focuses on developing a sociological view of institutions, the way they interact and the effects of institutions on society.[86] It both reacts against, and in some ways incorporates, agency theory, and its consideration of the impact of central management and divisional managers on institutional form.

Risk taking can be evident in any number of decisions taken by management, ranging from remuneration to accounting practices. The Tobin tax is a famous example of employing tax as a tool of corporate social responsibility. Developed by the economist James Tobin, who won a Nobel Prize for this work, the Tobin tax proposes to use financial market trading to benefit developing countries.[87] The proposal involves a suggested tax on all trade of currency across borders. The aim is to deter speculative capital flows. Governments would be attracted by the possibility of stemming such activity, and thus perhaps would assess the tax relatively happily. The proceeds from the tax would be earmarked solely for the benefit of developing countries.

The Tobin tax has been enormously successful from a variety of perspectives.[88] Besides its prestigious acknowledgement, it also has attracted the attention of corporate social responsibility advocates, intellectuals and political activists. In particular, it has been embraced by the French group Attac.[89] Its only failure, as such, is that it has yet to be adopted. Pearson has developed a proposal with the explicit objective of exploiting the potential of the Tobin tax for feminist objectives. Naming her project the Maria tax, Pearson has suggested that taxes could be levied on the foreign exchange of exports in proportion to the number of women in the workforce.[90] The funds collected could be reinvested in childcare,

86 Blom-Hansen suggests that 'when insights from policy network analysis are combined with the theoretical insights from "new institutionalism", it is possible to start providing explanations of policy networks and their impact on policy outcomes' ("'New Institutional" Perspective', at 690).

87 See J. A. Frankel and National Bureau of Economic Research, *How Well Do Foreign Exchange Markets Function: Might a Tobin Tax Help?* (Cambridge, MA: National Bureau of Economic Research, 1996).

88 The Tobin tax has received particularly strong support from S. George: '[The wealthiest countries] *should take the lead in designing equitable international taxation systems*, including a Tobin Tax on all monetary and financial market transactions ...' ('Globalizing Rights?', in *Globalizing Rights: The Oxford Amnesty Lectures 1999* (Oxford University Press, 2003, p. 31), emphasis in original).

89 D. Green and M. Griffith, 'Globalization and its Discontents', (2002) *International Affairs* (*Royal Institute of International Affairs 1944–*), 49–68.

90 Pearson, 'Feminist Responses'.

pensions, and women's health care, among other things. Pearson emphasises that it would be important to levy the taxes on governments, as opposed to industries, to sidestep the problem that employers might complain that it is too expensive to hire women.

Pearson suggests that the 'promotion of gender equality' could be a goal of the Tobin tax proposals (if adapted) as well.[91] Pearson proposes that taxes could be levied on the foreign exchange of exports in proportion to the number of women in the workforce.[92] Then, the funds collected could be reinvested in childcare, pensions and women's health care,[93] among other things.[94]

While the potential of tax and corporate social responsibility may at first glance appear most evident in the arena of tax avoidance, Pearson's Maria tax proposal demonstrates that the potential of this connection is richer than might first appear. The point is not simply that, for example, legislative efforts to curb tax avoidance serve the objectives of corporate social responsibility. It is that tax can be used as a tool to assist corporations in their efforts to act in a socially responsible way, without moving too far beyond the stakeholder model.[95] Tax law is one of the most powerful regulatory forces of international trade. The connection between tax law and the corporate social responsibility movement is both powerful, and ripe with potential for gender equality. The question with which this chapter ends is, what should we look at next? How should the tax, corporate social responsibility, gender equity connection be exploited to benefit the cause of gender equality?

There is the possibility that campaigns to eliminate tax havens, which benefit wealthy corporations, could provide a venue for 'feminist activism on gender-equitable taxation'.[96] Indeed, as arguments for the extension of gender budgeting from domestic concerns to a wider, international platform are beginning to take root,[97] the role of tax in corporate social responsibility is beginning to receive more attention.[98] Discussing this

91 *Ibid.*, at 31. 92 *Ibid.*, at 32. 93 Pearson, 'Feminist Responses'. 94 *Ibid.*

95 As Brudney first acknowledged in 1982, it is often easier for the independent director to monitor compliance with tax law, than it would be to monitor compliance with 'corporate social responsibility', more generally. V. Brudney, 'The Independent Director – Heavenly City or Potemkin Village?', *Harvard Law Review*, 95 (1982), 597–660. Similarly, a 2004 note in the *Harvard Law Review* observed that '[t]he 'independent director' has long been one of the great hopes of American corporate governance' ('Developments in the Law: Corporations and Society', *Harvard Law Review*, 117 (2004), 2169–2295, at 2181.

96 Çeagatay, 'Gender Budgets', at 22. 97 Pearson, 'Feminist Responses', at 33.

98 David F. Williams, 'Tax and Corporate Social Responsibility' (10 December 2007) *Tax Journal* 10.

rising popularity, Williams stresses that 'CSR must be distinguished from corporate philanthropy such as donations to charitable or community causes, which relates to the distribution of profits rather than to the manner in which they are earned'.[99] It is a 'way of doing business' for companies, as opposed to an 'add on' to normal business activities, and thus there is no reason why the principles of corporate social responsibility should not extend to management of the tax liability of a business.[100] The identification of a 'fair' tax payment by a business is described by Williams as a highly subjective issue, who suggests that many businesses will feel that they will know a fair tax payment 'when they see it'.[101]

Williams identifies potential engagement between tax and corporate social responsibility (CSR) in these areas: transfer pricing, tax arbitrage, tax havens, relations with tax authorities, and 'tax education, debate and community action'.[102] These are quantifiable objectives, and may be distinguished from the 'inadequate normative criteria' that typically plagues the evaluation of the outcomes of corporate behaviour.[103] Thus, traditionally, '[f]or social impacts, (e.g. ... payment of taxes ...) it is a question of whether firms adhere to public policy, the law, and ethical expectations'.[104] Williams has identified the possibility of something pragmatic, something more.

Within the corporate social responsibility literature, there are attractive arguments for pragmatic approaches to social objectives, through taxation, as a medium.[105] It is suggested that governments, in some instances, may need to make difficult choices, between using tax to collect revenue, or using tax to effect desirable social outcomes.[106] Within these choices, the government is both a regulator and a primary stakeholder – i.e., 'one

99 Williams, 'Tax'. 100 *Ibid.* 101 *Ibid.* 102 *Ibid.*

103 Diane L. Swanson, 'Addressing a Theoretical Problem by Reorienting the Corporate Social Performance Model', *Academy of Management Review*, 20 (1995), 43–64, at 51.

104 *Ibid.*

105 In this vein, Alain Verbeke and Chris Coeck also present pragmatic possibilities, and underscore the popular 'belief that taxes provide stronger incentives than conventional physical regulations (such as minimum environmental norms to be respected' ('Environmental Taxation: A Green Stick or a Green Carrot for Corporate Social Performance?', *Managerial and Decision Economics*, 18 (1997), 507–16, at 507).

106 Considering the impact of taxation upon polluters in particular, Verbeke and Coeck conclude that '[i]f behavioural effects are more important to the government than financial income, any reduction in pollution volumes will be seen as a contribution to the effectiveness of the environmental taxation system and environmental policy in general' (*ibid.*, at 515).

without whose continuing participation the corporation cannot survive as a going concern' – in part because the corporation must pay taxes to it.[107] Once the government assumes the possibility of a dual role, and acknowledges it may not always be completely in control of the corporation, however, other, not necessarily positive, possibilities emerge. For example, if the government is 'just' another stakeholder, then there is a possibility that corporate social responsibility could function to outsource functions that should rest with government – such as policing pollution, or ensuring economic equality– to business.[108]

This is a danger, but it is not inevitable. Indeed, when traditional enforcement mechanisms fail the state, the corporate social responsibility movement may present a viable alternative to the classic, socio-legal 'gap problem'.[109] The corporate social responsibility movement in some ways is founded upon the real entity view of the corporation, which supports the idea of the government as another stakeholder. [110] Yet it is also founded upon a sense of responsibility, owed from the corporation to the stakeholder (which may be the government), and not the other

107 Max B. E. Clarkson, 'A Stakeholder Framework for Analyzing and Evaluating Corporate Social Performance', *Academy of Management Review*, 20 (1995), 92–117 , at 106.

108 In a well-known article in the *New York Times Magazine* from 1970, Friedman suggested that stakeholder theories of corporate social responsibility constituted 'theft', 'political subversion', and an illegitimate tax on 'owners, employees and customers'. Joshua D. Margolis and James P. Walsh, 'Misery Loves Companies: Rethinking Social Initiatives by Business', *Administrative Science Quarterly*, 48 (2003), 268–305, at 272, discussing M. Friedman, 'The Social Responsibility of Business Is to Increase Its Profits', *New York Times Magazine*, (1970), 32–126. Margolis and Walsh suggest that 'Friedman did not deny the existence of social problems; he simply claimed that it's the state's role to address them' ('Misery', at 272).

109 Avi-Yonah explains that '[t]he ultimate success of the real entity view resulted from the fact that it gave more power to management than the other views, and that both legal commentaries and courts were ultimately solicitous of the welfare of corporations (that is, corporate management). Reuven S. Avi-Yonah, 'Corporations, Society, and the State: A Defense of the Corporate Tax', *Virginia Law Review*, 90 (2004), 1193–1255, at 1233. M. J. Phillips explains that '[t]he real entity theory assumes many forms, but common to them all is the claim that corporations are real, naturally occurring beings with characteristics not present in their human members' ('Reappraising the Real Entity Theory of the Corporation', *Florida State University Law Review*, 21(4) (1994), 1061–1122, at 1062). The real entity theory would give support to the idea of the government as just another stakeholder.

110 Avi-Yonah also draws attention to a 1932 *Harvard Law Review* article by Dodd, suggesting that the real entity theory is 'the foundation' for corporate social responsibility ('Corporations, Society', at fn. 190, citing E. M. Dodd, Jr., 'For Whom Are Corporate Managers Trustees?', *Harvard Law Review*, 45 (1932), 1145–63).

way around.[111] Additionally, the corporate social responsibility movement problematises the expectation of harm from a corporation, against its stakeholders[112] – again, not the other way around. If harm does occur, corporations may redress this either through policies informed by the CSR movement; or, interestingly, by paying taxes, to fund programmes that deal with the harm.[113] From the perspective of gender, economic equality, the former option is preferable; but, as Avi-Yonah has acknowledged, '[t]his requires considering the debate on corporate social responsibility'.[114]

111 In what is described as a 'famous paper' by M. Bradley *et al.*, Dodd argues that '[a] sense of social responsibility towards employees, consumers, and the general public thus may come to be regarded as the appropriate attitude to be adopted by those in business' ('The Purposes and Accountability of the Corporation in Contemporary Society: Corporate Governance at a Crossroads', *Law and Contemporary Problems*, 62 (1999), 9–86, at 42, citing Dodd, Jr., at 1160). Bradley *et al.* do emphasise, however, that 'communitarians look for evidence in support of Dodd's assertion and come away disappointed' (*ibid.*, at 42).

112 Thus, '[d]iscussions of externalities and contract failure may explain – but not explain away – the fact that corporations often harm or exploit many in society who have a stake in their activities' (Bradley, *et al.* 'Purposes and Accountability', at 42).

113 Avi-Yonah is both instrumentalist, and hopeful, and presents the note open which this chapter will draw to a close. He argues that '[g]iven that we do not want government to tell corporate management directly how to run their business (that idea was tried and failed in the socialist economies), only the tax law can directly reach these types of activities, which are the ultimate source of corporate power accumulation' ('Corporations, Society', at 1244). He proffers that '[i]t is interesting to consider ... that for-profit corporations should be taxed because their management choose not to address problems they could help solve and therefore create more work for the state' (*ibid.*, at 1245).

114 Avi-Yonah, 'Corporations, Society', at fn. 237.

5

Tax policy in context

Dealing with complex systems

The previous chapter sought a place for considerations of tax policy, women and the law within the corporate social responsibility literature. It referred to 'tax law' alternatively as an instrument, or as a topic, but did not engage with the style or substance of this sort of legislation. This chapter seeks to begin such engagement, and starts with the important question of style. Just as this book has acknowledged that bureaucracy is never a side issue in tax law,[1] so the same may be observed of the length, style and sheer complexity of fiscal legislation.

The complexity of tax legislation is a global problem,[2] with specific impact upon women, for several reasons. First, complexity makes it more difficult for tax legislation to achieve its goals.[3] Second, although tax legislation largely aims to be collected both fairly and efficiently, it also anticipates the variations in response to the legislation by taxpayers.[4] This

1 See above p. 000.

2 G. Warskett, *et al.*, 'The Complexity of Tax Structure in Competitive Political Systems', *International Tax and Public Finance*, 5 (1998), 123–51, at 123: '[m]odern tax systems in democratic states are complex and remain so despite the admonition of reformers'. For a discussion of tax complexity in a generalised context (although US law is the primary focus), see also L. Kaplow, 'How Tax Complexity and Enforcement Affect the Equity and Efficiency of the Income Tax', in J. Slemrod (ed.), *Tax Policy in the Real World* (Cambridge University Press, 1999).

3 See generally Kaplow, 'How Tax Complexity and Enforcement Affect the Equity and Efficiency of the Income Tax', and K. Krause, 'Tax Complexity: Problem or Opportunity?', 28 (2000), *Public Finance Review*, 395. This goes beyond the point that, if tax legislation is complex, then implementation and enforcement are difficult. For example, changes to tax legislation can impact, by way of example, directly upon a family's decision to have children, even when increased fertility in the population is not the intention of the legislation; and, perhaps, might not have been viewed as desirable. See L. A. Whittington, 'Taxes and the Family: The Impact of the Tax Exemption for Dependents on Marital Fertility', *Demography*, 29(2) (1992), 215–26, generally, and at 223 specifically.

4 Paul M. Hirsch suggests that 'the twin institutional goals of obtaining tax revenue both equitably (through redistribution) and efficiently (through monitoring and equal enforcement)

not only potentially attracts further complexity; it also produces unpredictable, and not necessarily positive, repercussions among taxpayers.[5] Tax complexity can reinforce existing inequities in tax systems, and create new ones. In the United Kingdom, the tax law rewrite programme presents perhaps a striking example of some success in addressing this problem,[6] although there have been accomplishments in reducing tax complexity in Australia as well.[7] The US perhaps has been less successful in this area, but not for lack of effort.[8] It is probably safe to posit that few of the tax systems considered in this book are satisfied with the levels of clarity and accessibility of their fiscal legislation.[9]

One challenge simplification projects face is a failure to appreciate the full complexity of policy variation among programmes addressing women in the welfare state.[10] Objectives that give rise to the tax expenditure – the identification of need – may be less receptive to the structures of tax. Indeed, tax policy, especially if implemented through tax expenditures, may be blamed as a source of complexity.[11] This also may be an unfortunate consequence of instrumentalist tendencies within the corporate social responsibility movement, as discussed in the preceding chapter. If tax is viewed as an easy route to direct action, the legislation itself may bend under expectations.

have long occupied game theory economists (such as Nobel laureate William Vickrey)' ('Sociology Without Social Structure: Neoinstitutional Theory Meets Brave New World', *American Journal of Sociology*, 102 (1997), 1702–23, at 1712, fn. 6).

5 *Ibid.*

6 *See* the website for the Tax Law Rewrite Programme (at: www.hmrc.gov.uk/rewrite/).

7 See generally S. James and I. Wallschutzky, 'Tax Law Improvement in Australia and the UK: The Need for a Strategy for Simplification', *Fiscal Studies*, 18 (1997), 445–60.

8 This is explored in J. Slemrod, 'Which is the Simplest Tax System of Them All?', in H. J. Aaron and W. G. Gale (eds.), *Economic Effects of Fundamental Tax Reform* (Washington, DC: Brookings Institution Press, 1996). A good resource for tax simplification efforts in the US is found at: http://tax.aicpa.org/Resources/Tax+Advocacy+for+Members/Tax+Simplification/.

9 See generally Warskett, *et al.* 'Complexity of Tax Structure'.

10 See A. Orloff, 'Gender in the Welfare State', *Annual Review of Sociology*, 22 (1996), 51–78, generally, and 56, specifically.

11 E. S. Clemens and J. M. Cook argue that tax expenditures are '[o]ne important mechanism for generating commitments of constituents to policies involves altering the costs and benefits of a particular line of action' ('Politics and Institutionalism: Explaining Durability and Change', *Annual Reviews in Sociology*, 25(1) (1999), 441–66, at 456). See also Sheldon D. Pollack, who has argued, '[c]omplexity does not enter the tax code so much out of malevolence as through misguided reform efforts and excessive demands made on tax laws as the vehicle for implementing public policy ...' ('Tax Complexity, Reform, and the Illusions of Tax Simplification', *George Mason Independent Law Review*, 2 (1994), 319–58, at 321).

Pollack states the case starkly, and insists that '[t]he dilemma that we may very well confront is that the more we attempt to do through the tax [law] – whether to achieve a "more perfect justice"[12] or implement social economic policies – the more we end up making the tax laws even more complex'.[13] It is clear that there are important problems associated with complexity, and that a complex body of fiscal legislation is not simply a boon for tax lawyers. Rather, it is a direct barrier to accessibility. Fundamentally, complexity may hinder a taxpayer's ability to understand what the law requires;[14] and obstruct, where present, the state's project of equality.

The obstructive complexity of national tax laws has attracted the attention of legal theorists trying to discern why tax laws are 'complex and remain so despite the admonitions of many tax reformers'.[15] Some legal theory has attempted to fashion a pattern out of this randomness, through the techniques offered by the natural science theories of dynamic systems/complexity theory. This chapter will explain why dynamic systems theory has proved so attractive to writers interested in complex legislation, and consider the potential for economic gender equality within these theories. In the second part of this chapter, the (older) dynamic systems theory movement will be placed within the (newer) context of critical tax theory. Both sections will focus upon the implications of these theories for the effectiveness of tax policy that targets and engages with women.

Response one: complexity and systems theory

In a vast literature, dynamic systems theory, in particular, has been deployed as part of attempts to discern how complexity in legislation

12 The symbolism of the feminine contributes to the formation of culture in a simultaneously interactive and predominant way. As Marjorie E. Kornhauser explains: 'While a universal Justice may exist in theory, in reality "Justice" is replaced by culture-bound "justices" – particularistic and contextual – rooted in the societies which they shape and which, in turn, shape them' ('Equality, Liberty, and a Fair Income Tax', *Fordham Urban Law Journal*, 23 (1996), 607, at 608).

13 Pollack, 'Tax Complexity'.

14 Tax complexity may 'undermine the capacity of the citizen/taxpayer to comprehend the legal obligations imposed ...' (*ibid.*, at 322.) Elisabeth S. Clemens suggested that '[t]axes have been ignored for the same reason that it turns out to be so fascinating: taxes are obscenely complex' ('Good Reasons to Stop Avoiding Taxes', *Law and Social Inquiry*, 24 (1999), 517–31, at 518).

15 Warskett, *et al.*, 'Complexity of Tax Structure', at 123.

happens.[16] Dynamic systems theory originates from applied mathematics, and is used to described the otherwise confusing behaviour of complex 'dynamical' systems.[17] Dynamic systems theory and chaos theory consider long-term behaviour of complex systems, and attempt to identify those aspects of systems that are unlikely to change, or to remain static, during the longer term. The attractiveness of dynamic systems theory for legal scholars has been the potential of building a complex 'law and society system' that understands, and is able to anticipate, complexity in rules.[18]

The objective of scholars, most notably Ruhl, who have employed dynamic systems theory in legal analyses, is to attempt to understand the modern administrative state.[19] This section will consider these analyses, to determine if one of the 'fixed points' of dynamic systems theory impacts upon the role of women in the economy. Much work in this genre is focused on environmental law, the proliferation of which in the US has interesting parallels for fiscal legislation, and for women. The question explored in dynamic systems engagement with environmental law is why, when there is so much law trying to prevent it, does pollution continue? Additionally, when pollution is relatively easy to quantify, why has it proved so difficult to produce clear rules addressing the problem?

Ruhl presents the example of how complexity is produced by the competing definitions, in the US, of the term 'discarded material'.[20] In a 1996 article, he explained that Congress had defined solid waste in the Resource

16 Ruhl is an important writer in this tradition. See, among others: 'Law's Complexity: A Primer', *Georgia State University Law Review*, 24 (2008), 885–911; 'Complexity Theory as a Paradigm for the Dynamical Law-and-Society System: A Wake-up Call for Legal Reductionism and the Modern Administrative State', *Duke Law Journal*, 45 (1996), 849–927; 'Fitness of Law: Using Complexity Theory to Describe the Evolution of Law and Society and Its Practical Meaning for Democracy', *Vanderbilt Law Review*, 49 (1996), 1406; 'Thinking of Environmental Law as a Complex Adaptive System: How to Clean Up the Environment by Making a Mess of Environmental Law', *Houston Law Review*, 34 (1997), 933; and J. B. Ruhl and H. J. Ruhl, 'The Arrow of the Law in Modern Administrative States: Using Complexity Theory to Reveal the Diminishing Returns and Increasing Risks the Burgeoning of Law Poses to Society', *UC Davis Law Review*, 30 (1997), 405–82; J. B. Ruhl and J. Salzman, 'Mozart and the Red Queen: The Problem of Regulatory Accretion in the Administrative State', *Georgetown Law Journal*, 91 (2002), 757.

17 An excellent introduction is provided in D. G. Luenberger, *Introduction to Dynamic Systems: Theory, Models, and Applications* (New York, NY: Wiley, 1979).

18 J. Rudd, 'J. B. Ruhl's Law-and-Society System: Burying Norms and Democracy under Complexity Theory's Foundation', *William and Mary Environmental Law and Policy Review*, 29 (2004), 551–632.

19 See Ruhl and Ruhl, 'Arrow of the Law'.

20 Ruhl, 'Complexity Theory', at 881.

Conservation and Recovery Act[21] to include 'discarded material', but the Environmental Protection Agency (EPA) has taken over two pages of the Code of Federal Regulations, many pages of the Federal Register and hundreds of pages of internal agency guidance to define the term.[22] Ruhl reports that few lawyers, even among the most experienced in environmental law, fully comprehend what the EPA's rules mean.[23] Additionally, this is not an isolated example in US environmental law. In over thirty years of the EPA's existence, it 'has amassed well over ten thousand pages in the Code of Federal Regulations'.[24]

Ruhl considered complexity theory as a means of clarifying why a single legal term, requiring only a definition, could lead to such a vast amount of material. He is not alone in turning to a form of systems theory out of, primarily, frustration. In 1989, Luhmann famously turned to systems analysis, in part, out of frustration with a lack of inquiry being made into the interaction of sociology and the administration of justice.[25] Similarly, LoPucki turned to what she described as 'a set of principles arguably applicable to various kinds of systems, including physical, biological, and social systems', looking for explanations of complexity.[26] She warned, however, that she found results only at 'broad levels of generality'.[27] She discouraged turning to systems theory for solutions to complexity, or in search of diagrams for simplicity, because at the level of specificity required for most legal reform, systems theory has little to offer.[28]

In a similar vein to LoPucki, Ruhl has suggested that, when things look bad, it may be a bad idea to legislate. Rather, it may be preferable to work with what exists, than to try something new. The response of agencies to crisis is often typified by quick (and, therefore, generally crude) measures aimed at preconceived 'wrongdoers' such as industrial polluters.[29] He presents the examples of the Clean Water Act (CWA),[30]

21 Resource Conservation and Recovery Act, 42 USC, s. 6901, PL 94–580 (US).

22 Ruhl, 'Complexity Theory', at 881. 23 *Ibid.* 24 *Ibid.*

25 N. Luhmann, 'Law As a Social System', *Northwestern University Law Review*, 83 (1988) 136, at 136–7.

26 L. M. LoPucki, 'The Systems Approach to Law', *Cornell Law Review*, 82 (1997), 479–521, at 483–4.

27 *Ibid.*

28 *Ibid.* LoPucki writes that Ruhl 'appl[ies] "dynamical systems theory" to law by loose analogy to purportedly find implications for legal structuring' (*ibid.*, at 484ff.). LoPucki also suggested (in 1997) that systems theory has been applied to law 'only rarely', and cites Luhmann and Ruhl as the sole two examples (*ibid.*). As of the writing of this book, it was possible to suggest that systems theory had become more popular.

29 Ruhl, 'Complexity Theory', at 882–3.

30 Clean Water Act 1972, PL 92–500, 86 Stat. 816 (US).

and the Clean Air Act (CAA),[31] both of which were enacted in the US in the early 1970s. The acts focused attention for the first time on 'end-of-pipe' pollutant emission control strategies.[32] Ruhl explains that 'we found out later, however, that what was no longer coming out the pipes was going into the ground instead, and the Resource Conservation and Recovery Act (RCRA) was passed to address, among other things, land dispersal of pollutants'.[33] Both the CWA and CAA were appropriate responses to individual problems, but they failed to predict the responses to them. Thus, 'the dynamics of law-and-society system played a surprise on the narrowly targeted environmental efforts'.[34]

There are parallels between the efforts of gender budgeting, and the inquiries of the dynamic systems legal theorist. In many ways, both are attempting to discern the impact of rules,[35] ideally so as to be able to craft better rules. Gender budgeting involves producing significant amounts of information about processes, and dynamic systems theory involves attempting to understand the process. Both gender budgeting and dynamic systems theory 'understand' that, while it is tempting to think that the rule is at fault – that, for example, pollution is the product of inadequately crafted regulation; or that gender economic inequality is the product of poorly structured budgets, or badly written tax laws – whatever the status or structure of the rule, it does not exist independently of political and social processes.

The dynamic systems theory turn is part of a relatively recent, cultural convergence towards the physical sciences. For much of the twentieth century, science (particularly physical science, but also social sciences) was directed towards the reduction of phenomena to their smallest possible components.[36] The guiding notion was that if one knew enough about the way in which the smallest sub-atomic particles interact, there was nothing which one could not analyse or predict. A typical consequence of this scientific reductionism was that, during the 1960s and 1970s, a weather

31 Clean Air Act 1970 (84 Stat. 1676, Public Law 91–604); Clean Air Act of 1963, Air Quality Act of 1967, Clean Air Act Extension of 1970 and Clean Air Act Amendments 1977 and 1990 (US).

32 Ruhl, 'Complexity', at 882–3. 33 *Ibid.*, at 883. 34 *Ibid.*

35 P. S. Menell and R. B. Stewart have explained that 'the roots of the regulatory tradition lie in the fact that most people, including most public decision makers, do not understand either the ways in which social and economic systems function to produce pollution problems or the sophisticated market-based programs of control offered by theoreticians and experts' (*Environmental Law and Policy*, Boston, MA: Little, Brown, 1994, at p. 239).

36 A compelling summary of the twentieth-century 'complexity turn' is provided by J. Urry, 'The Complexity Turn', *Theory, Culture and Society*, 25 (2005), 1, at 4ff.

presenter would come on the TV in September and October and announce what sort of winter it was going to be.[37] When, the following April or May it was pointed out that the forecast had been no more accurate than a random choice from descriptions of the twenty previous winters, they said they knew, but that was because they didn't have powerful enough instruments or good enough data or because their predictive techniques were insufficiently refined.[38]

Mirroring this development in law was a move towards micro-management:[39] if statutes could be sufficiently convoluted they could exhaust every possibility.[40] In any case rules (including those promulgated by the EPA, and by tax agencies) multiplied. This has run alongside an interesting development in the US literature, suggesting that common law methods – organic development by judges of law – are best.[41] What happened in science – the reason we no longer have those long-range weather forecasts – is that dynamic systems theory developed. The theory is about finding patterns in randomness, embracing randomness, and focusing on the way in which components operate together as systems.

Perhaps predictably, the first applications in law of dynamic systems theory are in those areas of law which are about the areas of science in which it is deployed, and hence environmental law. There are three principle foci of dynamical system behaviour: chaos, emergence, catastrophe.[42]

First, chaos theory has devoted attention to cases of naturally occurring random events.[43] Chaos theory depends upon simple deterministic rules, which nonetheless produce highly complicated, random system

37 For an interesting discussion of this, see J. Berland, 'On Reading "the Weather"', *Cultural Studies*, 8 (1994), 99–114.

38 G. Kendall and G. Wickham explain that '[t]he weather is a well known example of a chaotic system: it is a system which is in principle predictable, but the possibility of prediction quickly disappears because there are so many variables that it is impossible for us to specify completely and correctly any momentary "weather-state"' (*Understanding Culture: Cultural Studies*, London: Sage, 2001, at p. 49).

39 See M. Herz, 'Judicial Textualism Meets Congressional Micromanagement: A Potential Collision in Clean Air Act Interpretation', *Harvard Environmental Law Review*, 16 (1992), 175.

40 H. L. A. Hart discussed the relative unforseeability of consequences and indeterminacy of language. See, among others: *The Ascription of Responsibility and Rights* (London: Harrison & Sons Ltd, 1948), at p. 173; 'Positivism and the Separation of Law and Morals', *Harvard Law Review*, 71 (1957), 593, at 602ff. (discussing 'command theory'); *The Concept of Law* (Oxford University Press, 1994, 2nd edn), chs. 5 and 6.

41 E.g. in R. A. Epstein, *Simple Rules For A Complex World* and M. A. Eisenberg, *The Nature of the Common Law* (Cambridge, MA and London: Harvard University Press, 1988).

42 Ruhl, 'Complexity Theory', at 875–7. 43 *Ibid.*

behaviour. Chaos theory only looks complicated because the rules are unknown.[44]

Second, emergence theory depends upon the appearance of unforeseen qualities from the self-organising interaction of large numbers of objects, which cannot be understood through study of any one of the objects.[45] Emergence theory depends upon the condition of the system as a whole.[46]

Third, catastrophe theory suggests that catastrophic events occur with a sudden qualitative change in a dynamical system brought about by a continuous change in a system variable. The idea is that catastrophes depend upon 'strange attractors'.[47] What links these three theories of dynamic systems behaviour is their deterministic randomness, which is when precise laws lead to apparently random behaviour which is in fact minutely organised. Ruhl's thesis is that US legal theory and legal institutions have been built upon premises which obscure the dynamical behaviour of the socio-legal system. Through complexity theory, he argues, it is possible to gain a deeper appreciation of the need for allowing dynamic, unpredictable processes in the socio-legal system to prosper. Ruhl insists that, in a sense, theorists have been doing this all along. Quoting Schauer, Ruhl argues that it is no accident that Fried, Nozick and Dworkin all use the same word – 'catastrophe' – to characterise the circumstances under which all bets are off, i.e. if there's a catastrophe, then rights do not exist.[48]

There are four implications of complexity theory for analysis of gender in tax policy. The first implication concerns rights theories, and the extent to which it is possible to determine the effect of legislation. Rights theories are generally subject to, at least some extent, dependence on this sort of determinism, however reductionist. The second implication concerns common law and regulation. Under complexity analyses, common law is preferred to statutory legislation, largely because, given that

44 An example in natural law would be the weather.

45 Ruhl, 'Complexity Theory', at 875–7.

46 An example in natural law would be a beehive.

47 An example in natural law would be bending metal, where if one bends metal to a certain extent, it will bounce back into shape, but if one pushes it just a bit further, it stays bent, or even breaks, and its content has been altered in a completely unpredictable way.

48 Ruhl, 'Fitness of Law', at 1472, fn. 251, citing F. F. Schauer, *Playing by the Rules: A Philosophical Examination of Rule-based Decision-making in Law and in Life* (New York, NY: Oxford University Press, 1991), at p. 177.

the common law changes slowly and incrementally, it is less prone to catastrophe. Whereas the common law may be 'more coupled than is the administrative state',[49] it is also 'fragmented',[50] and, as Beatson has written, '[t]he fragmented nature of the common law means that it can appear obscure and – in the ugly modern jargon – to lack transparency'.[51]

Complexity theory aims to determine the degree of specificity with which rules can usefully be written. A return to a preference for common law is an identifiable theme, because of its lack of catastrophe. Yet, on these terms, the end of apartheid might quality as a catastrophe. Additionally (the third point), there are difficulties with accounts of the rule of law and democratic theory, which make the judges our number one legislators. It was perhaps fairly predictable that if law stops polluters from discharging into the air or the ground, then they will discharge into the earth. This, essentially, is McBarnet's account of 'creative compliance', which 'uses formalism to avoid legal control, whether a tax liability or some regulatory obstacle to raising finance, effecting a controversial takeover or securing other corporate, or management, objectives'.[52] Finally, the fourth point is that there are other criticisms of the potential place of complexity theory in tax policy, particularly from the perspective of gender.

49 Ruhl, 'Complexity Theory', at 919.

50 J. Beatson, 'Has the Common Law a Future?', *Cambridge Law Journal*, 56 (2009), 291–314, at 298.

51 Beatson explains that '[w]here the law is changed by a judicial decision, the traditional working assumption upon which the common law proceeds is the declaratory theory of decision-making: the judges declare law but do not make it and the law is regarded as having always been what the judicial decision stated it to be. Where the change is effected by overruling an earlier decision, this is manifestly fictional. But where no decision is specifically overruled but a decision has the effect of changing what had previously been regarded as the law—changing the perception of what the law is—the position is less clear. This is what occurred in the rape and marriage and recovery of unlawfully exacted taxes cases and the latter case is somewhat difficult to square with the declaratory theory. There is also other older authority consistent with the view that even a change in the perception of the law has a constitutive element. In two cases a person who paid money which was due under the view of the law that changed as a result of later decisions was said not to be mistaken "at the time the money was paid ... the law was in favour of the [payee]. But the implications of this have not fed through into the theory of judicial change and there are still powerful voices favouring the declaratory theory of judicial law-making"' (*ibid.*, at 314, citing *Henderson* v. *Folkestone Waterworks Co.* (1885) 1 TLR 329; *Julian* v. *Mayor of Auckland* [1927] NZLR 453; *Derrick* v. *Williams* [1939] 2 All ER 559, 565, at fn. 125).

52 D. McBarnet and C. Whelan, 'The Elusive Spirit of the Law: Formalism and the Struggle for Legal Control', *Modern Law Review*, 54 (1991), 848–73, at 849.

The search for what is natural has been identified as an ideologically loaded task, and a distinctly gendered pursuit – what Lloyd identified as a search for the 'male' reason.[53] If Attenborough-esque nature programmes hint that the answer to why we are what we are has been right in front of our noses, in the example of animals, for ever, and that humans have been too blinkered to notice, then an obvious clash with feminism awaits.[54] Feminists challenge why we are stuck with what we have, and necessarily mistrust efforts to convince us why what we have is natural, or, inevitable.[55] Perhaps 'efforts to convince' is a strong way of characterising what nature shows are about. They are mostly, after all, presenting something to an audience, although since the 1960s, and the heyday of structuralism,[56] any pretensions to mere presentation tend to be discarded.

Complexity theory is elaborate. By its own admission, complexity theory leads to few answers, and on the question of tax policy for women, answers are needed. There are also anti-democratic dangers in complexity theory improperly executed, and conservative tendencies in any theory exhibiting preferences for the organic. Indeed, there is a general problem with the deployment in a legal context of arguments about what is and is not natural. The fundamental problem with borrowing theories from the natural sciences is that natural sciences do not deal with values. Catastrophe in the sense defined is not the same as disaster, and, indeed, sometimes radical, rupturing change is a good thing.

53 G. Lloyd, *The Man of Reason: Male and Female in Western Philosophy* (London: Routledge, 1993).

54 See B. Crowther, 'Viewing What Comes Naturally: A Feminist Approach to Television Natural History', *Women's Studies International Forum*, 20(2) (1997), 289–300.

55 See generally S. Haslanger, 'Feminism in Metaphysics: Negotiating the Natural', in Miranda Fricker and Jennifer Hornsby (eds.), *The Cambridge Companion to Feminism in Philosophy* (Cambridge University Press, 2000).

56 This is very much an embracing of the madness, as advocated by Ruhl, although complexity theory is hardly discoursive. It is rather an attempt at revisionist history, perhaps a return to the questions not answered (to the extent that answering questions was the point) by not even post-structuralists, but by *structuralists*: '[t]he great lesson of dynamical systems theory for law reform, therefore, is that it is the *system* that counts as much as the *rules*, and that we cannot effectively change only one variable of that equation and expect the others to remain static. *Ceteris paribus* doesn't exist. Our legal institutions, however, have become prolific producers of rules of conduct, and our legal theory has focused for the most part on divining the meta-rules to explain those rules. We need some attention to the system at the structural level' ('Complexity Theory', at 916–17).

Response two: tax policy theorised – critical tax theory

The 'old liberalism', as Dworkin explained, fought for equality before the law.[57] The struggle was organized against difference – different, meaning different treatment before the law, and different opportunities.[58] Dworkin explained that the consensus that was presumed to exist surrounding the implementation of New Deal 'liberal' policies no longer exists, which can lead to confusion among the self-selected group claiming the label of 'liberal'.[59] As taxes always have straddled the public–private divide, the approach to tax and to gender in this post-'old liberal' era was bound to be diverse, and a commonality of approach, or even of objectives, was not to be expected.

This classic, 'old liberalism' discourse, articulated by Dworkin in 1978, found its perfect expression almost twenty years later, by which time critical tax theory had become an important development in socio-legal discourse, and involved scholars who care about tax, women and otherness.[60] The purpose of this section is to find the place for feminist perspectives in critical tax scholarship. It hopes to pick up the point with which the previous section ended – the acknowledgement that radical, rupturing change is sometimes desirable, and may be desirable on the question of the interactions between women and tax law – and to review how the critical tax movement has presented a forum for these calls to action.

Critical tax theory was defined by Infanti and Crawford as a movement involving 'scholars who challenge the traditional claim that tax law is neutral and unbiased'.[61] As such it is necessarily a broad church, and has embraced a variety of feminist strategies. Livingston had suggested,

57 The term 'old liberalism' was famously used in R. Dworkin, *Liberalism* (orig. pub.) Stuart Hampshire (ed.), *Public and Private Morality* (Cambridge University Press, 1978), in J. Nida-Rumelin and W. Vossenkuhl (eds.), *Ethische und Politische* (Cambridge, MA: Walter de Gruyter, 1998), at p. 182.

58 *Ibid.*

59 *Ibid.* Liberalism is no longer presumed to emanate from one place, and thus Erik M. Jensen asked why 'feminist and critical race commentary' is 'spreading' to taxation ('Critical Theory and the Loneliness of the Tax Prof', *North Carolina Law Review*, 76 (1998), 1753).

60 This history is detailed in, among others: M. A Livingston, 'Reinventing Tax Scholarship: Lawyers Economists and the Role of the Legal Academy', *Cornell Law Review*, 83 (1997), 365 and 'Radical Scholars, Conservative Field: Putting Critical Tax Scholarship in Perspective', *North Carolina Law Review*, 76 (1997), 1791; the publication of Anthony C. Infanti and Bridget J. Crawford, 'Critical Tax Theory – An Introduction' (at: http://papers.ssrn.com/sol3/papers.cfm?abstract_id=1333799), and which promises to set the foundation for future generations of scholars hoping to engage with critical tax theory.

61 Infanti and Crawford, 'Critical Tax Theory'.

'[a]lthough the critical tax project crosses theoretical lines, it is typically perceived as raising issues of horizontal equity, that is, arguments that women or minorities are treated differently by the tax system than similarly situated white males'.[62] This may be the reason why critical tax scholarship is sometimes misunderstood. As Livingston explained, '[m]y own belief is that critical tax scholarship is more about vertical than horizontal equity, so that attacks by traditional scholars miss the point to a considerable degree'.[63] The starting point of critical tax scholarship is misunderstood; and, thus, '[t]he argument is not that women or minorities are treated differently from similarly situated white men, but that they are not similarly situated in the first place because of the historic real-world disadvantages that adhere to these groups'.[64] As a broad church, however, critical tax theory also has included scholarship with ambitions that are clearly pragmatic. Thus, for example, Crawford has suggested that 'solutions' might be found through 'the appropriation of conservative modes of analysis for left-oriented purposes'.[65] Crawford's proposal is strategic, and dependent upon identifiable goals, potentially achievable through the political process, yet as such requiring consensus.

Crawford's strategic approach has been complemented by what perhaps could be described as the scholarship of taxing choices, pioneered by Alstott. For example, Alstott has placed in context particular tax breaks for mothers in the workforce that, by definition, would not benefit mothers who stay at home as caregivers.[66] The provision at issue is individual filing of tax returns, which affords equal tax treatment to both members of a married couple.[67] In the US, if a married woman files a tax return separately, she will not be claiming, for example, tax breaks which may favour marriage, or indeed any benefits which could be afforded her tax status by virtue of her husband's income. This 'equal' treatment, Alstott explains, is achieved by taking a benefit away from women who work at home.[68] The feminist goal of assisting women's continuing transition to market work faces an 'inevitable' conflict with the needs of caregivers.[69]

First, examination of the ideologies behind tax systems and tax reliefs 'opens the way to a better understanding of the changing nature of family

62 Michael A. Livingston, 'Blum and Kalven at 50: Progressive Taxation, "Globalization", and the New Millennium', *Florida Tax Review*, 4 (2000), 731–68, at 757.

63 *Ibid.*, at 758. 64 *Ibid.*

65 B. J. Crawford, 'Outsourcing Intimacy: The Taxation of Powers of Attorney' (at: http://digitalcommons.pace.edu/cgi/viewcontent.cgi?article=1397&context=lawfaculty, at 52).

66 Alstott, 'Tax Policy and Feminism'. 67 *Ibid.* 68 *Ibid.* 69 *Ibid.*

life and of the changing position of individuals within families'.[70] The connection between the two is important. Typically, the state acknowledges first that a need articulated by the family is legitimate (i.e. childcare), and this acknowledgement paves the way for both financial and social support.[71] Problems can occur when the state acknowledges (in an extension of Alstott's 'taxing choices' jurisprudence) that two, perhaps mutually exclusive and potentially conflicting needs, are valid.[72] A good example of this is provided by the frequently occurring 'privacy trade-off'.

Second, financial privacy for women is impossible when their husbands control their finances and their taxes. Thus, in the UK, the 1986 Green Paper entitled 'Reform of Personal Taxation' emphasised that independent taxation of married women is essential for both their autonomy and privacy'.[73] Yet state-based efforts to assist women financially frequently require that, in the first instance, privacy is sacrificed. Indeed, privacy is a consistent concern behind efforts to address the problems of women, work, childcare and poverty. When WFTC[74] was first designed, for example, reservations were lodged as to whether, if this benefit were to be administered through employers, then would it be appropriate – indeed, would recipients be embarrassed – if the financial circumstances of employees were to be known in such detail by their employers?[75]

Critical tax theory does not reject formalism per se. As there is an important role for formalism in tax legal scholarship, so there is a place for formalism in comparative analyses of tax policy, women and the law. Put simply, if a tax provision explicitly discriminates along the lines of gender, it is important that this should be identified, and it is most likely

70 J. Pahl, 'Personal Taxation, Social Security and Financial Arrangements within Marriage', *Journal of Law and Society*, 13 (1986), 241–50, at 249.

71 'The recognition by the welfare state that certain social needs are legitimate creates a legal framework for social access' (Å. Gunnarsson, *et al.*, *Exploiting the Limits of Law: Swedish Feminism and the Challenge to Pessimism*, Aldershot: Ashgate, 2007, at p. 194). Additionally, N. Ginsburg observed that '[t]he terms "social policy" and "the welfare state" are virtually synonymous' (*Divisions of Welfare: A Critical Introduction to Comparative Social Policy*, London: Sage, 1992, at p. 1).

72 J. Plantenga and J. Hansen have argued that the drives both for women's financial independence from men, and to assist women's relative poverty, have produced 'theoretical stalemate' ('Assessing Equal Opportunities in the European Union', *International Labour Review*, 138 (1999), at 429).

73 R. Lister, 'Future Insecure: Women and Income Maintenance under a Third Tory Term', *Feminist Review*, 27 (1987), 9–16, at 15.

74 The Working Families Tax Credit, Tax Credits Act 2002.

75 This is discussed throughout Mumford, 'Marketing Working Mothers: Contextualizing Earned Income Tax Credits within Feminist Cultural Theory', *Journal of Social Welfare and Family Law*, 23(4) (2001), 411–26.

that a formalist analysis will reveal this. The two approaches need not be exclusive, although critical tax theorists proceed from the basis that identification of even implicit bias is more likely to be identified from a broader, contextual analysis.

Tax law is not immune from the tensions in other areas of law, although Weisbach has suggested that 'in tax law the problem seems to be worse'.[76] Weisbach suggested that '[o]ne explanation might be the tax law's focus on form, which allows taxpayers to change the application of the law to particular transactions without significantly changing their economics'.[77] He also predicted work that later would be undertaken by Braithwaite, suggesting that '[a]nother might be the culture of tax compliance, which seems to encourage manipulation'.[78] More controversially, Weisbach proffered that '[y]et another explanation is that the tax law is not special and the analysis given here applies more generally'.[79] Most importantly, Weisbach stressed that, interesting as these suggestions may be, none of them are particularly important. 'Whichever explanation is correct', Weisbach wrote, 'the effect is common in tax law'.[80]

Among other issues, critical tax law addresses the impact of tax law on distinct groups of taxpayers. A variety of important work has been done in this area, dealing with a range of issues. Moran, for example, has striven to '[s]et ... an agenda for the study of tax and Black culture' in the US.[81] She has disproved the proposition that 'the Internal Revenue Code is supposedly race neutral but class sensitive ...'[82] The impact of this mistaken presumption, Moran demonstrates, is damaging. Class-based reforms are politically controversial, and as a consequence 'political barriers to class-based reforms [prevent the achievement of] race justice'.[83] The questions of race and class need not be mutually exclusive. As Moran writes, '[i]f we believe that blacks suffer from a class problem we should ask what law can do to improve that problem'.

Feminist approaches to tax law have been developed by many different writers, although Alstott's 1996 *Columbia Law Review* article addressing feminist approaches to tax law in many ways set the stage for modern understanding of a legal, academic feminist tax agenda.[84] In this article Alstott drew attention to a number of developments. She stressed the

76 David A. Weisbach, 'Formalism in the Tax Law', *University of Chicago Law Review*, 66 (1999), 860–86.

77 *Ibid.*, at 869. 78 *Ibid.*, at 869–70. 79 *Ibid.*, at 870. 80 *Ibid.*

81 Beverly Moran, 'Setting an Agenda for the Study of Tax and Black Culture', *University of Arkansas at Little Rock Law Review*, 21 (1999), 779–94.

82 *Ibid.*, at 784. 83 *Ibid.* 84 Alstott, 'Tax Policy and Feminism'.

fact that there has been a dramatic increase in women's labour market participation in recent decades. Despite this, women continue to perform a disproportionate share of 'family labour', or the unpaid work of caring for children and other family members. This 'gendered division of family labour reduces women's wages, contributes to the high and disproportionate rate of poverty among single mothers, limits married women's autonomy within the marital household, and circumscribes women's life choices and social and economic power'.[85]

Although the breadth of critical tax scholarship, spanning over a decade, is remarkable, a common point within this literature is the acknowledgement that free markets have not always provided the best solutions for women.[86] In the presence of agreement upon a need to turn to the state, however, there will not necessarily be agreement upon the terms of this turn. For example, financial independence for women can mean both independence from state assistance, as well as freedom from financial dependence upon men.[87] The challenge is to forge the link between support for women, and support for a wider human community.[88] What however are the boundaries of this wider community, and is it necessary to delineate the distinctions between different types of legal culture?

By referring to 'legal culture' it may be implied that this is something that exists separately from popular, or other, cultures, which, even for tax law, is simply not the case.[89] Even if different elements of culture

85 *Ibid.*, at 2001. A report by the Organisation for Economic Co-operation and Development (OECD) on single-parent families warned that '[i]f working and non-working poor were both covered under a single system, then the seemingly inequitable differentiation between them could not be eliminated' (Y. Ergas, 'Child-care Policies in Comparative Perspective: An Introductory Discussion', in OECD (ed.), *Lone-parent Families: The Economic Challenge*, at pp. 215–16).

86 As Jeanne M. Dennis writes, '[t]aking the historical discrimination against women in the labor market as a starting point, feminist law and economic theory does not assume that free markets produce the best solutions. Therefore, a feminist approach to law and economic theory, like comparable worth, looks to state power to address market inequities' ('The Lessons of Comparable Worth: A Feminist Vision of Law and Economic Theory', *UCLA Women's Law Journal*, 4 (1993), 1–36, at 28).

87 The financial responsibility of men for financially dependent women and children historically has been used to justify male 'tax advantages'. See J. S. O'Connor, *et al.*, *States, Markets, Families: Gender, Liberalism and Social Policy in Australia, Canada, Great Britain and the United States* (Cambridge University Press, 1999), at p. 24.

88 Robin West, 'Jurisprudence and Gender', *University of Chicago Law Review*, 55 (1988), 1–72, at 15.

89 As B. Yngvesson explained, 'while the notion of popular legal culture appears in one sense self-evident, it is an inherently problematic concept, implying the existence of separate spheres of law rather than providing a more complex analysis of the ways legal culture

might appear to be unrelated, on closer examination, simply the fact of their juxtaposition may be meaningful.[90] This also applies to gender, its significance in legal and a wider culture, and, in particular, those aspects of tax law which may be perceived as 'gender issues'.[91]

In a relatively recent and very useful review of the modern state of critical tax scholarship, Crawford explained that 'critical tax scholarship does not take as its primary task a detailed rewriting of tax rules, nor does it emphasize the ways in which the tax law actually could favor disenfranchised groups'.[92] Rather, critical tax scholarship 'uncovers, reveals, and exposes bias in the face of arguments that the tax laws are value neutral'.[93] There are theoretical links between critical tax scholarship, and its steadfast refusal to adopt a positivist agenda, and cultural feminism.[94] Cultural feminism, which has been credited with the 'death' of radical feminism', advocates separateness based on an essentialist view of gender difference.[95] It has been criticised for advocating a retreat from political activism, towards a 'lifestyle'.[96] Critical tax scholarship and

is produced, and popular understandings of the law shaped' ('Inventing Law in Local Settings: Rethinking Popular Legal Culture', *Yale Law Journal*, 98 (1988), 1689–1709, at 1690).

90 D. Patterson argued that '[p]ostmodernity is exemplified in culture by the presence of "pastiche" – the juxtaposition of unrelated elements in various cultural forms' ('Postmodernism/Feminism/Law', *Cornell Law Review*, 77 (1992), 254–317, 258). Thus, by way of example, C. Lucia, engaging in analysis of the film *Adam's Rib*, observes that the character played by Katharine Hepburn is unable to escape her family 'recalculated under the power of property and tax law' ('Women on Trial: The Female Lawyer in the Hollywood Courtroom', in M. Fineman and M. T. McCluskey (eds.), *Feminism, Media, and the Law*, Oxford University Press, 1997, at p. 147).

91 Thus, '[i]s gender something with which we come into the world, or is it produced in our language or culture?' (*ibid.*, at 259).

92 Bridget J. Crawford, 'Tax Avatars' (2008) *Utah Law Review*, 793–833, at 832 (at: http://digitalcommons.pace.edu/cgi/viewcontent.cgi?article=1549&context=lawfaculty).

93 *Ibid.*

94 'Cultural feminism' has been defined in a number of different ways. For example: cultural feminism defines women as typically more oriented towards relationships and therefore, more caring than men. Cultural feminists assert that men usually view problems in terms of 'abstract rights', while women approach dilemmas in terms of 'real and complex relationships between people'. Women attempt to resolve conflicts through 'strategies that maintain connection and relationship'. Thus, the theory underlying cultural feminism is that by embracing the female voice, the law would come to recognise and respect the specifically feminine values of connection and caring over the male value of autonomy. Page McGuire Linden, 'Drug Addiction During Pregnancy: A Call for Increased Social Responsibility', *American University Journal of Gender and Law*, 4 (1995), 105–39, at 113.

95 V. Taylor and L. J. Rupp, 'Women's Culture and Lesbian Feminist Activism: A Reconsideration of Cultural Feminism', *Signs*, 19(1) (1993), 32–61, at 32.

96 *Ibid.*

cultural feminism have a negative in common: the absence of a pragmatic agenda.

Cultural feminism has been criticised for suggesting that gender is at the heart of all social problems faced by women.[97] Fiss has tempered this criticism with the suggestion that perhaps the term 'relational feminism' is to be preferred to cultural feminism, on the basis that the problem is not gender, on its own, but the way in which women relate to society, and society relates to women.[98] It is a two-way street. Another response to the essentialist criticism of cultural feminism is to rebrand this approach as an acceptance, or 'celebration'[99] of difference.[100] This allows 'cultural

97 Turnier *et al.* suggest that 'cultural feminism posits that gender alone can account for the different approaches made by men and women as solutions to social problems ...' (W. J. Turnier, P. Johnston Conover and D. Lowery, 'Redistributive Justice and Cultural Feminism', *American University Law Review*, 45 (1996), 1275–1322, at 1279). But cf. Wai Chee Dimock, who eloquently makes the point that social, metonymic foci on women are strong trends in both culture and literature: *Residues of Justice – Literature, Law, Philosophy* (Berkeley, CA and London: University of California Press, 1996), at pp. 84–8.

98 Owen M. Fiss suggests that the term 'relational feminism' is preferred to 'cultural feminism', and that '[l]ike the cultural feminists, the relationalists emphasize the ethic of care proclaimed by Gilligan and see women as having a special (though not exclusive) connection to this ethic, but differ on their understanding of the etiology of the tendency of women to value care more highly than men do. This tendency, they insist, stems not from biology – that women have the capacity to bear children – but rather is socially constructed' ('What is Feminism?', *Arizona State Law Journal*, 26 (1994), 413–42, at 425).

99 Lisa R. Pruitt, 'A Survey of Feminist Jurisprudence', *University of Arkansas at Little Rock Law Journal*, 16 (1994), 183–205, at 189.

100 This approach emerges as the most common understanding of the term 'cultural feminism', the origins of which often are ascribed to both Robin West and Carrie Menkel-Meadow. Robin West, 'Jurisprudence and Gender', *University of Chicago Law Review*, 55 (1988), 1–42; Carrie Menkel-Meadow, 'Portia in a Different Voice: Speculations on a Women's Lawyering Process', *Berkeley Women's Law Journal*, 1 (1985), 39–63. Examples of difference as a linchpin in legal cultural analysis include: Dorothy E. Roberts, who noted, '[i]t is now commonplace for feminist scholars to acknowledge the differences among women' ('Racism and Patriarchy in the Meaning of Motherhood', *Journal of Gender and the Law*, 1 (1993), 1–38); Robert R. M. Verchick, who suggests that it is because women are different, or special, through motherhood, that they tend to become environmental activists ('In a Greener Voice: Feminist Theory and Environmental Justice', *Harvard Women's Law Journal*, 19 (1996), 23–88, at 28). Simply, if pollution makes children sick, then mothers will act to protect their children. This twists Roberts' characterisation of work as a 'romanticized middle-class quest' for 'resistance of motherhood' into an ideology of instinct. Class also forms an important part of this analysis. R. Cherry explains that, in the US, '[t]raditionalists have consistently used the federal tax system to discourage middle class women from working' ('Rational Choice and the Price of Marriage', in K. S. Moe (ed.), *Women, Family, and Work: Writings on the Economics of Gender*, London: Blackwell, 2003, at p. 36). Verchick quotes Aurora Castillo of Mothers of East Los Angeles as explaining that '[i]f one of [our] children's safety is jeopardized, the mother turns into a lioness' ('In a Greener Voice', at 28, quoting Gabriel Gutiérrez,

feminism', itself, to be understood as a culturally appropriated concept, which is added to, and redefined, constantly.[101] This evokes what Minow characterised as the tripartite 'dilemma of difference'; i.e., is difference 'recreated' by discounting/counting it; and, if difference is discounted, then humans are rendered prisoners of a purportedly neutral past; or, if difference is emphasised, then is this only achievable through public neutrality – *but* empowerment of the private sphere with the discretion to rectify past injustice (and is this a good idea)?[102] As Minow points out, this is only relational – in her example, 'I am no more different from you than you are from me. A short person is only different in relation to a tall one.'[103]

For feminist legal scholars, this is, as Morgan has recounted, a debate which has probably 'absorbed the most energy'.[104] For example, do maternity-leave laws address historical, gendered workplace injustice, or do they further the belief that pregnancy is exclusively women's responsibility?[105] And, if pregnancy is exclusively women's responsibility, does this empower them, or disempower them? Feminist legal theory,

Mothers of East Los Angeles Strike Back, in R. D. Bullard (ed.), *Unequal Protection: Environmental Justice and Communities of Color* (San Francisco, CA: Sierra Club Books, 1994).

101 See Edward LiPuma's analysis of Bourdieu's account of culture, what constitutes it and how we experience it, in *Culture and the Concept of Culture in a Theory of Practice*, in C. Calhoun, E. LiPuma and M. Postone (eds.), *Bourdieu: Critical Perspectives* (Cambridge: Polity, 1993). Linda J. Lacey finds compelling 'the concept that women are shaped by their culture in certain ways' ('Mimicking the Words, But Missing the Message: The Misuse of Cultural Feminist Themes in Religion and Family Law Jurisprudence', *Boston College Law Review*, 35 (1993), 1–48, at 4).

102 Martha Minow, *Foreword: Justice Engendered*, *Harvard Law Review*, 101 (1987), 10, at 12–13.

103 *Ibid.*, at 13. To take Jenny Morgan's twist on this dilemma: 'are women the same as or different from men, or is this the wrong question'? ('Feminist Theory as Legal Theory', *Melbourne University Law Review*, 16 (1988), 743–59, at 743).

104 *Ibid.*, at 744.

105 *Ibid.*, at 744–5, and, among others: W. W. Williams, 'Equality's Riddle: Pregnancy and the Equal Treatment/Special Treatment Debate', *Columbia Law Review*, 86 (1986), 1118; S. Law, 'Rethinking Sex and the Constitution', *University of Pennsylvania Law Review*, 132 (1984), 955. Morgan refers to Gilligan's classic and often-cited work with the Heinz dilemma as a touchstone in her analysis – i.e., whereas Jake, an 11-year-old boy, quickly announces that Heinz should steal a drug he cannot afford to save his wife's life; conversely, Amy, an 11-year-old girl, while stressing that the wife should not be allowed to die, concludes that Heinz should find another way to get the money – perhaps get a loan – because 'he might have to go to jail, and then his wife might get sicker again, and he couldn't get more of the drug and it might not be good' ('Feminist Theory', at 747, citing C. Gilligan, *In a Different Voice: Psychological Theory and Women's Development*, Cambridge, MA: Harvard University Press, 1990). As Morgan notes, the Heinz dilemma

generally, perhaps began by accepting the system,[106] and questioning its operation and the exercise of its discretion, and then progressed to non-acceptance and epistemological analysis. The next step was acknowledgement of the dangers of epistemology, and the potential oppression of the general.[107] This is where cultural feminism and critical tax scholarship enter the discussion.[108]

The possibility of common ground in between critical tax law and its critics may be found in an unlikely place: the standard, liberalist account, the Rawlsian model of equality.[109] One key aspect of a pragmatic realisation of Rawls' social contract would be the constant correction necessary to maintain equality for all citizens.[110] This means that equality would not remain static, and would have to be policed. Progressive taxation is

provided strong support for theorists arguing that alternative dispute resolution is a feminist solution (*ibid.*, at 748–9, citing C. Menkel-Meadow, 'Toward Another View of Legal Negotiation: The Structure of Problem Solving', *University of California Los Angeles Law Review*, 31 (1984), 754; C. Menkel-Meadow, 'Portia in a Different Voice: Speculations on a Women's Lawyering Process', *Berkeley Women's Law Journal*, 39 (1987), 39–63, at 51). But cf., among others: D. R. Stallone, 'Decriminalization of Violence in the Home: Mediation in Wife Battering Cases', *Law and Inequality*, 2 (1984), 493.

106 Clare Dalton argued that feminist legal theorists understand the legal system 'broadly, as including the rules that constitute the formal body of law; the discourses in which those rules are situated, and through which they are articulated and elaborated ...' ('Where We Stand: Observation on the Situation of Feminist Legal Thought', *Berkeley Women's Law Journal*, 3 (1988), 1, at 2).

107 *Ibid.*, at 8. The 'oppression of the general' was explained by C. Weedon as follows, '[w]hatever else we do, we should be attractive and desirable to men, and, ideally, our sexuality should be given to one man and our emotional energy directed at him and the children of the marriage. This message comes to us from a wide range of sources, for instance, children's books, women's magazines, religion, the advertising industry, romance, television, the cinema and current tax and social security arrangements' (*Feminist Practice and Poststructuralist Theory*, Oxford: Blackwell, 1997, at p. 3).

108 For example, the 2007 case of *Spearmint Rhino Ventures* considered whether an agency relationship had developed between pole dancers and the owners of the Spearmint Rhino clubs, such that the clubs should be liable for VAT on the grounds that they were providing a service. The court ruled that such a relationship had not developed for, even though the dancers had to pay a fee to the club, this fee simply enabled them to 'ply their trade', and, crucially, they kept all of the money they earned for each dance they performed ([2007] STC 1252). A pragmatic analysis of this case from a feminist perspective would conclude that, as the issue concerned the tax liability of the club owners, and not the dancers, then there is no negative outcome for women from this decision. A critical tax analysis, or indeed a cultural feminist analysis, would have difficulty accepting that the dancers were indeed as autonomous as they are described in the text of this decision. The tax victory afforded to the club owners can be analysed as a link to a wider marketplace which primarily values women for their sexuality.

109 As established in J. Rawls, *A Theory of Justice* (Oxford University Press, 1999).

110 Donna M. Byrne, 'Progressive Taxation Revisited', *Arizona Law Review*, 37 (1995), 739–89, at 778.

the sort of corrective action, likely to maintain equality for all citizens,[111] envisioned within the social contract.[112]

There are a variety of responses to the question of progressive taxation, and its impact upon women.[113] In a sense pre-dating critical tax theory (perhaps commencing the era), a 1987 article by Kornhauser remains the standard point of reference for feminist arguments supporting progressivity.[114] This article demonstrates how many 1980s, Reaganomics-inspired criticisms of progressivity as anti-feminist were in fact standard progressivity critiques, retread. She exhorted that 'the choice of a flat or a progressive tax is still choice between opposing philosophies'.[115] The philosophies at issue are a sense of the 'common humanity', or the 'narrow vision of the self-interested man'.[116]

Similarly, Bankman and Griffith argued that '[t]raditional legal analysis of progressive taxation is flawed because it is not grounded in a theory of distributive justice'.[117] They conclude that 'under any welfarist social welfare function, and under reasonable assumptions regarding the components of individual utility and the nature of the economy, the optimal tax structure would redistribute income from the rich to the poor, although by means of a demogrant [or pure lump-sum transfer] rather than by graduated marginal rates'.[118] This is in the interest of all citizens, possibly – but what about women, specifically?

111 Byrne argued that, '[i]f the theoretical structure supporting progressivity is made of pillars such as equal distribution and distinctions between wealth arising from luck and ambition, perhaps the case for progressivity is not so uneasy' (*ibid.*, at 789). Elmer D. Fagan advocated a 'socio-political' theory as the best way of analysing the desirability of progressive taxation ('Recent and Contemporary Theories of Progressive Taxation', *Journal of Political Economy*, 46 (1938), 457–98, at 497–8). The socio-political theory acknowledges that '[i]n a world in which change is inevitable the criteria of welfare themselves cannot be static' (*ibid.*, at 496).

112 Byrne has suggested that '[a]ny system developed under Rawls's principles ... would require constant "correction" to maintain the ideals of equality'. She suggests that progressive taxation and wealth transfer taxes would enable this to happen, yet '[t]hat such "correction" might reduce the overall size of the economic pie is not such a concern for Rawls because the main goal is not a maximum pie overall, but maximum slices for those at the bottom' ('Progressive Taxation', at 778). See also, generally, S. L. Hurley, 'The Unit of Taxation Under an Ideal Progressive Income Tax', *Oxford Journal of Legal Studies*, 4 (2002), 157–97.

113 Alvarez and McCaffery, 'Gender and Tax', in Tolleson-Rinehart and Josephson, *Gender and American Politics*, at p. 92.

114 M. E. Kornhauser, 'The Rhetoric of the Anti-Progressive Income Tax Movement: A Typical Male Reaction', *Michigan Law Review*, 86 (1987), 465–523.

115 *Ibid.*, at 523. 116 *Ibid.*

117 Joseph Bankman and Thomas Griffith, 'Social Welfare and the Rate Structure: A New Look At Progressive Taxation', *California Law Review*, 75 (1987), 1905–67, at 1966.

118 *Ibid.*

Liberal political theory has been described 'male or masculine'.[119] Is there a place for gender equality within the Rawlsian social contract? Okin has raised the possibility of a 'constructive critique' of Rawls, which could find that place.[120] For example, the Rawlsian model of equality can have unpredictable results for the family, not least because of its assumption that 'heads of families' are gender neutral.[121] Okin has explained the proponents of standard, Rawlsian liberalism have never responded to feminist criticisms.[122] She engages the question 'feminism and liberalism: friends of foes?' directly,[123] and suggests that it is possible to defend liberalism against 'anti-liberal feminist critiques'.[124] Rawls devotes much of *Theory of Justice* to institutions and, especially, to taxation[125] – tax law could be the forum for the engagement which Okin advocates.

As a final word, this chapter will draw to a close with Okin, who suggests the possible terms of this discourse:

> Rawls simply states, without argument, that '[w]e wouldn't want' families to be regulated internally by principles of distributive justice ... But having spent much time thinking about justice and its applicability or lack of applicability to families, some of us are not sure that this is at all evident. We still ask: 'Why not?'[126]

119 S. M. Okin, 'Justice and Gender: An Unfinished Debate', *Fordham Law Review*, 72 (2003), 1537, at 1543.

120 J. Borison, 'Alice through a Very Dark and Confusing Looking Glass: Getting Equity from the Tax Court in Innocent Spouse Cases', *Family Law Quarterly*, 30 (1996), 123–72.

121 Okin, 'Justice and Gender', at 1547. For example, Stephen Kershnar analysed the stereotype of Rawls' theory, in which life is one big competition for primary goods, and suggested, '[g]iven that there is some evidence that stay-at-home mothers are happier than other women, it is not clear why trading this role for more primary goods makes someone's life go better or is demanded by rationality' ('For Discrimination against Women', *Law and Philosophy*, 26 (2007), 589–625, at 614). His suggestion is based on the assumption that the 'stay-at-home mother' has sacrificed primary goods, although her ability to stay at home will be enabled by somebody else's money, whether her partner or the state. Stay-at-home mothers may be 'happier' because they have been relieved of the competition for primary goods, not because (as Kershnar implicitly suggests) they have chosen caretaking over primary goods. They have both (although, perhaps, in the modern middle-class dilemma, possibly fewer primary goods than they otherwise would have). Finally, Cohen observed, '[f]eminists have noticed that Rawls wobbles, over the course of his writings, on the matter of whether or not the family belongs to the basic structure [of the principles of justice] and is therefore, in his view, a site at which principles of justice apply' ('Where the Action Is', at 4).

122 Although, interestingly, Rawls did respond, the generation of liberals his work influenced did not follow. Okin, 'Justice and Gender', at 1538–9.

123 *Ibid.*, at 1542–4. 124 *Ibid.*, at 1546.

125 *Ibid.*, at 1545 (referring to Rawls, Part II of *Theory of Justice*).

126 Okin, 'Justice and Gender', at 1567.

Okin is referring to the fact that Rawls draws clear lines between public–private spheres, although he does not explain why these lines should be drawn. Systems theorists would not challenge the existence of these delineations necessarily, but might attempt to discern patterns in the failure of the rules governing the public sphere to protect the economic interests of women, despite the varied initiatives of the welfare state. They might seize the statistics of gender budgeting with interest, and attempt to identify fixed points within chaos. Critical tax scholars, however, starting from the problem of the imperfect interaction between women and tax policy, might pragmatically suggest strategies for reform; or, taking a wider approach, identify the self-excluding choices presented to women through the 'tax state', even if those choices are not presented as self-excluding. The critical tax scholars will agree, however, that the problems have not arisen from 'neutral' tax policies. Ultimately, it is significant that Okin selects the arena of the family for her point of departure in a reconciliation process between Rawls and liberal feminism. The significance of this, in particular to the project of this book, will be explored in the following chapter, addressing the peculiar challenges of taxing women within the family unit.

6

Tax policy applied

Taxation of the family unit

Although this chapter follows on from the broad, theoretical boundaries of Chapter 5, and proceeds with analysis of women, tax policy and families, it does so with a focus that is specific to the UK. Chapter 2 of this book addressed the theoretical underpinnings of the issue of tax policy, and the challenges that may be associated with defining it. This set the foundations for Chapter 3, and its analysis of gender budgeting as an example of 'tax policy in action'. The premise of gender budgeting is that tax policy, as embodied in the Budget, impacts upon women; and, thus, it is necessary to discern the details of this (economic) impact. Gender budgeting will produce these details, and it will be necessary to make sense of them; this argument, eventually, led to Chapter 5's interaction with 'tax policy theorised', and its analyses of the contributions of (dynamic(al)) systems theory (specifically, on the question of tax complexity) and, more generally, critical tax theory on the questions surrounding women, tax policy and the law. This analysis was preceded, however, by Chapter 4's consideration of the contribution of the corporate social responsibility movement to this book's project. This chapter acknowledged that the diffusion of power does not end at the boundaries of government. The corporate social responsibility movement is in many ways an answer to creative compliance; it is an attempt to hold businesses accountable to more than their shareholders, and to investigate the potential benefit from engaged and aware corporate practices to a wider, stakeholder society. Chapter 5 on tax policy theorised, however, acknowledged the difficulties of defining these benefits. It ended by observing that it is in the arena of the family that expectations from tax law, especially towards women, become especially difficult to articulate and to define.

The present chapter, on tax policy applied, will continue with the question of the family; and, in doing so, will turn clearly and directly to the UK. One reason for this focus is a single case. The famous *Arctic Systems* case,[1] holding that a tax arrangement through which a wife received dividends as a shareholder in the family business, thus attracting the accusation by the Revenue that the wife was a settlor to an arrangement in which she had no real business interest, should be allowed to stand, has invigorated wider interest in the relationship between women and the tax system.[2] This chapter will consider this case, and other aspects of the UK tax approach to issues concerning families, in particular, over the past two decades. Particular attention will be devoted to how aspects of this approach have changed, and how these changes have engaged with evolving societal values.[3]

The principle of independent taxation, under which spouses may opt to be assessed for tax purposes outside of the family unit, was one focus of the literature which responded to the *Arctic Systems* case,[4] and thus will be addressed within this chapter. Independent taxation in some ways serves as a continuing complication of efforts to resolve questions

1 *Jones* v. *Garnett* (*Inspector of Taxes*), [2007] UKHL 35; [2007] 1 WLR 2030 (the *Arctic Systems* case).

2 Among this vast literature, see, among others: J. Freedman, 'Why Taxing the Micro-business Is Not Simple – A Cautionary Tale from the "Old World"' (5 2006, at: http://search.austlii.edu.au/au/journals/JATTA/2006/5.html), arguing that '[t]he message to tax policy makers, therefore, is to examine small businesses, especially micro-businesses in their social and family context. Understand what drives them and that they are not simple'; Glen Loutzenheiser, 'Income Splitting and Settlements: Further Observations on *Jones* v. *Garnett*' (2007) 6 *British Tax Review* 693–716; Glen Loutzenheiser, 'Jones v. Garnett: High Court Gives Taxpayer the Cold Shoulder', *British Tax Review*, 4 (2005), 401–11; R. Kerridge, '*Jones* v. *Garnett* (*Arctic Systems*): Another Way of Getting to the Same Result', *British Tax Review*, 5 (2007), 591; Anne Redston, 'Income Sharing: The Nelsonian Option', *British Tax Review*, 6 (2007), 680–6; Anne Redston, 'Small Business in the Eye of the Storm', *British Tax Review*, 5 (2004), 566–81. The implications of this case were also considered in the Mirrlees Review: C. Crawford and J. Freedman, 'Small Business Taxation: A Special Study of the Structural Issues Surrounding the Taxation of Business Profits of Owner Managed Firms' (21 April 2008, at: www.competition-law.ox.ac.uk/tax/documents/Dimensions_Tax_Design_MR2008.pdf, or www.ifs.org.uk/mirrleesreview/press_docs/small_businesses.pdf, at 22–3, on the IFS website).

3 The chapter will argue that the relationship between the tax system and societal values is interactive. This chapter, and this book, has benefited enormously from the publication in 2007 of the IFS Report, written by Tracey Bowler, on the taxation of the family in the UK. Tracey Bowler, *Taxation of the Family*. She restricted her topics of study to income tax, capital gains tax, inheritance tax and stamp duties (*ibid.*, at 1).

4 Freedman, 'Why Taxing the Micro-business Is Not Simple': 'The central feature creating this problem is the ability of micro-businesses to incorporate and thus transform income from labour into income from capital. Within a family context but where the regime is one of independent taxation of spouses, there are many conflicts of policy and practicalities'. See also Crawford and Freedman, 'Small Business Taxation', at 23.

concerning taxation of what Freedman describes as family 'micro-businesses'.[5] Although the Revenue's lack of success in *Arctic Systems* to some extent put these fears to rest, there exists the question of whether the pursuit of this case indicates that the principle that a married woman should be allowed by the tax system to declare her own income – that, for tax purposes, a husband does not own all of his wife's income – is under threat from existing or future anti-tax avoidance legislation.

This chapter considers these and other queries surrounding the *Arctic Systems* case within the context of some standard arguments of feminist theory. The issues within tax law, and the place of *Arctic Systems* within recent social, political and legislative developments are addressed. This chapter is structured in four parts. First, *Arctic Systems* will be placed in a contemporary context, and considered within the context of the child-centric focus that has developed in taxation and benefits in the UK. Second, the connection between independent taxation and the *Arctic Systems* case will be explained. In particular, the chapter will consider the modern, child-centric focus in the UK tax and benefits system and its implications within a system based upon independent taxation. The question of independent taxation will be approached from two perspectives: it will be analysed as a feminist achievement, but also within the context of tax avoidance. That a clash is perceived to exist between the achievement of feminist objectives in the tax system, and the control of tax avoidance, goes some way towards highlighting some fundamental problems in the way the tax system is organised. It will be argued that acknowledging the inconsistencies in this organisation is important to women, and important to tax law.[6]

In the third section, the tax system is considered from the perspectives of both inducement to and discouragement against marriage, and both of these perspectives are linked to points emphasised by the *Arctic Systems* case. This section contains consideration of the elements of joint responsibility, and unpaid labour. Finally, the chapter concludes with a section addressing the relationship between tax law and family law. *Arctic Systems* has produced a range of important tax scholarships, addressing the details of the tax system, and how these details should or should not be amended in response to this case. While this chapter will refer to and is informed

5 Freedman, 'Why Taxing the Micro-business Is Not Simple'.

6 As Oliver Oldman and Ralph Temple insisted, '[r]esponsible and rational development of tax law demands that problems of policy, administration and law be faced rather than avoided or ignored' ('Comparative Analysis of the Taxation of Married Persons', *Stanford Law Review*, 12 (1960), 585–605, at 605).

by this literature, the intention is not to replicate these arguments here. Rather, the intention is to connect issues, highlighted by this case, with a wider literature.

Introduction to the *Arctic Systems* case: the issues

In the UK, before 1988, a wife's self-reported income was automatically included with that of her husband for tax purposes. Independent taxation afforded wives the option to have marriage ignored for tax purposes, and for wives to be assessed for tax separately.[7] The progress of *Jones* v. *Garnett*, could be described as an explosion of tensions that had been building since 1988, when independent taxation was introduced. The case concerned Arctic Systems, an IT firm owned by husband and wife, Geoff and Diana Jones.[8] The company claimed a turnover of nearly £100,000, but Geoff Jones paid himself a salary of £6,520 for running the business, while his wife drew £3,600 for administrative work.[9] The couple shared the remaining amount in dividends, which allowed them to pay less tax and national insurance.[10]

The Revenue contended that Mr Jones' decision to allocate a substantial portion of dividends to his wife was an 'arrangement', and 'not a transaction at arm's length because Mr Jones would never have agreed to the transfer of half the issued share capital, carrying with it an expectation of substantial dividends, to a stranger who merely undertook to provide the paid services which Mrs Jones provided'.[11] The statute in issue was s. 660A of the Income and Corporation Taxes Act 1988,[12] which provides that:

> (1) Income arising under a settlement during the life of the settlor shall be treated for all purposes of the Income Tax Acts as the income of the settlor and not as the income of any other person unless the income arises from property in which the settlor has no interest.

The use of s. 660A may have been surprising, but signs that it was coming had been evident since at least 2004, when equal splitting of income for spouses ceased, and was replaced by the requirement that 'distributions will be taxed according to each spouse's actual entitlement where one

7 Finance Act 1988, s. 104. 8 [2007] 1 WLR 2030, at p. 2032.

9 Lord Hoffmann commented that 'The latter is accepted to have been a reasonable figure for Mrs Jones's services but the former figure is, given the company's receipts, plainly less than Mr Jones could have earned in the market' (*ibid.*).

10 *Ibid.* 11 *Ibid.*, at p. 2033.

12 Now rewritten by s. 622 of Income Tax (Trading and Other Income) Act 2005.

spouse is beneficially entitled to all of the shares'.[13] Although the Joneses won on this issue in the House of Lords, the controversy seems likely to continue. As Gammie[14] stressed, both the Court of Appeal and the House of Lords (apparently following on with the tradition of deadlock, started in the commissioners) were evenly divided as to whether the Jones' tax arrangement in fact should be categorised as a settlement.[15]

The impact of child centrism

This case has rejuvenated interest in the connection between independent taxation, families, unpaid labour – in short, the intersections between women, tax policy and the law. Few of the issues highlighted by the *Arctic Systems* case have been resolved, and as tax advisors await either further legislation[16] or further litigation, this chapter will argue that consideration of some developments in feminist theory highlights that many of these questions require fundamental reconsideration of the economic foundations of the family. The difficulty of taxing the family unit, when much of the labour performed by women, in particular, is unpaid, is emphasised. This chapter concludes that ultimately a choice will have to be made as to the objectives that should be pursued when families are taxed. The proposal is that a choice which reflects the unequal economic position of women should be considered.

Modern practices concerning the taxation of the family unit are child centric, but it does not necessarily follow that problems concerning the unequal economic position of women have been resolved by this focus. It does mean, however, that the tax system no longer necessarily highlights the inequities that can exist for women within marriage.[17] Before the introduction of independent taxation, the tax system was obviously unequal. Now, it is no longer as obvious, but the reaction to

13 J. Whiting, 'Finance Act Notes: Employment-related Aspects, etc. – Sections 78–82, 85 and 91–92', *British Tax Review*, 5 (2004), 480, at 485.

14 Malcolm Gammie, QC, who represented Mr Jones.

15 M. Gammie, 'Reflections on *Jones* v. *Garnett*', *British Tax Review*, 6 (2007) 687, at 687.

16 Crawford and Freedman, 'Small Business Taxation', at 22.

17 By contrast, marriage works for men. As Nancy E. Shurtz explained, '[e]ven those in our culture whom we have been conditioned to emulate – "successful" men who embody the positive traits of self-reliance, industriousness, and material affluence – are found to be happier, healthier and more prosperous in a state of connection (marriage) than those who are not' ('The Theory of "Taxing Men"', *Southern California Review of Law and Women's Studies*, 6 (1997), 485, at 492).

Arctic Systems – indeed, perhaps the fact of the case itself – indicates, at the very least, that marriage, women and taxation still demand attention.

The interaction between women, tax and marriage in the UK could be described through the analogy of a dimming light. In the period between the introduction of the Married Women's Property Act in 1882,[18] and the introduction of independent taxation of women in 1988, the dissonance between the ethos of the nineteenth-century statute, and the continuing requirement that a wife's income should be combined with her husband's for tax purposes, was glaring. The effect was a spotlight on the economic inequality of marriage.[19] The inequality could be described as fostered and even produced by the tax system; or, alternatively, it could be portrayed as an existing, societal inequality which was revealed by the tax system. The point is that it was evident.

It is noteworthy that the married couple's allowance, which essentially involved the tax system rewarding husbands for marriage, was not immediately repealed in 1988, when independent taxation was introduced.[20] This is surprising, because the married couple's allowance might have been viewed as contradictory to the purpose of independent taxation.[21] Nonetheless, enthusiasm for the married couple's allowance had dwindled,[22] and by the 1993 Budget Norman Lamont introduced important changes to the allowance.[23] Effectively, the allowance changed

18 Eventually, the Married Women's Property Act 1964.

19 As Martin Daunton wrote: '[e]ven when women had the right to own their own property, and to be taxed on their earnings in some circumstances, the Inland Revenue continued to insist that the incomes of husband and wife were aggregated in order to calculate the marginal tax rate' ('What Is Income?', in John Tiley (ed.), *Studies in the History of Tax Law*, at p. 13).

20 N. Lee points out that the married couple's allowance might also have been viewed as contradictory to both the Sex Discrimination Act 1975 and the Equal Pay Act 1970: 'The Effect of the Human Rights Act 1998 on Taxation Policy and Administration', *eJournal of Tax Research*, 2 (2004), 155–82. Taxation and social security law were specifically excluded from the Sex Discrimination Act of 1975: S. Atkins, 'The Sex Discrimination Act 1975: The End of a Decade', *Feminist Review* (1986), 57–70, at 58. According to Atkins, '[t]hese omissions have shackled the effectiveness of the law since its inception' (*ibid.*).

21 *Ibid.*

22 Lee suggests that a new era was afoot, such that (in 2005) she wrote that '[s]ince the beginning of the 1990s, successful attempts have been made to weed out such discrimination from the UK tax system' ('Effect of the Human Rights Act 1998', at 155).

23 In an interim report for the IFS, S. Adam and G. Loutzenhiser suggested that although '[t]he main policy provisions for married couples – the married couple's allowance in Income Tax and the married women's reduced rate in NICs – are gradually disappearing', nonetheless '[i]ntegration may provide an opportunity to deal them a death blow, but if desired they could be retained in a merged system' ('Integrating Income Tax and National Insurance: An Interim Report', in *Institute for Fiscal Studies* (December 2007), at p. 52).

into a tax credit, and was reduced in value, first, to 20 per cent of its original value; and, later, down to 15 per cent, then 10 per cent; and, now, has been abolished.[24] From the century-long persistence of joint taxation after the Married Women's Property Act, to the lingering of the married couple's allowance, the tax and benefits system has seemed particularly resistant to economic equality within marriage, even in the face of political will to effect change.

As the next section will discuss, after the introduction of independent taxation, a feminist objective had been achieved,[25] but the focus on the individual meant that women's economic status in the tax and benefits system was still highlighted. Women and men were both objects of attention of the tax system. The development of a focus on the child by New Labour shifted this attention, and carried with it an element of loss for feminist objectives. This is not to argue that child centricism and feminism are mutually exclusive, or that the tax credits system is necessarily unsuccessful. The expansion of the tax credits system, for example, did not increase labour market participation of women living in poverty.[26] Increased support for childcare through the tax system is a clear New Labour accomplishment that could be described as correspondent with feminist goals.[27] What was lost with the development of a child-centric focus, however, was the highlighted position of women's inequitable position in the market. The light was finally dimmed, and the terms of the discourse had shifted.

History offers little evidence of a need to use the tax and benefit system to encourage women to take care of their children, so the child-centric

24 Himmelweit described the persistence of the married couple's allowance to 2000 as a 'relic' of the joint taxation system. Himmelweit, 'Making Visible the Hidden Economy: The Case for Gender-impact Analysis of Economic Policy', at 65, fn. 8. The allowance has now been replaced with a single person's allowance, described by Lee, 'Effect of the Human Rights Act 1998'.

25 'Feminists and others considered it a great victory for women when, in 1989, the taxation system was reformed so that everyone declared and paid tax on their own individual incomes' (Himmelweit, 'Making Visible the Hidden Economy', at 61).

26 This is a conclusion of research reported at R. Blundell, *et al.*, 'Labour Market Impact'. See also M. Brewer, *et al.*, 'Did Working Families' Tax Credit Work? The Impact of In-work Support on Labour Supply in Great Britain', *Labour Economics*, 13 (2006), 699–720, which also considers the impact of the WFTC in combination with other aspects of the tax and benefits system.

27 See the response of Lorraine Dearden to the key elements of the government's '10-year Strategy for Childcare, which largely focuses on increased maternity leave, the nursery education grant, and reforms of the childcare element of the working tax credit' ('PBR Analysis: Childcare Strategy', December 2004, at: www.ifs.org.uk/publications/3196).

focus was in some ways misplaced. Barbara Castle's[28] faith that child benefit[29] would be well spent if entrusted to mothers is but one testament to this. Child benefit combined both child centricism and women-focused objectives. The introduction of independent taxation, however, was different. It was motivated by the social advantages that would be achieved by encouraging women's fiscal independence.[30] It was a lobbying victory of the UK's Women's Budget Group;[31] and, once achieved was hailed both for the financial independence for women it fostered,[32] and for the fiscal privacy now afforded to women.[33]

Children were not an important part of the rearrangement of the tax system away from the focal point of the married couple, towards the individual. That changed, however, when the New Labour policy of 'supporting families through supporting children'[34] was pursued in large part through the tax system. Children were targeted through the universal child tax credit and childcare tax credits,[35] which entailed another reorientation of the tax system, away from tax allowances, and towards tax credits. This was a significant shift, because while tax allowances inherently favour the better off, tax credits and benefits target support at the lower end of the income distribution. Indeed, tax credits have more in common with welfare payments than with any aspect of the tax system.[36]

28 Who was famously averse to the label of feminist, actively resisting the title in the 1950s, although coming to an 'apologetic' or 'qualified' position on feminism in the 1970s. Amy Black and Stephen Brooke, 'The Labour Party, Women, and the Problem of Gender, 1951–1966', *Journal of British Studies*, 36 (1997), 419–52, at 438. Castle sponsored the Equal Pay Act 1970.

29 *Per* the Child Benefit Act 1975 (repealed by the Social Security Act 1986).

30 See discussion throughout A. Dilnot, P. Johnson and G. Stark, 'Tax Policy and the 1991 Budget', *Fiscal Studies*, 12(2) (1991), 23.

31 See Himmelweit, 'Tools for Budget Impact Analysis: Taxes and Benefits' (2005) ['Herramientas para análisis del impacto del presupuesto: Impuestos y beneficios'], UNIFEM–OECD–Nordic Council Conference on Gender Responsive Budgeting, Brussels, October 2001 (at: www dgic be/en/topics/gender/himmelweit.html).

32 As predicted in K. O'Donovan, 'Should All Maintenance of Spouse Be Abolished?', *Modern Law Review*, 45 (1982), 424, at 429.

33 Also predicted in J. A. Kay and C. Sandler, 'The Taxation of Husband and Wife: A View of the Debate in the Green Paper', *Fiscal Studies*, 3(3) (1982), 173–87.

34 Budget speech 1998 (at: http://archive.treasury.gov.uk/budget/1998/chxstat2.htm).

35 See discussion at Sylvia Bashevkin, 'From Tough Times to Better Times: Feminism, Public Policy, and New Labour Politics in Britain', *International Political Science Review/Revue internationale de science politique*, 21 (2000), 407–24, at 418.

36 See N. Lee, 'The New Tax Credits', *Journal of Social Security Law*, 10 (2003), 10 7–52; J. Lewis, 'Gender and Welfare Regimes: Further Thoughts', *Social Politics: International Studies in Gender, State and Society*, 4 (2002), 160–77; J. Lewis, 'Gender and Welfare State Change', *European Societies*, 4 (2002), 331–57; J. Millar, 'From Wage Replacement to

Bowler has considered the impact of the individualistic reorientation of the tax system after the introduction of independent taxation. Her work suggests that, despite the recent child-centric focus,[37] the focus of the tax system upon individuals, regardless of family, persists.[38] She also qualifies, however, that there are 'significant exceptions' to this approach.[39] She explains that these exceptions include income election rules for jointly held property, the tax avoidance rules on settlements; capital gains tax exemptions for transfers between spouses/civil partners, and, the inheritance tax exemptions for transfers between spouses/civil partners both before and after death.[40] It was of course the avoidance rules on settlements that were directly at issue in the *Arctic Systems* case, as a later section in this chapter will explain.

Earned income tax credits, through which the tax system provides financial support to citizens in connection with the structures of employment, have attracted scholarly attention in both the US and the UK. Although much of this literature does not identify itself explicitly as within the tradition of critical tax scholarship, it displays features that could be described as evocative of that literature.[41] Largely, the focus of this literature is the increase in market participation by mothers, as a result of the tax credits. The evidence indicates that, in this, the credits have been relatively successful. In the US, the Earned Income Tax Credit

Wage Supplementation: Benefits and Tax Credits', in J. Millar (ed.), *Understanding Social Security* (Bristol: Policy Press, 2003); H. Land, 'Spheres of Care in the UK: Separate and Unequal', *Critical Social Policy*, 22 (2002), 13–32, at 15.

37 Winnie Chan suggested that the early Blair years saw a movement away from strengthening marriage, and a development towards assisting families with children, 'Women, Childcare and Taxation', *Kings' College Law Journal*, 10 (1999), 71–92, at 71. Chan warned that such programmes suffer from a lack of flexibility, as there is 'no single, best answer' for parents (*ibid.*, at 72). Additionally, Chan urged that support should be provided for parents, regardless of whether or not the parents are employed in the paid marketplace (*ibid.*, at 73).

38 Bowler, *Taxation*, at p. 5. 39 *Ibid.* 40 *Ibid.*

41 Writing of the US Earned Income Tax Credit, J. K. Scholz suggested that the credit 'plays a central role in public policy as it affects the working poor' ('The Earned Income Tax Credit: Participation, Compliance, and Antipoverty', *National Tax Journal*, 47 (1994), 63–87, at 80). Similarly, analysis of what might be described as classic women-focused tax expenditure programmes in Canada, such as childcare subsidies, revealed that such programmes actually were more likely to be accessed by, and to benefit generally, men. N. D. Polikoff notes that '[a]lthough the individual has been the basis for calculating tax liability in Canada since the inception of personal income taxation in 1917, for the most part American law has recognized a husband and a wife as a single taxable unit since 1948' ('Ending Marriage as We Know It', *Hofstra Law Review*, 32 (2003), 201–32, at 209, fn. 52, citing N. J. Knauer, 'Heteronormativity and Federal Tax Policy', *West Virginia Law Review*, 101 (1998), 129–234, at 144). Finally, see also Young, *Women, Tax and Social Programs.*

did appear to increase the overall labour market participation of single women with children.[42] Women who already had jobs, however, did not appear to increase their overall working hours due to the credits.[43] In the UK, analysis of predictive models (which simulated likely results) suggested that the credits would produce an increase in labour for single mothers, but a drop in market participation for married women.[44] The increase in reliance on earned income tax credits in the UK under the Blair administration responded to the absence of a national childcare policy, and in some sense transplanted the issue to tax law.[45] It also addressed the problem that, in particular, single mothers face in the workplace, such that it is only financially worthwhile for them to take on jobs that are relatively well paid.[46]

Tax credits encourage perceptions of women as actors within the economy that are not necessarily in harmony, however, with their own self-perceptions.[47] Tax credits may appear to increase the economic choices available to single mothers, for example, but whether these choices are in fact desirable is less clear.[48] Tax credits in some ways are premised on the ideas that women are 'held back' from the market by the 'expense' of their children;[49] and that the opportunity of paid work for mothers

42 N. Eissa and J. B. Liebman, *Labor Supply Response to the Earned Income Tax Credit* (Cambridge, MA: National Bureau of Economic Research, 1995).

43 *Ibid.* 44 Blundell, *et al.*, 'Labour Market Impact'.

45 Neither the UK nor the US have an official, 'national childcare policy', unlike some other European countries: K. England, *Who Will Mind the Baby?: Geographies of Childcare and Working Mothers* (London: Routledge, 1996), at p. 3.

46 A study of both the UK and the Netherlands revealed that, given the interaction of the tax and benefits system with the cost of childcare, it is only worthwhile financially for single mothers to take well-paid jobs, for which most are unqualified: A. van Drenth, *et al.*, 'Sources of Income for Lone Mother Families: Policy Changes in Britain and the Netherlands and the Experiences of Divorced Women', *Journal of Social Policy*, 28 (2000), 619–41, at 624. Intriguingly, Macdonald argues that 'Germany treats single parents as workers, the United Kingdom treats them as mothers ...' ('Gender and Social Security', at 13).

47 'What becomes apparent as one surveys the literature is the existence of a continuing asymmetry between the way of women's being and the way they are perceived legislatively and economically' (Hilda Kahne and Andrew I. Kohen, 'Economic Perspectives on the Roles of Women in the American Economy', *Journal of Economic Literature*, 13 (1975), 1249–92, at 1279).

48 Barbara R. Bergmann, 'What Policies Toward Lone Mothers Should We Aim For?', *Feminist Economics*, 10 (2004), 240–6.

49 Lewis identified this gap in the policy discourse. She wrote: 'In Britain and America there has been active debate about the fate of children in lone-mother families; however attention has effectively centred on the welfare dependency of their mothers. What has been absent is a commitment to the social inclusion of lone-mother families, whose welfare depends on there being universal, citizenship-based entitlements to benefits and services' ('The "Problem"', at 198).

in the public marketplace may be purchased by the government through financial investment, administered through the tax system.

According to Chow and Berheidee, analyses of the social science literature addressing the family and work reveal three different models: the separate sphere model, the spillover effects model and the interactive model.[50] Within the separate sphere model, the family generally is the woman's domain, and the paid marketplace is the man's. The structures of both environments are drawn along gender essentialist lines – the home is supposed to be a woman's domain and 'sanctuary'.[51] The presence or absence of a romantic relationship between parents is also very important in determining the lines that divide the two domains.[52] The separate sphere model denies that either the private domain of the home or the public sphere of the paid marketplace have much to do with each other, whereas the second model acknowledges that the effects of one sphere may 'spill over' into the other.[53] Finally, the interactive model is described as a feminist agenda, and acknowledges the 'intimate relationship' between family and work.[54]

The separate sphere model would appear to underpin many policies of the welfare state, although lines are not clearly drawn, and clashes sometimes occur. For example, conflict exists between the operation of the UK tax credit system and the principles underpinning other aspects of the tax system, given that the family unit is assessed as a household. Additionally, the WFTC (now Child Tax Credits)[55] and the Disabled

50 E. N. L. Chow and C. W. Berheide, 'The Interdependence of Family and Work: A Framework for Family Life Education, Policy, and Practice', *Family Relations*, 37 (1988), 23–8, at 24–5.

51 *Ibid.*, at 24.

52 In *R.* v. *Taleb*, a woman avoided a custodial sentence (on the grounds of her family responsibilities) yet received a 'painful' financial penalty on the basis of her failure to disclose on a tax credits application that she was living with the father of her children. Her penalty was based on a written confession, which read, in part: 'The initial reason for not including [my partner] is that we were no longer in a sexual relationship. We were in a relationship in that we were partners, as part of the family unit, for the benefit of the children' ([2007] EWCA Crim 2193 CA (Crim Div)). The penalty imposed was indeed 'painful', and the substance of this case included consideration of whether the penalties imposed were to excessive (the court concluded that they were).

53 Chow and Berheide, 'Interdependence of Family and Work'. 54 *Ibid.*, at 25.

55 Tax credits have had an interesting legislative path in the UK. Although they have been around for a number of years, modern tax credits were introduced in Tony Blair's administration with the Tax Credits Act 1999. This legislation introduced the WFTC which, in an intriguing change of nomenclature, was later repealed by the Tax Credits Act 2002. Thus, in April 2003 WFTC, DPTC and children's tax credit were replaced by two new tax credits, called Child Tax Credit and Working Tax Credit. The aim was simplification, as it was promised that '[t]hese new tax credits will provide support to a wider range of people through a single framework'.

Person's Tax Credit (DPTC) both rely on 'social security definition of income', as opposed to definitions of income found in tax law.[56]

The sometimes confused presentation of the WFTC was a product of efforts in the early days of New Labour to court middle-class voters.[57] These voters were credited with assisting Blair's overwhelming first election win as prime minister, and thus, Bashkevin has suggested, fostered a resistance against substantial change in policy direction.[58] The year 1997 may not have been the moment for the introduction of significantly redistributive tax policies, but generally there is little consensus among women on the question of whether government should encourage mothers receiving benefits to work in the marketplace, or assist them in staying at home.[59] Similarly, there is little consensus among politicians on this question, and no obvious trends among MPs based on gender.[60]

Language was important from the beginning in the New Labour amendment of the tax/benefit system. The working families' tax credit, as it was initially named, was an initial attempt to state plainly that families who 'worked' would be given credit against tax. The renaming to the Child Tax Credit and the working tax credit was perhaps part of a process in which, as a report for the Institute for Fiscal Studies suggested, 'presentation' is of utmost importance.[61]

56 CCH [¶160–020] '"New Tax Credits" – Antecedents and Policy Issues'. The problems stem from the fact that '[i]ncome from capital, for most benefits, is assessed by reference to a "tariff income" scale which bears no relation to commercial rates of return on investment'. See also S. Ganghof, who explains that '[w]hile taxation of capital income is very costly, creating incentives to lower marginal tax rates, the high overall tax burden on labour makes it difficult to reduce tax rates on labour incomes' ('Globalization, Tax Reform Ideals and Social Policy Financing', *Global Social Policy*, 5 (2005), 77–95, at 77). Additionally, 'income from capital is broadly based on income actually received'. CCH [¶160–020] '"New Tax Credits"'. Finally, 'investment income which is tax exempt is generally not counted for tax credits' (*ibid.*).

57 'Tony Blair tried to nurture a respectable, achieving, middle-class image within Labour, and to hone a political rhetoric that emphasized individual duty and fiscal prudence' (Sylvia Bashevkin, 'From Tough Times to Better Times: Feminism, Public Policy, and New Labour Politics in Britain', *International Political Science Review/Revue internationale de science politique*, 21(4) (2000), 407–24, at 408).

58 *Ibid.*, at 420.

59 Angela McRobbie, 'Feminism and the Third Way', *Feminist Review*, 64 (2000), 97–112, at 98.

60 Philip Cowley and Sarah Childs, 'Too Spineless to Rebel? New Labour's Women MPs', *British Journal of Political Science*, 33(3) (2003), 345–65, at 356: 'On the variables that better explained voting during the parliament – such as the tax/spend scale or the socialist/*laissez-faire* scale – there is no noticeable differences between the new women and their male colleagues'.

61 Andrew Dilnot and Julian McCrae, 'Family Credit and the Working Families' Tax Credit', Institute for Fiscal Studies (1999) (at: www.ifs.org.uk/bns/bn3.pdf, at 16).

Thus, by refocusing the debate on the child (as opposed to the parents, as with 'working families'), New Labour perhaps sidestepped an element of a presentation that had not been working for them. There was some criticism in the media at the time that the tax credits were muddled on many fronts, including class. The basis of some attacks included the suggestion that all mothers, including those who could afford not to work, were being encouraged to employ caretakers. The end of traditionalism that Giddens identified[62] is not uniform. Some mothers may appreciate financial assistance to work outside of the home, and some may appreciate financial assistance to stay at home. Giddens would describe this as part of the birth of individualism (the follow-up to the end of traditionalism)[63] which by its nature will produce difference.[64]

Tax credits for childcare by their nature will attract the attention of politicians, because as tools of policy change they appear to be so efficient.[65] Education, social inclusion, the economy – all of these factors are implicated with a single legislative tool.[66] From this perspective, it is surprising that childcare was described as a 'neglected' area of fiscal and social policy.[67] The challenge for the government is to choose which of the new individualists it will support. By its nature it cannot support the cause of individualism or the end of traditionalism, but it can support some commonalities among identified groups of individuals. Other groups will lose out with these choices.[68]

New Labour identified itself publicly with the socialist philosophy of R. H. Tawney,[69] the historian of early British capitalism whose analyses were of much interest to 'British Marxist circles', and beyond.[70] Tawney

62 Addressing this directly, McRobbie suggested that the end of traditionalism need not necessarily dictate the end of socialism ('Feminism', at 98).

63 A. Giddens, 'Living in a Post-traditionalist Society', in U. Beck (ed.), *Reflexive Modernisation: Politics, Tradition, and Aesthetics in Modern Social Order* (Cambridge: Polity Press, 1995).

64 McCaffery addressed the question of traditionalism in a US context: 'Working mothers are a fact of life in America today. A tax system set against them is set against marriage for those who cannot afford tax's burdens and toward stress for the vast numbers who live and work under its antiquated rules' ('Women and Taxes', at 22).

65 Stephen J. Ball and Carol Vincent, 'The "Childcare Champion"? New Labour, Social Justice and the Childcare Market', *British Educational Research Journal*, 31(5) (2005), 557–70, at 558.

66 *Ibid.* 67 *Ibid.*

68 McRobbie, 'Feminism', at 98, discussing Ruth Lister's contribution to this debate.

69 Mark Bevir, and David O'Brien, 'New Labour and the Public Sector in Britain', *Public Administration Review*, 61(5) (2001), 535–47 at 536.

70 David Ormrod, 'R. H. Tawney and the Origins of Capitalism', *History Workshop* [1984], 138–59, at 139.

defined 'freedom' as the power to choose between alternatives.[71] Tawney explained that, once a man has identified what he needs to survive (from physical to intellectual needs), then 'freedom consists in the opportunity secured by him, within the limits set by nature and the enjoyment of similar opportunities by his fellows, to take the action needed in order to ensure that these requirements are satisfied'.[72] Tax credits can be politically marketed thus as affording parents the 'freedom' to enter the marketplace.

Child tax credits are very much a hybrid, and in some ways straddle the boundaries between the tax system and the welfare state. In the UK, a working parent may be entitled to either the Child Tax Credit, or the Working Tax Credit, or both.[73] Tax credits are an obvious starting point in a book addressing women and tax law. At their most basic, they are tax legislation, addressing women and wages, but they are also politically friendly ways of redressing either failures of the market, or wider, societal failures to consider the link between the marketplace and unpaid labour.[74]

71 R. H. Tawney, 'English Politics Today: We Mean Freedom', *Review of Politics*, 8(2) (1946), 223–39, at 224.

72 *Ibid.* A classic example of Tawney's work is presented with a study he conducted of 'boy labour', which concluded that laws permitting adolescents to work were potentially damaging both to the children involved and the economy itself. R. H. Tawney, 'The Economics of Boy Labour', *Economic Journal*, 19(76) (1909), 517–37, at 535ff. This study, conducted in 1909, displays equal concern both for the status of the child workers and the status of the economy – a harmonised approach which unsurprisingly would make itself attractive to late 1990s, early New Labour rhetoric. His greatest fame however is as a historian (and champion of adult education) whose concern would be more likely to rest with the 'boy labourer', than the market. He is, after all, famous for writing 'freedom for the pike is death to the minnow'. Tawney, *Equality London* (London: Unwin, 1931), at p. 238.

73 This section relies on the legislation referred to, and the discussion and explanation provided in Child Poverty Action Group, *Welfare Benefits and Tax Credits Handbook* (Child Poverty Action Group 2007/2008 – '*Handbook*'), starting at p. 1193. Although tax credits may be administered with other benefits, the rules for calculating them are separate. The child tax credit is intended for low-income families with responsibility for a child under 16, or under 20 if the parent is engaged in a full-time, approved educational programme. The working tax credit is also based on a family's income, and is distributed to families who work sixteen hours or more a week, and have a child. It is also available to taxpayers without children, who have a disability which makes it difficult to get a job; or, who qualify for what is described as a fifty-plus element; or, who work thirty hours or more a week, and are over 25. Child benefit is ignored as income for the purposes of both the child tax credit and the working tax credit (*Handbook*, at p. 1196).

74 Alstott described tax credits as politically friendly assistance, which 'help the working poor while avoiding conundrums of welfare'. They have the benefit of being viewed as both 'pro work' and 'pro family'. They are also, as Graetz has acknowledged, a form of 'direct subsidy', with the detraction that they crowd the US tax code ('Implementing a Progressive Consumption Tax', at 1631).

Weisbach and Nussim explain that there are two basic theories underpinning the combination of tax systems with government spending: the comprehensive base theory, and the theory of tax expenditures.[75] The comprehensive base theory argues that, because broad tax bases are easiest for governments to manage, spending programmes are best kept separate from the tax system, thus to preserve the tax base.[76] The theory of tax expenditures 'recognize[s] the functional equivalence of putting a programme in the tax programme or somewhere else'.[77] Both approaches, however, tend to conclude that important government policies should not always be administered through the tax system.[78]

The reason for this is not that tax advantages do not belong in association with children. The US, in particular, tends to associate tax advantages with children, at both ends of the socio-economic scale,[79] if not so much towards the middle of the scale.[80] In the UK, children are associated with tax advantages as well, especially within the context of the family unit.[81] Complications arise from the fact that, within a family unit, tax advantages may be structured so as to discourage a second earner.[82]

In the UK, tax credits have been around for a long time. The child tax credit was the successor to the working families' tax credit, which was the successor to family credit, which succeeded family income supplement.[83] Apparently, family income supplement was introduced as a precursor to a then-anticipated tax credit scheme, which did not materialise.[84]

75 David A. Weisbach and Jacob Nussim, 'The Integration of Tax and Spending Programs', *Yale Law Journal*, 113 (2004), 955–1028, at 957–8.

76 *Ibid.* 77 *Ibid.*, at 958. 78 *Ibid.*, at 957–8.

79 D. T. Ellwood and J. B. Liebman explain it thus: 'Low income families with children receive large tax benefits from the Earned Income Tax Credit, while high income taxpayers receive large tax benefits from dependent exemptions (whose value is greater to those in higher tax brackets' ('The Middle-class Parent Penalty: Child Benefits in the US Tax Code', in James M. Poterba (ed.), *Tax Policy and the Economy* (Boston, MA: MIT Press, 2001), at p. 1).

80 They explain that 'middle income parents receive substantially smaller tax benefits associated with children' (*ibid.*).

81 D. Sainsbury observed that 'when qualifying conditions for tax benefits involve an income ceiling, it is usually family income that determines eligibility. Accordingly this sort of benefit introduces familialism into systems of individual taxation. Refundable tax credits are also biased against a second earner, creating huge disincentives if the earnings convert a tax refund into a liability to pay taxes' (*Gender and Welfare State Regimes*, Oxford University Press, 1999, at p. 258).

82 *Ibid.*

83 Pat Strickland, 'Working Families' Tax Credit' (House of Commons Library, 9 April 1998), at p. 7.

84 *Ibid.*

Interestingly, a proposal in 1985 to institute the family credit as a tax credit was opposed on the grounds that money would be transferred from men to women.[85] Presently, the modern child tax credit grew to be the quintessential New Labour tool for addressing women, work and families through the tax system.

Tax credits became popular beyond the borders of the UK in the 1990s; and, indeed, beyond the limits of the transatlantic, Clinton–Blair policy exchange under which they appeared to flourish. Efforts to use the tax system to influence the workplace choices of mothers were developed in France during this time,[86] as well as in Australia, Canada[87] and Ireland.[88] The changes to the French system were interesting, because they appeared to represent a shift away from a previous, post-Second World War policy of using the tax system to encourage mothers to stay at home, such that the French 1950s have been referred to as the 'golden age of familialism'.[89] Ireland, by contrast, appears never to have experienced a 'golden age of familialism'; indeed, perhaps the reverse, with a strong reliance on the market to redress socio-economic problems.[90] Post-Second World War,

85 *Ibid.*

86 In the late 1990s: 'in 2001, in addition to a reform of unemployment insurance designed to intensify job search, the French government introduced a form of negative income tax (Prime pour l'Emploi), a completely new type of policy intervention in France' (C. Erhel and H. Zajdela, 'The Dynamics of Social and Labour Market Policies in France and the United Kingdom: Between Path Dependence and Convergence', *Journal of European Social Policy*, 14 (2004), 125–42, at 135). Erhel and Zajedla identified the links between French and UK policy: 'Two principal measures linked it closely to the British orientation: first, a selection process among minimum-wage beneficiaries, so as to identify those able to work; second, provision of a subsidy for employers who hired people who had been minimum-income beneficiaries for at least two years' (*ibid.*, at 138). They conclude that 'recent changes in social and employment policies have led to converging trends through differing institutional paths (the main policy innovation in the UK was the minimum wage, while in France it was the principle of a negative income tax)' (*ibid.*).

87 Writing about Australia, the UK, Canada and the US, O'Connor *et al.* predicted that '[t]he 1990s likely will be remembered as a period of contentious restructuring of state social provision – one in which issues of gender were quite marked' (*States, Markets, Families*, at p. 1).

88 Child tax allowances, introduced in 1944, have existed as long as the Irish state. M. Daly and S. Clavero, *Contemporary Family Policy: A Comparative Review of Ireland, France, Germany, Sweden and the UK* (Dublin: Institute of Public Administration 2002), at p. 22.

89 In France, after the Second World War, '[t]he generous family benefits system established after the war included special benefits for housewives; the tax code, too, gave fiscal advantages to mothers at home. The 1950s became what historian Antoine Prost has called the "golden age of familialism"' (K. J. Morgan, 'The Politics of Mothers' Employment: France in Comparative Perspective', *World Politics*, 55 (2003), 259–89, at 275.

90 B. Nolan and T. M. Smeeding conducted a research study in Ireland concluding that, interestingly, 'Ireland has lower than average poverty reduction policies and a fairly high rate of overall relative poverty while its strong economy (not its tax–benefit policy) is

the UK may not have experienced a 'golden age of familialism', but it did develop a strong concept of the obligations of government to society in the form of the welfare state,[91] in ways which echoed, for example, the Nordic countries (which developed a much more extensive welfare system).[92] The US and Italy present different cases in point. While direct financial assistance support for childcare is described as 'limited', for example, it is the case that tax policy has helped to encourage the expansion of the number of US childcare placements available.[93] Similarly, in Italy, tax benefits are limited, but on the basis of a woman's place within a family unit (and vary according to whether she is married, divorced or cohabiting).[94]

The post-Second World War era has been significant in many countries. By way of (comparative) reference, the fundamentals of the tax system in the US were established before women entered the workforce in large numbers.[95] In that country, and despite the remarkable increase in numbers of women in the workplace over the twentieth century, women have made no economic progress compared to men since 1960.[96] This lack of progress has occurred within a marketplace that governments have

mainly responsible for the level of overall inequality that is evident' ('Ireland's Income Distribution in Comparative Perspective', in paper prepared for the 28th General Conference of the International Association for Research in Income and Wealth, Cork, Ireland: Maxwell School of Citizenship and Public Affairs, Syracuse University, 2004, at: www.iariw.org/papers/2004/smeeding.pdf, at 3).

91 As M. Bevir explains, '[f]or much of the post-war period, social democrats saw the Keynesian welfare state as a means of realizing these commitments. The state would promote equality by demand management, welfare provision, and progressive taxation' ('Narrating the British State: An Interpretive Critique of New Labour's Institutionalism', *Review of International Political Economy*, 10 (2003), 455–80, at 463).

92 In the Nordic countries, 'the market also supports generous welfare state arrangements, since it widens the tax base as well as limits the needs for social intervention' (J. Vogel, 'European Welfare Regimes and the Transition to Adulthood: A Comparative and Longitudinal Perspective', *Social Indicators Research*, 59 (2002), 275–99, at 281).

93 O'Connor, *et al.*, *States, Markets, Families*, at p. 5.

94 R. Trifiletti explains that, in Italy, '[a]s for tax benefits, women are considered lone parents, and therefore favoured, only if they are unmarried or widows, but not if they are divorced or separated mothers with cohabiting children' ('Southern European Welfare Regimes and the Worsening Position of Women', *Journal of European Social Policy*, 9 (1999), 49, at 60).

95 This is discussed throughout M. Abramovitz, *Taxes Are a Woman's Issue: Reframing the Debate* (New York, NY: Feminist Press at the City University of New York, 2007).

96 V. R. Fuchs, 'Women's Quest for Economic Equality', *Journal of Economic Perspectives*, 3 (1989), 25–41, at 25. Fuchs defines economic 'well-being' as 'access to goods and services (market and nonmarket) and leisure'. Fuchs explains that, '[i]n the labor market, occupational segregation is still widespread, women are much more likely than men to work part-time, and they still earn much less for each hour of work. In the home, women continue to provide the bulk of the childcare and nonmarket services' (*ibid.*).

shaped and controlled. As Dennis stresses, 'government shapes the market by establishing trade policies and tax systems, and by exercising control over the currency'.[97]

In the UK, however, Hakim has argued that studies have proved that the 'myth of rising employment' for women is 'demonstrably untrue'.[98] For example, Hakim challenges the common assumption that women's employment rates have risen steadily since the Second World War: 'all change in the post-War period has consisted of the substitution of part-time for full-time jobs, and the substitution of married women for single women workers, largely as a result of the abolition of the marriage bar'.[99] On the issue of the commitment of women's commitment to their careers, Hakim refers to research demonstrating that, when asked, women tended to express greater concern and commitment to family and home life, than to their jobs.[100] Similarly, Hakim criticises the idea that part-time work is an undesired option for women who, burdened by childcare responsibilities, have no other 'choice'.[101]

A clear theme among the vast tax credit literature is that the value of tax credits can be found in the fact that they encourage parents to work in the paid market, for the good of their children. There are other ways of achieving this result in a tax system than with tax credits. For example, studies have suggested that a decrease in rates of taxation leads to higher labour force participation by women.[102] A range of research from around

97 Dennis, 'Lessons', at 15.

98 C. Hakim, 'Five Feminist Myths about Women's Employment', *British Journal of Sociology*, 46 (1995), 429–55, at 431.

99 'There was absolutely no increase in the volume of female employment, measured in full-time equivalent numbers, from World War Two up to 1987 in Britain' (*ibid.*, at 432–5).

100 *Ibid.* 101 *Ibid.*, at 436.

102 N. Eissa, 'Taxation and Labor Supply of Married Women: The Tax Reform Act of 1986 as a Natural Experiment' (at: www.gsb.columbia.edu/ipd/pub/WP_5023.v5_TaxReformAct(Eissa)_1986.pdf, at 24). Intriguingly, the availability of independent taxation also may play a part in this. For example, additional research has proved that '[i]n countries where husbands and wives are taxed separately, women's employment does not generally increase couples' marginal income tax rate as much as in countries (such as the United States) where a couple's earnings are jointly taxed, although the total effect depends on the specific tax structure' (T. van der Lippe and L. van Dijk, 'Comparative Research on Women's Employment', *Annual Review of Sociology*, 28 (2002), 221–41, at 233). Presumably, this increase in taxation would impact upon the desirability for married women to work outside of the home. On this subject, also see A. P. Simester and W. Chan, arguing that taxing the household as a unit would have the effect of discriminating against women, as it 'uprate[s] the *commencing* marginal rate of the secondary income earner to the highest rate payable on the spouse's income' ('On Tax and Justice', *Oxford Journal of Legal Studies*, 23 (2003), 711–26, at 711). Thus, '[g]iven that the secondary

the world has established the dramatic impact that tax policy can have on both economic and private choices made by the family. In this situation, however, a number of factors may be at play. For example, presumably, if employers have more funds available to them because of lower rates of taxation, then they will be able to afford more employees, if they are comparatively low paid. Additionally, the probability that it will be economically 'worth it' for mothers to work outside of home will increase.

Tax credits, unlike manipulation of tax rates, are predicated upon visions of the ideally motivated worker, or perhaps the ideal mother. Tax credits also clearly, blatantly, abandon the myth of neutrality in tax provisions.[103] The hope is that they will encourage women to work, although the majority of women raising young children in the UK are, in fact, employed.[104] Discussions of tempting mothers into the marketplace are thus outdated, and reference an antiquated image of the mother torn between work and home. For the majority of women, the choice has been made. Discussions of whether or not the choice *should* be made inevitably neglect the important consequences of this choice,[105] and are unhelpful.[106]

income earner is generally female, and that the labour supply of secondary income earners is relatively sensitive to marginal tax rates, this switch substantially increases the disincentives for women to work' (*ibid.*, at 711–12). Finally, the availability of separate taxation for couples also can affect both the cost of women's part-time employment and the number of women in paid employment. R. A. Rosenfeld and G. E. Birkelund conducted a 2002 research study, which concluded that 'policy can affect the cost of women's employment. Where couples are taxed separately (as in Sweden), women's employment does not generally increase a couple's marginal income tax rate as much as when a couple's earnings are taxed jointly, although the total effect favouring full-time or part-time work will depend on the specific tax structure' ('Women's Part-Time Work: A Cross-National Comparison', *European Sociological Review*, 11(2) (2002), 111–34, at 116).

103 As R. Johnson explains, 'ostensibly neutral tax provisions are premised on domesticity's version of the ideal worker, and function as a mechanism of discipline' ('Law and the Leaky Woman: The Saloon, the Liquor Licence, and Narratives of Containment', *Continuum: Journal of Media and Cultural Studies*, 19 (2005), 181–99, at 183). Johnson is referring specifically to the context of motherhood. A 'neutral' tax provision would not impact upon a mother's decision to work outside of the home, and is thus premised 'on domesticity's version of the ideal worker'; in other words, the focus is upon the 'ideal worker', or ideal mother, who presumably would prefer to work at home.

104 H. Davies, *et al.*, 'Forgone Income and Motherhood: What Do Recent British Data Tell Us?', *Population Studies*, 54 (2000), 293–305, at 305.

105 And, as Johnson would argue, 'function as a mechanism of discipline' ('Law and the Leaky Woman', at 183).

106 Among other consequences, the refrain that one faces a difficult choice, long after the choice has been made, can foster doubt – from both the mother and her employer, both of whom may worry that the mother's presence in the workplace is 'difficult'.

The male breadwinner–female housewife model continues to constitute the foundation of the tax and benefits system in the UK,[107] and elsewhere.[108] Variations apart from this model are inevitably problematised, and the point at which a legal system problematises the public impact of a private choice reveals much about the system itself.[109] In a tax system based upon the foundation of the male breadwinner–female housewife model, taxing the male *and* female breadwinners' model might require a reconsideration of the foundations of the system itself. Thus the question is not whether the tax system should evolve to accommodate changes in society. Rather the question is whether the tax system, based on an outdated model, may actively prevent or hinder changes that otherwise might benefit society.

If a tax system is based on the female housewife model, then employing the tax system to encourage women into the marketplace is bound to cause confusion and difficulty unless that foundation is reconsidered. The incentive (tax credit) risks being quarantined from the rest of the tax and benefit system as a form of directed support, or tax expenditure. It is a portion of the budget reserved for women, but not otherwise a true part of the fiscal state, supporting and interacting with the economic engine of the paid marketplace. If the ultimate plan is to abandon the tax expenditure at the point, by way of illustration, when mothers have exchanged state benefits for paid employment, and then to leave these mothers as active market participants, then the plan is almost bound to fail.[110] Without more, the tax system will remain based on the male

107 See H. Land, explaining that '[t]he state provided support for ... family care by making the male breadwinner–females housewife model the foundation of the tax and benefits system' ('Spheres of Care in the UK: Separate And Unequal', *Critical Social Policy*, 22 (2002), 13–32, at 14).

108 For discussion of the male breadwinner model in German taxation, see discussion above, at pp. 00–0. M. Burk suggested in *Ms Magazine* that 'few of us realize that the [US] tax code has always favored men over women, especially those with stay-at-home wives' ('A Feminist Tea Party?: Time to Start Righting the Tax System's Wrongs', in *Ms Magazine*, spring 2007).

109 Land's observation (in 'Spheres of Care') is directed at the UK, but it speaks directly to McCaffery's work with the tax problems caused in the US by the two-worker family. See discussion below, at pp. 00–0.

110 But cf. Hakim, 'Five Feminist Myths', who has sought to demonstrate that there are 'feminist myths' about women and employment. First, women are perceived to be entering the marketplace in ever increasing numbers (*ibid.*, at 430). Second, women are supposed to be as committed to the paid marketplace as men (*ibid.*, 432). Third, difficulties in securing affordable or appropriate childcare are presented as the main barrier to women's employment. Finally, there is an assumption that part-time jobs, to which women are attracted for a variety of reasons are *poor quality* (*ibid.*, at 431,

breadwinner–female housewife model. As the tax system interacts with the market, it will undermine efforts by the market to evolve beyond this model. The new, women market workers will be similarly undermined.

The next step is to identify the means by which the foundations of the tax and benefits system might be changed. A starting point for the relationship between tax and benefits is that governments would wish to encourage economic circumstances through which taxpayers are in a position to pay more of the former, and, of the latter, to receive fewer. In some ways thus receipt of benefits is a classic moment of problematisation, and Philipps, in particular, has warned that it is important to challenge the reduction of benefits discourse. She warns that '[f]eminists need to intervene in these tax policy debates to ensure that the principle of valuing women's care giving work is not appropriated for agendas that are less concerned with gender equality than with reducing social welfare expenditures or resisting women's entry into markets'.[111] By referencing 'resisting women's entry into markets', it would appear initially that Philipps is referring to policies which differ, for example, from the UK's child tax credit, the aim of which is to encourage women specifically into the marketplace. Her reference to 'reducing social welfare expenditures' resonates, however, for this initiative, and for the earned income tax project generally.[112]

While placing the male breadwinner model at the heart of the tax and benefits system causes inexorable problems, it is not as clear what should replace it.[113] Individualisation in tax and benefits is a growing trend in

emphasis added). See also, generally, B. Pettit and J. Hook, 'The Structure of Women's Employment in Comparative Perspective', *Social Forces*, 84 (2005), 779–801.

111 Lisa Philipps, 'Taxing the Market Citizen: Fiscal Policy and Inequality in an Age of Privatization', *Law and Contemporary Problems*, 63 (2000), 111–32, at 131.

112 Giddens specifically referred to cost as a reason to reconsider the spending and government investment patterns of the National Health Service (NHS). Anthony Giddens, 'Risk and Responsibility', *Modern Law Review*, 62 (1999), 1–10, at 7, 9 and 10. He linked his sociological economic theories explicitly with a New Labour agenda, in a way perhaps evocative of what Schumpeter described as Beveridge's endorsement of Atlee's welfarist state. Schumpeter, 'English Economists and the State-managed Economy', *Journal of Political Economy*, 57(5) (1949), 371–82. (In this fascinating article, Schumpeter reviews the leading socio-economists in England at the time, and details how many of them became involved with Atlee's plan for a welfare state.) This is a moment for attention, as Philipps advocates, and also a potential opportunity.

113 As T. M. Smeeding observed, 'Of course, the relationship between antipoverty spending and reductions in poverty is complex. No one kind of program or set of programs are conspicuously successful in all countries' ('Poor People in Rich Nations: The United States in Comparative Perspective', *Journal of Economic Perspectives*, 20 (2006), 69–90, at 87).

the EU, in particular, although an increasing proliferation of means-testing appears to risk reversing this trend in some instances.[114] There are also tendencies of privatisation in identifiable form, since the 1990s tax credit expansion era. As Philipps memorably warned (in 2000), '[a] new emphasis on privatization is rippling through many fields of state policy in various countries'.[115] This tendency appeared to be based upon a general assumption that private choices are preferable to those encouraged by public regulation.[116] The ability of privatisation to achieve changes which are both long-lasting and far-reaching, however, is restricted.[117]

Philipps' concerns echo the Teubnerian warning that '[w]e live in a time of increasing disenchantment with the goals, structures and performance of the regulatory state'.[118] This, Teubner explained, was partly due to a 'more general concern with the effects of welfare-regulatory intervention'.[119] Whereas the nineteenth century gave us formalism in the law, the twentieth-century disillusionment with this gave rise to the 'rematerialization' of the law.[120] Much of the theory in this area derives from the 1970s, when truly targeted critiques on what came to be described as the welfare state were developed.[121] This was a development from the Marxist critiques of the 1960s, with a women-centred focus.[122] This developmental link is probably best summarised by Mackinnon's famous

114 Land explains that '[t]ax and benefit systems across the EU have moved hesitantly and unevenly towards the individualization of reliefs and benefits, although the growing emphasis on means testing and tax credits in the UK – based on the couple as the unit of assessment – is reversing this trend among lower income families' ('Spheres of Care', at 15).

115 Philipps, 'Taxing the Market Citizen', at 111. Within this context, however, as Philipps explained, '[t]he restructuring of tax policy to foster a more privatized social and economic order is often overlooked as an example of this pattern'.

116 L. Philipps, 'Tax Law and Social Reproduction: The Gender of Fiscal Policy in an Age of Privatization', in Brenda Cossman and Judy Fudge (eds.), *Privatization, Law, and the Challenge to Feminism* (University of Toronto Press, 2002), at p. 41.

117 S. B. Boyd, *Challenging the Public/Private Divide: Feminism, Law, and Public Policy* (University of Toronto Press, 2002), at p. 22. C. Hood has suggested that it might be possible to 're-privatize' tax law enforcement in the UK ('Privatizing UK Tax Law Enforcement?', *Public Administration*, 64 (1986), 319–33).

118 G. Teubner, 'Substantive and Reflexive Elements in Modern Law', *Law and Society Review*, 17 (1983), 239–86, at 239

119 *Ibid.*, at 240.

120 *Ibid.* Additionally, historically, truly 'anti-statist' positions do not have a long history with British feminists. M. McIntosh, 'Feminism and Social Policy', in Christopher Pierson and Francis G. Castles (eds.), *The Welfare State Reader* (Cambridge: Polity Press, 2006), at p. 123.

121 *Ibid.*, at p. 120. 122 *Ibid.*, at p. 121.

observation that '[s]exuality is to feminism what work is to Marxism: that which is most one's own, but which is most taken away'.[123]

If the Married Women's Property Act sounded the call for independent taxation of women, by 1920 it was a clear and delayed feminist objective. The 1920 Royal Commission on Taxation[124] 'heard plenty of evidence about the taxation of women'.[125] Lilian Knowles was the only woman on the Commission.[126] The Commission concluded that a married couple should continue to be employed as 'the basis of the income tax unit', with a 'powerful' dissent by Dr Knowles.[127] She argued that this approach was iniquitous, because married women's property legislation required that women should be treated as individuals, and, additionally, husbands frequently maintained complete control over financial decisions within a family.[128]

While husbands may still maintain financial control in families, other aspects of family financial life have much changed in the twenty-first century. The tax system has become a reflection of societal changes as to what constituted the definition of a family. The previous section explained that marriage is no longer at the centre of what constitutes a family; rather, the linchpin of a child appears at the heart of the tax system's vision of family unity. Yet the kind of family which the tax system is prepared to recognise as surrounding the child has changed dramatically as well. An allowance is now also paid to unmarried couples with children, single parents and (for a limited period) to divorcing or separating couples. Gordon Brown's expressed intention, as Chancellor, 'to make our primary

123 C. A. MacKinnon, 'Feminism, Marxism, Method, and the State: An Agenda for Theory', *Signs*, 7 (1982), 515–44, at 515.

124 A. C. Pigou reported that the objective of the Commission was: '[t]aking the income tax as it is and assuming that the amount of money raised by it at present will have to be maintained, how can the various anomalies and unfairnesses and complications of the tax, which have necessarily grown up with its growth, be best cured or palliated, so as to make this tremendous engine of revenue – probably the most powerful that the world has ever known – more equitable and less burdensome, but not less effective, than before' ('The Report of the Royal Commission on the British Income Tax', *Quarterly Journal of Economics* (1920), 607–25, at 607).

125 N. Brooks, 'The Irrelevance of Conjugal Relationships in Assessing Tax Liability', in *Tax Units and the Tax Rate Scale* (at: http://law.harvard.edu, 1996).

126 *Ibid.*

127 K. A. Lahey, 'The Benefit/Penalty Unit in Income Tax Policy Diversity and Reform' (Law Commission of Canada 2000, at: http://epe.lac-bac.gc.ca/100/200/301/lcc-cdc/benefit_penalty_unit-e/lahey.html).

128 *Ibid.*, citing Dr Lillian Knowles, 'Reservation', in *Report of the Royal Commission on Taxation*, p. 151.

aim that of supporting families through supporting children',[129] also had other objectives.[130] Yet the tax system now is based on the idea that any adults, or single adult, who commit(s) to a child financially has/have formed a family.

Independent taxation

In the UK, joint taxation of a married couple's income ended on 6 April 1990, after which date husbands and wives have had the option to be taxed separately.[131] Although the UK tax system has become an interesting expression of Alstott's 'no exit obligation',[132] it is important not to lose sight of the socio-economic changes introduced by independent taxation, despite the distraction of the modern child-centric focus. Among the many changes augured by independent taxation, studies have established that the switch led to a significant amount of reallocation of family assets.[133] On the whole, many family assets were transferred to women, who tend to be in a lower tax bracket. This, as will be discussed, in many ways would have set the stage for the *Arctic Systems* case. This study suggests that it became popular to assign capital to women not because of a change in societal attitudes, or perhaps because of a connection to increased market activity, but because of tax efficiency. The tax system has incorporated the approach of a business reality test as a challenge to tax-motivated transactions, so a clash was perhaps inevitable.

The tax system has proved capable of adaptation in other areas, however, to accommodate exceptions to the independent taxation principle. For example, Bowler has described the tax credits system as representing an important exception to the model of independent taxation.[134] More

129 House of Commons Debates, 17 March 1998 (pt. 8), col. 1108.

130 The Treasury took the initiative in many areas associated with gender equality and mainstreaming under Brown's chancellorship, including the WFTC, the national minimum wage and other initiatives associated with the 'New Deal' (J. Squires and M. Wickham-Jones, 'New Labour, Gender Mainstreaming and the Women and Equality Unit', *British Journal of Politics and International Relations*, 6 (2004), 81–98, at 85).

131 *Per* Finance Act 1989.

132 A. Alstott, *No Exit: What Parents Owe Their Children and What Society Owes Parents* (New York, NY: Oxford University Press, 2004).

133 See M. Stephens and J. Ward-Batts, 'The Impact of Separate Taxation on the Intra-Household Allocation of Assets: Evidence from the UK', *Journal of Public Economics*, 88(9–10) (2004), 1989–2007.

134 T. Bowler, 'Taxation of the Family', Tax Law Review Committee Discussion, Paper No. 6, April 2007, p. 5.

accommodation may yet be required, however, and indeed Bowler warns that '[t]he definitional issues arising from the tax credit system will be increasingly important if the tax system moves away from only recognising couples who are married/civil partners'.[135] This issue appears urgent in light of the number of mothers who choose to have children either with a cohabitant,[136] or as a lone parent.

There is some element of anti-independent taxation discord apparent in the literature. In 1999, Dench reported that '[a]rticles have appeared in the British press arguing for an end to the independent taxation of wives in order to help reduce poverty'.[137] Dench's reaction to these criticisms is robust, suggesting that 'there are other ways to meet this goal that do not revitalize coverture'.[138] The prospect of its repeal has not been entertained seriously at any political level. Rather, the debate appears to concern the extent of accommodation, much as occurred with the administration of the tax benefits system, that is appropriate. This debate occurs most often in the context of tax avoidance.

The family business occupies an interesting position in cultural lore. It conjures images of the small trader, the sort of economic actor whom, it is assumed, is crucial to the health of an economy. A small trader actually makes something, and is therefore productive and useful. If the small trader has the support and contribution of a family to the success of the business, then this can only be assumed to have, potentially, positive consequences. Family businesses will consist of workers who are uniquely dedicated to the success of the enterprise. There may be little danger of clock-watching, and an assumed unity of purpose. As small businesses are supported by the tax system – for example, through capital allowances, a purpose of which is to support businesses in the dangerous, early years of operation, perhaps before a profit reasonably may be anticipated – one might assume that the case for extending such support to the small family business is even stronger. As Freedman warns, '[t]here is a tendency to believe that because small businesses do not involve as many people as large businesses and because the sums of money concerned are lower, that

135 *Ibid.*

136 Which may not necessarily mean a lone parent, as Bowler estimated that, in 2004–5, 10 per cent of all cohabiting families were step families (*ibid.*, at p. 2).

137 G. Dench (ed.), *Rewriting the Sexual Contract* (London: Institute of Community Studies, 2007), at p. 8.

138 *Ibid.*

their affairs should be simpler'.[139] This sort of reasoning is, she stresses, 'mistaken'.[140]

The complex issues raised by the family business initially might be approached from a comparative perspective, beginning with the position of the employee. An employee, to start, enjoys far fewer tax benefits than a trader, or an independent contractor. It is much more difficult, for example, for an employee to deduct expenses from earnings[141] than it is for a trader. Additionally, employees might receive any one of a variety of modes of support for their employment from family members. This might range from organising elaborate events to entertaining colleagues, to proof-reading reports before they are submitted to an assessor at work. These examples specifically exclude the traditional forms of contribution from the sphere of unpaid labour (ordinary cooking and laundering clothes, for example), so as deliberately to emphasise that there are some duties which a family member might perform for a relative, which it may be assumed would not receive (nor expect) any degree of relief or support from the tax system if that relative is an employee.[142]

The justification for a higher test of deductibility for employees, than for traders, is that traders are required to supply the infrastructure within which they perform the activities which will lead to a profit. They might therefore reasonably be presumed to have more expenses. By contrast, an employee enjoys an infrastructure that is provided through the workplace, and is paid for by the employer. Within the model of comparison between the trader and the employee, there is greater scope for recognition of a wider range of activities supporting the trader. The trader has scope to create his or her own individual infrastructure, and to receive recognition for this self-creation through the tax system, as long as the test of 'wholly and exclusively' test is satisfied.

The existence of this flexibility, combined with the presumed self-interest of relatives to the effort to reduce the tax liability of a family

139 J. Freedman, 'Why Taxing the Micro-Business Is Not Simple – A Cautionary Tale from the "Old World"', *Journal of the Australasian Tax Teachers Association* (2006) (at: http://search.austlii.edu.au/au/journals/JATTA/2006/5.html).

140 *Ibid.*

141 Employee expenses must be wholly, exclusively and necessarily connected with the effort to acquire earnings, whereas trading profits need only be wholly and exclusively connected with a trade.

142 This is a standard element of feminist economic discourse: i.e. analysing the effectiveness of tax and benefit provisions in light of the unequal distribution of unpaid labour between men and women. For example, Himmelweit emphasised the importance of 'unequal division of caring responsibilities by gender' in her analysis of the WFTC ('Making Visible the Hidden Economy', at 50).

member, leads to the suspicion with which the Revenue may view the tax structure of the classic family business. Far from the premise that it may be relevant to consider even greater tax concessions for the family business, tax law has structured a number of tests for the examination of tax reliefs claimed by family members in such an enterprise. For example,[143] a taxpayer is unable simply to assign a portion of income to a spouse or civil partner, so as to be able to take advantage of his or her marginal rates. Similarly, a taxpayer is unable to assign income or assets (such as shares) to children, because settlements legislation[144] precludes the assignment of wealth if it may reasonably be argued that the recipient did not contribute to the efforts to produce the wealth.

The issues in *Arctic Systems* in comparative context

The motivation for this sort of legislation has been the idea of unfairness; i.e., that it is unfair for some tax advantages to be available to small businesses, but not to employees. This is an idea that Redston has examined at length.[145] Among other arguments, Redston asks: 'why is it *unfair* for employees to be in a worse position than small business proprietors, but *fair* for them to be in a worse position than those who transfer property or savings to their spouses?'[146] Put differently, why has the tax system problematised some comparisons, and not others?

Redston works through the policy justifications for treating separate classifications of taxpayers, comparatively, differently, but maintains criticism of the government's 'policy periscope' for small family businesses.[147] She suggests that there are 'other, more appropriate comparators', but also warns that the government 'should also recognise that placing income allocation under a microscope is likely to cause disproportionate complexity and uncertainty for small family businesses'.[148] This is an important point, as it acknowledges that comparing relationships which exist in the marketplace, with relationships formed within the private sphere, is likely to prove awkward.

The nature of this uneasy relationship has been explored in related literature, addressing joint and several liability for spouses in the US tax system. This literature deals directly with the problems caused by assessing private relationships within the realm of public standards. The

143 As will be discussed below, at pp. 00–0. 144 Also discussed below, at pp. 00–0.
145 In Redston, 'Income Sharing', 680–6. 146 *Ibid.*, at 681. 147 *Ibid.*, at p. 686.
148 *Ibid.*

US introduced joint taxation of families in 1948.[149] The result, as Valentine and Fleischman describe, is that '[t]he majority of married persons in the United States file a joint income tax return with their spouses because this generally provides a lower combined tax liability'.[150] They warn that '[u]nfortunately, many spouses are not aware of the concept of *joint and several liability*, which mandates that both spouses are liable for any unpaid tax liability in total'.[151] Among other consequences, '[t]his means that the IRS [Internal Revenue Service] can collect the total tax liability from either spouse'.[152]

The wives who may fall foul of such a principle are in some ways the reverse of Mrs Jones, one of the litigants in *Arctic Systems*. It is important in this context to distinguish between what the Revenue was unhappy about, and what it attacked.[153] Essentially, the Revenue conceded that although Mrs Jones was entitled to some of the profits, she in fact had received too many of them. There were few other options available to the Revenue: it was s. 660A, or nothing. The principle considered in the US joint and several liability literature is also the reverse of the post-independent taxation literature. It is interesting, by comparison, to consider the outcome of a campaign *for* joint taxation. Nonetheless, there are some theoretical parallels.

Joint taxation was introduced in the US in response to two cases. The 1930 US Supreme Court case *Poe* v. *Seaborn*[154] ruled that, in community property states, spouses are taxed as if each has earned one half of the couple's total income, so both husband and wife are taxed under the same marginal rate.[155] This means that each spouse is individually liable for one-half of the community property income, regardless of which spouse actually earns the income, and whether or not a joint or separate return is filed.[156] Also in 1930, the Court ruled, in *Lucas* v. *Earl*,[157] that the

149 In the US, joint filing is presented as a privilege of and incentive towards marriage (Knauer, 'Heteronormativity').

150 Sean Valentine and Gary Fleischman, 'Ethical Reasoning in an Equitable Relief Innocent Spouse Context', *Journal of Business Ethics*, 45 (2003), 325–39, at 325.

151 *Ibid.* (emphasis in text). 152 *Ibid.*, at 325.

153 I am grateful to Anne Redston for drawing the significance of this distinction to my attention.

154 *Poe* v. *Seaborn*, 282 US 101 (1930) (US).

155 Sara LaLumia, 'The Effects of Joint Taxation of Married Couples on Labor Supply and Non-wage Income', in press, corrected proof *Journal of Public Economics*, 92 (7) (July 2008), 1698–1719, at 5.

156 See Martin Silver, 'Spousal Liability for Federal and State Taxes' (at: www.wsba.org/media/publications/barnews/archives/2000/mar-00-spousal.htm).

157 *Lucas* v. *Earl*, 281 US 111 (1930) (US).

contracts which divide income between spouses are not recognised for the purposes of tax.[158] The introduction of joint taxation in 1948 would have alleviated the position of spouses in community property states.[159] Despite this, its introduction was not welcomed by everyone.

The impact of joint taxation in the US produced some results which would have appealed to the IRS. As LaLumia explains, after the introduction of joint taxation, the incentive for husbands to shift income to wives was removed, thus there was a marked decline in the US in the number of wives with 'non-wage income'.[160] LaLumia however also draws attention to a 1942 letter to the *New York Times*, addressing a pre-1948 proposal to introduce joint taxation:

> To those who know the long struggle of women in this country to own property, to control their earnings, to be guardians of their children, to move out of the subject class, this measure is a symbol. It represents the defeat of a major principle of our way of life.[161]

Acknowledging the negative symbolism of joint taxation, LaLumia suggests that 'while the worst fears of joint taxation have been unrealized, indeed joint taxation does affect wives' labor supply and non-wage income'.[162] Interestingly, however, she also emphasises that '[t]here is no evidence that husbands' labor supply and non-wage income were significantly affected by joint taxation'.[163]

Thus LaLumia's research suggests that wives are affected most seriously by joint taxation. Similarly, Jones' research builds upon this premise, and refers to the insidious impact of gendering in the tax system, particularly on the question of income splitting. She warns that '[t]he pervasive discussion of gender roles and relationships that surround ... decisions [as to implementing income splitting] ... should be exposed and thought of in terms that go beyond definitions of income, assertions about political credit, and concerns about administrability'.[164]

158 See discussion at LaLumia, 'Effects of Joint Taxation', at 4.

159 This is a regime found in some US states, under which most property acquired during a marriage (with various exceptions – for example, for some gifts) is owned jointly by both spouses and is divided upon divorce or death.

160 LaLumia, 'Effects of Joint Taxation', at 4.

161 *Ibid.*, at 21, quoting Florence Guy Seabury, 'Letter to the Editor', *New York Times* (25 May 1942).

162 *Ibid.* 163 *Ibid.*

164 C. C. Jones, 'Split Income and Separate Spheres: Tax Law and Gender Roles in the 1940s', *Law and History Review*, 6 (1988), 259–310, at 296.

Seaborn is one of the most famous cases in US tax law,[165] and is typically a starting point there for discussions of taxation of the family. The existence of widespread income splitting in the US, before this case, has been dismissed by Ventry as a 'legal fiction', which ultimately did not impact upon the 'ownership equals taxability' principle which continues to underpin taxation of the family unit.[166] Ventry argues that the principle is 'good law',[167] largely because it removes the 'false barometer' of marriage as the basis of taxation in US law.[168] In common law, 'nearly all' control of property is located with the husband.[169] Ventry suggests that statutory changes to this common law principle did not fully alleviate patriarchy; and, indeed, that the true status of gender equality in marriage lies 'somewhere in between' the common law and the statutory positions.[170] The value of *Seaborn* is that it 'challenged definitions of taxable income deviating from strict legal title'.[171] Additionally, the decision was 'a definitive blow to the position that control determined ownership'.[172] This principle is not applied 'uniformly' by the IRS, however, because it is denied to same-sex families.[173]

In the UK, Williamson has drawn attention to the situation in which a husband or partner has under-declared his business profits and is facing a self-assessment enquiry.[174] He explains that an upward adjustment of his profit figure will result in a reduction in the couples' tax credit award, since the trading income on which the award is based will mirror the profit. In Williamson's example, the wife or female partner is unaware of the self-assessment enquiry, and also does not know that the award of child tax credit, on which she depends to support her children, is at risk. Williamson warns that, in this example, the couple will probably have run up an overpayment of tax credits, which they will be expected to repay. That will be the joint responsibility of the couple, even though the original misdeclaration was made by the husband. Additionally, '[b]ecause their liability is not only joint, but joint and several, the female partner will remain liable even if the male partner becomes bankrupt or absconds'.[175] The Revenue would then have the option of pursuing the female partner for all or some of the debt.

The closest parallel to joint and several responsibility (if not liability) for tax in the UK arises from the 'joint ownership' claim of couples to tax

165 Dennis J. Ventry, Jr., 'Saving Seaborn: Ownership as the Basis of Family Taxation', *SSRN eLibrary* (2009), at 3.

166 *Ibid.* 167 *Ibid.* 168 *Ibid.*, at 7. 169 *Ibid.*, at 18.

170 *Ibid.*, at 19. 171 *Ibid.*, at 72. 172 *Ibid.*, at 73. 173 *Ibid.*, at 3.

174 Robin Williamson, 'Private Lives', *Tax Journal* (2005), 17–18, at 17. 175 *Ibid.*

credits.[176] Each parent is jointly and severally responsible to the Revenue for overpayment of tax credits, and for the accuracy of information presented to the Revenue to support the claim. A problem can arise if one parent is less than honest with another about financial circumstances – which, in the event of relationship breakdown, is not a difficult possibility to imagine.[177]

There are some protections available to the female partner in terms of criminal liability. If she were charged a penalty for fraud or negligence under the tax credits legislation, the female would be protected by statute against having to pay, provided that she did not know, and could not reasonably be expected to have known, of the male partner's default.[178] However, she has no such protection in terms of civil liability. The Revenue may choose to proceed simply on the basis of which parent is more likely to be able to repay the money.

The problem with this example is that a family has been designated for tax purposes, on a child-centric basis, despite either discord or dishonesty. The reason why joint and several liability has persisted in the US is that, as the tax code does not apply to a suspect class of persons, its application to different classes of taxpayers has not been subject to a high level of scrutiny.[179] This is also the case in Canada, and this situation was predicted to continue after the adoption of the Charter.[180] As Woodman explains, '[t]he fact that the classifications [in income tax legislation] may have a disparate and adverse impact on women or minorities is immaterial' in Canadian law.[181]

In a UK-specific context, independent taxation enables privacy for each member of a couple (or for co-parents), but this privacy can have negative results, when it assists someone inclined to be less than forthright with a partner. As a variety of research has established, independent taxation reverberates through a tax system, and often produces a range of unanticipated consequences. For example, the availability of independent taxation can affect the cost of women's part-time employment.[182] In fact, during the 1980s in Sweden, there was a marked movement among women

176 *Ibid.* 177 *Ibid.* 178 *Ibid.*

179 Faye Woodman, 'The Charter and the Taxation of Women', *Ottawa Law Review*, 22 (1990), 625, at 631–2.

180 *Ibid.*, at 632. In the late 1960s, Canada started taxation of the family as a unit, following the recommendation of the Report of the Royal Commission on Taxation. Harvey E. Brazer, 'The Report of the Royal Commission on Taxation', *Journal of Finance*, 22 (1967), 671–83, at 674.

181 Woodman, 'The Charter', at 632.

182 Rosenfeld and Birkelund 'Women's Part-time Work', at 116.

from part-time to full-time employment, driven in part by the availability of independent taxation and wider tax reform.[183] There is no denying the importance of independent taxation to families, as its availability (or not) can impact upon the economic choices that they make.

Independent taxation is not yet very old in the UK, but its impact is beginning to be understood. Independent taxation acknowledges individuals within a tax system, and in some ways is thus accompanied by a requirement of complexity.[184] It follows that, the more individuals that exist within a tax system, the greater the number of circumstances to consider. This is not to suggest that considering every family (whether or not there are children) as a single unit, as a producer of 'household income', would be any easier. Indeed, as Nelson rightly notes, the entire question is 'a little bit strange'.[185]

This is because:

> [t]he notion of 'the household' as a unit supposes that households can be uniquely and discretely identified, and, if notions of tax equity 'across households' are to be well-defined, they have identifiable welfare levels. The language of 'the individual' as a unit tends to focus attention on adult earners as the only tax-relevant human beings, with notions of dependency and other aspects of human relations pushed into the background.[186]

A child-centric focus would be easier within a system that offers independent taxation, as it encourages less of a focus upon 'adult earners'. The 'identifiable welfare level' in the modern UK welfare state is the well-being of the child. There is less clarity in aspects of the tax and benefit system where children are not involved, except the encouragement to enter the

183 This is the conclusion of the study detailed in Marianne Sundstrom, 'The Growth in Full-time Work among Swedish Women in the 1980s', *Acta Sociologica*, 36 (1993), 139–50. Later, in the early 1990s, Sweden introduced a drastic reform of its tax system, which extended the number of taxpayers included in the tax base, and significantly reduced the marginal rate. See S. Steinmo, 'Globalization and Taxation: Challenges to the Swedish Welfare State', *Comparative Political Studies*, 35 (2002), 839–62, at 839. The leading writer in this area is Åsa Gunnarson. See, especially, 'Exploring the Limits of Law: Swedish Feminism and the Challenge to Pessimism', in Gunnarson *et al.* (eds.) (Aldershot: Ashgate, 2007).

184 Although, in the joint taxation system in the US, research still supports the desirability of at least considering each spouse differently. A US study from 1984 stressed the difficult position of secondary earners (so often wives) within the tax system, concluding that 'optimal tax rates on secondary workers in the family are much lower than those on primary earners' (see M. J. Boskin and E. Sheshinski, *Optimal Tax Treatment of the Family: Married Couples*, NBER Working Paper No. 368 (also Reprint No. r0468, at: www.nber.org/papers/W0368.pdf).

185 J. A. Nelson, 'Tax Reform and Feminist Theory in the United States: Incorporating Human Connection', *Journal of Economic Studies*, 18(5–6) (1991), 11–29, at 11.

186 *Ibid.*

marketplace, with the attendant assumption that the marketplace is best equipped to deal with social and economic problems. The tax system assumes the role of enabler, of entrance provision to the marketplace, as opposed to providing solutions for problems directly. It may be that the UK system assumes the role of enabler more easily than other systems (such as, by way of comparison, the US), as it has fostered for decades a more cooperative, and perhaps less heavy-handed, relationship with taxpayers.[187]

This section has included comparative consideration of some of the issues raised by questions concerning independent taxation in a variety of countries in an effort to expose the challenges inherent in one system to the insights of the literature in another system. It has done so however with an eye on the dangers of comparative analyses of these sorts of aspects of tax systems, even as between European countries. Such research, for example, seldom reveals that one sort of tax provision is clearly, identifiably linked with the achievement, or not, of a positive social objective.[188] Additionally, even if countries have a bias in common between tax systems, it will not necessarily follow that the reasons behind these biases are similar.[189]

The importance of acknowledging comparative difference is evident in the EU response to calls for independent taxation. The European Commission issued a memorandum in 1984, recommending fully independent taxation for women throughout Europe.[190] Meehan and Collins described the UK efforts six years later as falling 'short' of these recommendations, yet 'at least partially positive'.[191] It is notable that, as Farmer and Lyall

187 R. Mason and L. D. Calvin suggested in 1978 that 'England's less rigid policies foster a willingness to cooperate with tax officials at the expense of rendering enforcement procedures redundant' ('A Study of Admitted Income Tax Evasion', *Law and Society Review*, 13 (1978), 73–89, at 77). Conversely, in the US, a 1976 study concluded that although not as many Americans were looking for 'free lunches' as first might be expected, ultimately it was not clear that, despite this willingness to pay more in taxes if needed, most study participants really understood how taxes and funding actually worked.

188 Indeed, '[t]he comparative analysis of ... European tax systems has shown that nominal or formal categories of "individual" or "joint" taxation systems can not clearly be associated with the denial or the concession of tax relief within the breadwinner model' (I. Dingeldey, 'European Tax Systems and their Impact on Family Employment Patterns', *Journal of Social Policy*, 30 (2001), 653–72, at 668).

189 For example, Nelson has written that '[o]ne reason for the bias of the [US] tax code towards the traditional one-earner couple is no doubt an ideological one. It is no secret that many current US political conservatives and religious fundamentalists believe that the maintenance of civilization depends on the maintenance of the traditional patriarchal household' ('Tax Reform', at 26).

190 E. Meehan and E. Collins, 'Women, the European Union and Britain', *Parliamentary Affairs*, 49 (2001), 221–34, at 225.

191 *Ibid.*

have explained, '[a]lthough both the Parliament and the Economic and Social Committee called for the submission of a draft directive on the matter, no such proposal has been put forward'.[192] Independent taxation might have been thought to have been a relatively simple subject matter for a directive, but the response to EU initiatives in this direction would suggest otherwise.

Tax law extracts money from the paid marketplace, but is also often used as a tool to influence choices made within the unpaid market. The use of settlements legislation against Mrs Jones may be characterised as an effort by the Revenue to insist that her efforts to support her husband's work should not be brought within the paid market. This argument fails, however, in light of the fact that Mrs Jones did not argue that her husband rewarded her with shares in recognition of her activities supporting the home; nor did Mr Jones insist that he was in some sense paying her for being a housewife. Rather Mrs Jones argued that she was a skilled administrator, and that she brought these abilities to her husband's work – put simply, if Mrs Jones were not available to provide administrative support to Mr Jones' business, then it would have been necessary to hire someone else. The use of the settlements legislation against this argument – indeed the thread linking the line of settlements jurisprudence analysed in *Arctic Systems* – implies that family members are immediately suspect if the suggestion is that they have contributed to a relative's work. This is an argument which demands analysis within the wider context of economic inequality and gender. This, essentially, would require a different *Arctic Systems*. What if the issue in this case had concerned compensating women for unpaid labour?

Incentives: the tax system as inducement/deterrent to marriage

The question now is whether the tax laws should not be re-examined in the light of changing social mores, particularly to the extent that the status quo penalises marriage as against cohabitation. The fact that the Law Commission is considering whether family law should now prescribe rights and obligations for unmarried couples might send a signal to those responsible for tax policy.[193] Historically, support for

192 P. Farmer and R. Lyal, *EC Tax Law* (New York, NY: Oxford University Press, 1994), at p. 33.

193 As Pahl argued, '[i]t is not possible to isolate families from the social and economic contexts in which they are located: inequalities within the family can easily be translated into inequalities in wider society, and *vice versa*' ('Personal Taxation', at 249).

the institution of marriage from the UK tax system has been mixed.[194] Currently, as this section will explain, the introduction of the Civil Partnership Act 2004 (CPA 2004), while primarily an accomplishment representing progress in the cause of equality for same-sex relationships, also may represent a strengthening of support for marriage[195]

By 2005, Bowler estimated that 43 per cent of births in the UK were 'outside of marriage'.[196] This represented a rise in single parent families from 18 per cent in 1971, to 28 per cent in 2006.[197] Despite the fact that successive governments have attempted to encourage the institution of marriage, Bowler argued that it was 'undoubtedly the case' that marriage was decreasing in popularity, at the same time that the number of couples choosing not to marry was increasing.[198] Her recommendation, however, is that '[r]eal relationships should matter, and yet the tax law should be marriage-neutral'.[199]

Should the tax system encourage men and women to get married?[200] Independent taxation is a feminist achievement perhaps because it

194 In 1953 (two years before the Royal Commission), Carter explained that: 'The historical growth of State Aid has followed two quite diverse lines, working slowly down through tax policy, and more haltingly up through new expenditure programmes. On the one hand relief has been given to taxpayers with family responsibilities, but the "elementary canon of financial equity" seems to have been interpreted to mean if a person did not pay tax (or only paid in small amounts), he did not need family aid (or only in small amounts). On the other hand, where the earning parent has been unable adequately to support his family due to illness, injury or unemployment, aid has been forthcoming. Between the two extremes, the average family supporter continues to be in a very unfavourable position compared with his neighbours who are not so burdened' ('Income-tax Allowances', at 227).

195 See N. Barker, 'Sex and the Civil Partnership Act: The Future of (Non) Conjugality?', *Feminist Legal Studies*, 14 (2006), 241–59, arguing that the CPA 2004 is based upon a return to a conjugal model for families, with significant potential for the treatment of cohabiting families. See also C. F. Stychin, 'Not (Quite) a Horse and Carriage: The Civil Partnership Act 2004', *Feminist Legal Studies*, 14 (2006), 79–86, for examination of some of the issues.

196 Bowler, 'Taxation of the Family', at 2.

197 *Ibid.* In 2006, Bowler estimated that one in four children in the UK lived with a single parent.

198 *Ibid.*, at 3.

199 Patricia A. Cain, 'Heterosexual Privilege and the Internal Revenue Code', *University of San Francisco Law Review*, 34 (2000), 465–95, at 495.

200 The UK tax system aims positively to encourage taxpayers either to get married, or to form a civil partnership. This was confirmed in the interpretation of the CPA 2004 in the recent case of *Burden* v. *United Kingdom* (13378/05) ECHR (Grand Chamber), 29 April 2008 (2008) 47 EHRR 38, [2008] STC 1305 in which the European Court of Human Rights confirmed the freedom of a Member State to encourage social stability by providing tax incentives to form families. It is worth nothing though that, in practice, other elements of the tax system, notably capital gains tax on main residences, works in

encouraged financial separation for women away from the family, which is not a locus of gender equality.[201] Given this, one approach to *Arctic Systems* is to stop expecting so much from it. The portrayal by the Revenue of Mrs Jones' work for the company may have been objectionable, but at least that portrayal, in the final analysis, lost in court. The position of family workers such as Mrs Jones may be uncertain in the face of further response from the Revenue, but there have always been examples of tax legislation which target married couples specifically, so this is nothing new.[202]

A perplexing aspect of this area of the tax system is that it appears unable to prevent the imposition of a marriage penalty,[203] at both ends of the economic spectrum,[204] despite perceived widespread political support for marriage as a social institution. Research has established a surprisingly clear link between tax incentives and the decision to marry, so any marriage tax penalty, at the least, would present a confusing message.[205]

the opposite direction – and in tax credits, being married gives rise to an assumption of shared income, whereas single parents with partners are in a position to ignore any contributions from their partners.

201 See, among others: K. M. Baber and K. R. Allen, *Women and Families: Feminist Reconstructions* (New York, NY: Guilford Press, 1992); P. H. Collins, 'It's All in the Family: Intersections of Gender, Race, and Nation', *Hypatia* (1998), 62–82; G. Pascall, *Social Policy: A Feminist Analysis* (London: Tavistock Publications, 1986), at p. 13.

202 Bowler, 'Taxation of the Family', at 5. For example, married couples are prevented from transferring either income or assets so as to take advantage of different marginal rates (*ibid.*). Additionally, married couples are treated as 'connected persons' at various points in tax legislation, so as to preclude the possibility of a transaction at market value. Married couples, effectively, are considered to be incapable of a market value transaction in these circumstances.

203 As J. Alm *et al.* explained, '[a] marriage penalty or subsidy occurs when a change in marital status generates a change, negative or positive, in disposable income' ('Policy Watch: The Marriage Penalty', *Journal of Economic Perspectives*, 13 (1999), 193–204, at 194). One of the consequences of the marriage penalty, which the Tax Reform Act of 1986 aimed to eliminate is that, if it did not exist, many married women would work longer hours. This is the conclusion of the study detailed in Deenie Kinder Neff, 'Married Women's Labor Supply and the Marriage Penalty', *Public Finance Review*, 18 (1990), 420–32.

204 D. T. Ellwood wrote that '[a]t a time when removing marriage penalties in tax policy affecting higher income families is a popular notion, it seems strange to ignore marriage penalties for those at the bottom of the income range' ('The Impact of the Earned Income Tax Credit and Social Policy Reforms on Work, Marriage, and Living Arrangements', *National Tax Journal*, 53 (2000), 1063–1105, at: www.hks.harvard.edu/inequality/Summer/Summer00/papers/Ellwood.PDF, at 40).

205 In fact a 1996 study found that couples in England and Wales were delaying marriage by one year to avoid the impact of a marriage penalty. A. M. G. Gelardi, 'The Influence of Tax Law Changes on the Timing of Marriages: A Two-country Analysis', *National Tax Journal* 49(1) (1996), 17–30, at 27–8. There is an interactive element to marriage subsidies, or penalties, and the number of people who select this option. Indeed, a 1996

The message has not become any clearer in the UK with the passage of the CPA 2004. Although the CPA 2004 has been criticised both for encouraging gay and lesbian couples to follow a heteronormative model, and for offering little beyond the rights available before its enactment,[206] it also represents an important success. Between December 2005 and September 2006,15,700 couples registered as civil partnerships.[207] Each of these couples found themselves to be in the position that now could be described as analogous, for purposes of tax, to a heterosexual married couple. Significant, and stigmatising, time and effort would no longer be required to manage the tax system so as to be able to achieve results that, for heterosexual couples, come automatically.[208] This is an important result.[209]

The CPA 2004[210] only starts a process towards inclusiveness, but it is a start. Queer theory provides a forum for exploring the value of this start, and its significance for marriage, as well as the gender equality project.[211] Among the important insights offered are that marriage has always been

study concluded that changes to the 'married man's allowance' in the 1968 Budget led to significant changes in marriage patterns, thus 'add[ing] to the stream of research showing that tax law can distort behavior and is not neutral to taxpayers' decision making processes' (Alm, *et al.*, 'Policy Watch', at 200, discussing Gelardi, 'Influence of Tax Law Changes').

206 R. Auchmuty, 'Same-sex Marriage Revived: Feminist Critique and Legal Strategy', *Feminism and Psychology*, 14 (2004), 101–26.

207 Bowler, 'Taxation of the Family', at 2.

208 As Cain explained, '[t]o the extent long-term, committed, same-sex couples are similarly situated to married couples, this exclusion not only results in a denial of benefits, but also imposes costs in the form of stigma by communicating that same-sex relationships are less worthy and less valuable. The exclusion also imposes costs by requiring additional time and money to be spent by gay and lesbian taxpayers in order to determine or alter the consequences of the exclusion' ('Heterosexual Privilege', at 495).

209 The literature indicates that the absence of legislation such as the CPA 2004 impacts upon self-esteem and feelings of social inclusion. For example, Infanti insists that, in the US, 'the Code stigmatizes gays and lesbians and attempts to force them into the closet' ('The Internal Revenue Code as Sodomy Statute', *Santa Clara Law Review*, 44 (2004), 763–804, at 765). See also K. Brooks and D. Parkes, 'Queering Legal Education: A Project of Theoretical Discovery', *Harvard Women's Law Journal*, 27 (2004), 89–136, at 118–19: 'One student described the alienating experience of learning taxation law in a US law school. She claimed to understand that "couples" means "heterosexual couples". None of these rules will ever apply to me'. As Cain argued, in the US '[t]here is no rational justification for such differential treatment in a world in which civil unions are otherwise treated the same as marriage' ('Federal Tax Consequences of Civil Unions', *Capital University Law Review*, 30 (2002), 387–408, at 408).

210 Civil Partnership Act 2004.

211 As Knauer persuasively argues, '[q]ueer theory does not get sidetracked by bare claims of equality or a gender-based analysis that ignores issues of sexual orientation. It offers a perspective from which to consider the marital regime in toto' ('Heteronormativity', at 234).

about economic power; and, intriguingly, about preventing concentrations of power between men, as marriage forced them into family units.[212] Additionally, this literature makes it clear that civil partnerships are not immune from the confusion (illustrated by the marriage penalty) surrounding the taxation of married couples.[213]

One analysis of the enactment of the CPA 2004 is that it removed barriers to the tax advantages of marriage for some families. Another approach to this legislation suggests that the CPA 2004 actively encourages more families to choose the institution of marriage/civil partnership through the offer of tax incentives. In this interpretation, tax is thus relied upon to influence families to choose marriage, a decision in which a government might have decided not to intervene. Recognition of same-sex spouses has tax benefits for the state, in that it may assist redistribution of resources, and preclude tax discrimination in favour of heterosexual couples.[214] Although successive governments in the UK have declined to consider whether or not the tax system should place marriage at an advantage,[215] and despite the confusion of the marriage tax penalty, marriage (and now civil partnerships) have received economic protection and encouragement from the state through taxation.[216]

Cohabiting couples largely are treated by the tax system as single persons. The tax consequences for cohabiting couples are mixed. They hold onto their double private residence exemptions and avoid being the target of anti-avoidance provisions targeted specifically at them, but they also

212 K. A. Lahey writes that '[s]ome of the first tax policies designed to promote heterosexuality and discourage sharing economic power with same-sex partners were enacted by Augustus in Rome from 30 BC to AD 14' (*Are We 'Persons' Yet?: Law and Sexuality in Canada* (University of Toronto Press, 1999), at p. 221). Lahey's contribution to this field is immense, and has influenced many of the writers discussed in this chapter.

213 Cain demonstrates that lesbian couples suffer in the US both because rules are clear, and because rules are unclear: 'Taxing Lesbians', *Southern California Review of Law and Women's Studies*, 6 (1996–7), 471, at 481. Lesbians clearly cannot benefit from shifting the tax burden to the lower-earning partner (*ibid.*, at 475). It is unclear how gifts between couples will be taxed (*ibid.*, at 476). Add to this mix the fact that 'a substantial number' of lesbians are likely to have children, and the stage for institutional conflict appears set (*ibid.*, at 474).

214 As Boyd explained, 'where public moneys are involved (for example, income tax benefits), an appropriate redistribution of resources between heterosexual and gay/lesbian taxpayers may result from the recognition of same-sex spouses' ('Family, Law and Sexuality: Feminist Engagements', *Social and Legal Studies*, 8(3) (1999), 369–90, at 378).

215 Bowler, 'Taxation of the Family', at 6.

216 It makes tax sense to marry. Bowler argues that, primarily because of the capital gains tax and inheritance tax advantages, the tax system favours married couples and civil partners (*ibid.*, at 5–6).

(without children) will not enjoy allowances. In 2006–7, the Law Commission published a report, *Cohabitation: the Financial Consequences of Relationship Breakdown*, which among other objectives aimed to publicise the fact that there is no concept in English law of 'common law marriage', and thus cohabiting couples should take enormous care when planning their financial futures.[217]

Despite significant public frustration at its delay,[218] in December 2008, the Cohabitation Bill[219] was introduced in the House of Lords as a Private Member's Bill by the Liberal Democrat peer, Lord Lester of Herne Hill.[220] The tax changes promised are not great, as '[c]ohabiting couples are treated as unconnected individuals for taxation purposes and as such cannot, for example, benefit from various reliefs and exemptions in the taxation system available for spouses and civil partners'.[221]

This should be viewed in light of the fact that there is a wide literature discussing marriage, and its socio-economic impact upon women.[222] This literature has been drawn upon by, in particular, Deech, who has made a strong case for denying legal recognition of cohabitation on the grounds of 'individualism'.[223] One of the reasons that women are poorer than men is because they spend more of their time engaging in unpaid labour.[224] The act of income splitting[225] by independent contractors and

217 Catherine Fairbairn, '"Common Law Marriage" and Cohabitation', in Home Affairs Section (ed.), House of Commons 2 January 2009, at p. 1.

218 Paul Lewis (reporting), 'Cohabitation Law Delay "Shoddy"' (at: http://news.bbc.co.uk/1/hi/programmes/moneybox/7285193.stm).

219 Cohabitation Bill, [HL] 2008–9.

220 Fairbairn, '"Common Law Marriage"', at p. 1. 221 *Ibid.*

222 See, among others: L. J. Waite, 'Does Marriage Matter?', *Demography* (1995), 483–507; L. Thompson and A. J. Walker, 'Gender in Families: Women and Men in Marriage, Work, and Parenthood', *Journal of Marriage and the Family* (1989), 845–71, at 850–1; and, generally, L. Sargent, *Women and Revolution: A Discussion of the Unhappy Marriage of Marxism and Feminism* (London: South End Press, 1981).

223 R. L. Deech, 'The Case against Legal Recognition of Cohabitation', *International and Comparative Law Quarterly*, 29 (2008), 480–97. Deech explains that '[i]ndividualism lends itself well to the achievement of the equality of women: it requires the treatment of the family as a collection of individuals with separate and independent rights and avoids treating the family as a unit, a treatment which is bound to suppress the personal needs of the less prominent members, usually the women, and focus on the head of household' (*ibid.*, at 481).

224 See J. C. Gornick, 'Gender Equality in the Labour Market: Women's Employment and Earnings', *Gender and Welfare State Regimes* (1999), 210–42; B. Jordan, *Trapped in Poverty?: Labour-market Decisions in Low-income Households* (London: Routledge, 1992).

225 Although asset transfers may be the single greatest tax incentive to marriage, since 2004, married couples and civil partners have been precluded from income splitting in its purest form. Bowler, 'Taxation of the Family', at 7, citing s. 282A(4A) Income Corporation and Taxes Act 1988.

their families could be recharacterised as an effort by Mr Jones to bring more of his wife's activities out of the unpaid marketplace, and into the paid marketplace. There could be benefits for the Revenue, and by extension the government, in shifting its view of income splitting as tax avoidance, and as a necessarily bad thing.

The current, post-'third way' position is to merge tax with benefits, and thus to involve the tools of paid activity (tax is such a tool) with the arena of poverty (in which benefits exist).[226] Women and their children overwhelmingly outnumber men in this arena. This approach does not necessarily assist the tax system. The difficulty of distinguishing whether legislation in question is actually a benefit, or a tax, can add yet another layer of confusion upon an already confused body of tax law. The coherence and clarity of tax law can suffer in this. By converse, accepting that men in self-employment will use the corporate vehicle to compensate their wives for the vast and varied amount of labour they will engage in to support their paid activities is, at the least, a clear approach.

A clear approach is not necessarily a desirable approach for the Revenue. But it is worth asking exactly why it was easier to challenge a wife's contribution to a family business, as opposed to the contribution of anyone else.[227] If it is accepted that labour occurs within households, and that households contribute to economic output, why is the concept of household income 'a little bit strange'?[228] One reason why women's finances in particular tend to be considered within the 'household' is that, when their labour is considered in proportion to the income they receive, there is in fact a discrepancy between their labour and their income. As a great deal of women's efforts tend to be invested in unpaid labour within a unit that easily, if roughly, could be defined as the household, a common focus on such a categorisation was perhaps inevitable.

226 Mumford, 'Marketing Working Mothers', at 411.

227 In the Mirrlees Review, Crawford and Freedman warned that '[t]his is a question that needs addressing in a holistic way, looking at the rules on family taxation, small business taxation and capital transfers between spouses in the round' ('Small Business Taxation', at 23).

228 J. A. Nelson, 'Tax Reform and Feminist Theory in the United States: Incorporating Human Connection', *Journal of Economic Studies*, 18(5–6) (1991), 11–29, at 11. This is because '[t]he notion of "the household" as a unit supposes that households can be uniquely and discretely identified, and, if notions of tax equity "across households" are to be well-defined, they have identifiable welfare levels. The language of "the individual" as a unit tends to focus attention on adult earners as the only tax-relevant human beings, with notions of dependency and other aspects of human relations pushed into the background' (*ibid.*).

A 1981 study addressed this issue, and concluded:

> that wives working outside the home react to higher levels of taxation by reducing their market hours and increasing their home production time. In fact, the hypothesis cannot be rejected that wives completely reallocate time lost from the labor market to nonmarket production in an attempt to restore household real income. The authors conclude that the production loss from progressive taxation is usually overstated, though wives may lose through depreciation of their market skills and society loses to the extent that specialization in the economy declines.[229]

These statistics operate however on the presumption that it is possible to separate a woman's paid and unpaid labour, and a woman's income, from her household, and it is in fact notoriously difficult to do this. A system which allowed incorporated, family businesses to shift wealth via dividends to other family members ostensibly for the tax benefit, but within a wider context of recognition for unpaid labour that families provide to support activities within the paid marketplace, is not immune from the challenges of the engulfment principle, mentioned earlier. It, too, presumes that it may be possible to identify things which in fact are difficult to discern. It is also open to challenge on other grounds. 'Maximum slices for those at the bottom',[230] as Byrne argued, will not cover taxpayers such as Mrs Jones. This context is important, however, because it explains some assumptions upon which the tax system is founded. Kershnar's analyses[231] emphasise the divide between the paid and unpaid markets. The competition for primary goods is constructed as the only market which matters. The market itself is also composed entirely of individuals, and the family unit is presented simply as a forum from which one may escape the pressures of the competitive marketplace. These are presumptions which may be assumed to have influenced the system of taxation.[232]

229 Janet C. Hunt, *et al.*, 'Taxation and the Wife's Use of Time', *Industrial and Labor Relations Review*, 34 (1981), 426–32, at 426ff.

230 Donna M. Byrne, 'Progressive Taxation Revisited', *Arizona Law Review*, 37 (1995), 739–88, at 778.

231 S. Kershnar, 'For Discrimination against Women', *Law and Philosophy*, 26(6) (2007), 589–625, at 614.

232 Johanna Niemi-Kiesiläinen explains that, '[t]heoretically, the construction of entirely individual duties through income tax and individual social rights based on earnings-related social security schemes are rooted in an underlying assumption of the individual as autonomous' ('Economic Dependence and Self-support in Family, Tax and Social Law', in Eva-Maria Svensson, Anu Pylkkänen and Johanna Niemi-Kiesiläinen (eds.), *Nordic Equality at a Crossroads: Feminist Legal Studies Coping with Difference* (Aldershot: Ashgate, 2004), at p. 149).

The US tax legal theorist Boris Bittker wrote in 1975 that '[a] persistent problem in the theory of income taxation is whether natural persons should be taxed as isolated individuals, or as social beings whose family ties to other taxpayers affect their taxpaying capacity'.[233] From Bittker's perspective, 'family ties' are an encumbrance (without the negative connotations), which prevent a taxpayer from earning as much as he otherwise might. Given the extent to which a family may prevent a taxpayer – and, Bittker would have argued, regardless of the gender of the taxpayer – from earning more, it is fair to allow those encumbrances to be taken into account by the tax system.[234]

This section will draw to a close with Bittker,[235] for it is proposed that his insight into the 'next steps' for the problem of intra-family income shifting are immensely relevant in the post-*Arctic Systems* era in the UK. Bittker suggested that 'tax theorists have excessively downgraded the importance of legal rights within the family, and [it] may be that a swing of the pendulum is in the offing'.[236] He also warned that 'theoreticians, whatever their backgrounds, cannot "solve" the problem of taxing family income'.[237] Ultimately, he suggests 'the expert must give way to the citizen'.[238] This conclusion has much relevance for the problem at issue in this chapter.

Is it possible to arrange the tax system in such a way as to acknowledge the unpaid labour that family members will invest to support the efforts of one of their own in the paid marketplace? Or, must the issue remain whether or not this kind of arrangement is an illegitimate effort by a taxpayer to avoid his taxes by overrepresenting the significance of a family member's contribution to his business?[239] It may be necessary, as Bittker

233 B. I. Bittker, 'Federal Income Taxation and the Family', *Stanford Law Review*, 27(6) (1975), 1389, at 1391.

234 He argued that both the US Congress and its Treasury need to balance any number of factors determining the extent to which a system is fair, but the most important factor is 'society's assumptions about the role of marriage and the family' (*ibid.*, at 1392).

235 Who, in 1975, related the following story: '[d]uring a 1963 discussion at the Brookings Institution of a forthcoming book on federal taxation of the family, a participant commented: "I don't think that 27 economists should have been assembled to address themselves to problems which are really partly anthropological, partly sociological, partly anything except what we have competence in". In point of fact, some of the "27 economists" at the Brookings convocation were lawyers, but their expertise in matters anthropological and sociological was probably not enhanced by either their legal training or their innocence of economics' (B. I. Bittker, 'Federal Income Taxation and the Family', *Stanford Law Review*, 27 (1975), 1389–1463, at 1463).

236 *Ibid.*, at 1392. 237 *Ibid.*, at 1496. 238 *Ibid.*

239 It is important to stress at this point that the Joneses vigorously contested the suggestion that the value of Mrs Jones' contribution was in any way overrepresented, [2007] 1 WLR 2030, 2032, para. 3: 'Mrs Jones did the book keeping, dealt with the bank and the

suggested, for the expert to give way to the citizen, and for the citizens at that juncture to make a choice. The choice will concern whether the tax system should take the opportunity to value and acknowledge unpaid labour.

Tax and family law

'Fairer unit or tax on virtue?' – thus began a 1960 *Stanford Law Review* article by Oldman and Temple including a comparative analysis of the taxation of marriage.[240] The title is an interesting tease, suggesting that a tax on marriage is in some ways also a tax on women, 'the fairer sex'. Taxes which impact upon, discourage or encourage[241] marriage certainly impact upon the economic well-being of women, so the tease is evocative.[242] While it is important not to exaggerate our expectations of the promise of taxation for economic inequalities supported through marriage,[243] there are also serious problems in continuing to assume that there is a 'common purse' in marriage, and the challenge for the tax collection authority is simply to devise the appropriate levy for that purse.[244]

Looking for the 'common purse' presumption

Two cases, in particular, present evidence of the 'common purse' presumption in English tax law. The first, the 1959 *Emery* case, presents a

insurance company, paid tax and VAT and attended to correspondence. This took four or five hours a week.'

240 Oldman and Temple, 'Comparative Analysis', at 585.

241 This can have important class implications. As I. Montanari explained, '[s]ince marriage subsidies predominantly take the form of tax allowances which are always regressive in character, the class dimension is here intermingled with the gender dimension ...' ('From Family Wage to Marriage Subsidy and Child Benefits: Controversy and Consensus in the Development of Family Support', *Journal of European Social Policy*, 10 (2000), 307–33, at 307).

242 In 1977, C. D. Harbury and D. Hitchens suggested that the three most important factors for determining the wealth of women both in the UK and the US were 'inheritance, marriage and "entrepreneurship"' ('Women, Wealth and Inheritance', *Economic Journal*, 87 (1977), 124–31, at 124).

243 In a 1983 analysis of the US system, D. R. Feenberg suggested that 'no positive income tax system can achieve the simultaneous goals of marriage neutrality, horizontal equity, and progressivity ...' ('The Tax Treatment of Married Couples and the 1981 Tax Law', National Bureau of Economic Research 1983, at: www.nber.org/papers/w0872.pdf, at 44).

244 Feenberg contended that it was unfair to treat married couples as a unit because there was no 'common purse', wives rarely had any control over the family finances, and married women's property legislation required that women be treated as individuals by the state for all policy purposes (*ibid.*).

good example of the sort of asset transfer the courts have typically sought to discourage, on the basis of a presumed common purse in marriage. In this case, the plaintiff brought an action against his wife, a US citizen, claiming that shares held in US companies in her name were held by her in trust for them both jointly.[245] The court held that the husband had transferred the shares into his wife's name to avoid payment of US tax, and in those circumstances a court of equity would not help him to rebut the presumption of advancement.

The second, the 1946 case of *Nugent-Head* v. *Jacob*,[246] concerned the income tax liability of a woman who lived separately from her husband. The case turned on whether a strict interpretation of the word 'separate' was supportable. It might have been assumed that the Revenue would be keen to support a literal reading of the term, thus establishing that the taxpayer was living with her husband for the purposes of tax,[247] but, as the case involved income from possessions located abroad, the facts were a bit more complicated than this. This was a highly controversial case at the time, and the subject of an interesting amount of academic commentary.[248] Although the couple were separated by the husband's overseas military service, the House of Lords held that they nonetheless were not living separately because 'there had been no rupture of marital relations'.[249]

The case[250] considered the circumstances under which 'a married woman living in the United Kingdom separate from her husband' could be assessed to income tax on trading profits separately from that of her husband. The issue largely concerned the remittance basis of taxation for a foreign resident, as the income in question arose from properties maintained by the wife in the US. The court, however, focused upon statutory construction; for, as Viscount Simon lamented in this case: '[i]t is much to be regretted that the present statute law defining in what cases a married woman is herself liable to income tax, and in what cases the liability to

245 *Re Emery's Investment Trust* [1959] 1 All ER 577, *per* Wynn-Parry, J.

246 *Nugent Head* v. *Jacob*, [1948] AC 321; [1948] 1 All ER 414; 64 TLR 127; 30 TC 83; [1948] TR 23; [1948] LJR 759; (1948) 92 SJ 193.

247 J. A. Coutts, 'Income Tax Liability of Married Women', *Modern Law Review*, 12 (1949), 110–12, at 110.

248 'Divorce Cruelty LCBG', *Modern Law Review*, 10 (1947), 198–203; Raoul P. Colinvaux, 'Income Tax Liability of Married Women', *Modern Law Review*, 11 (1948), 346–7; and Coutts, 'Income Tax Liability'.

249 [1948] 1 All ER 414, at 416; [1948] AC 321, at 324 *per* Viscount Simon.

250 [1948] AC 321.

tax on her income falls on her husband instead, is not stated in plain and unambiguous language'.[251]

The facts involved a US woman who lived in England with her British husband. The wife remained ordinarily resident in London during the periods in question, while her husband served abroad in military service. Although there was no question but that the husband and wife had a 'very happy'[252] marriage, the court in *dicta*[253] elected to consider the financial obligations of a husband towards a wife from whom he has decided to separate. This (deemed) analogous situation was considered relevant to the question of whether or not the taxpayer wife in this was 'living with' her husband.[254] The *Nugent-Head* court held that the wife was indeed 'living with' her husband for the purposes of tax, on the basis that there had been 'no rupture of marital relations', despite the fact that they had lived apart for three years.[255] This had the consequence that the wife was assessed under the provision that 'the profits of a married woman living with her husband shall be deemed to be the profits of the husband, and shall be assessed and charged in his name, and not in her name or the name of her trustee'. Thus, the tax was assessed to her husband (an advantage to the family under the circumstances of the remittance basis),[256] a victory for the taxpayer.

The Court of Appeal also had engaged in criticism of the language of the legislation addressing the tax status of women who lived separately from their husbands, complaining as to the 'extraordinary ambiguity of the language ... and the statutory history of that language shows how the reluctance of the Inland Revenue to see any Parliamentary change made

251 [1948] AC 321, at 322. Colvinaux later wrote that 'no one would dispute Viscount Simon's lament' ('Income Tax Liability', at 347).

252 *Jacob*, at 323.

253 For example, *ibid.*, at 324.

254 *Ibid.*, at 325.

255 *Ibid.*, at 324.

256 Recall that the income would now be that of her husband, who is not resident in the UK for the purposes of the remittance basis. This is explained in Note, 'Income Tax Liability', at 200. (The author of this note was revealed in a later edition of *Modern Law Review* to be Raoul P. Colvinaux – 'Income Tax Liability', at 347.) It is worth pointing out that the legislation in question – Income Tax Act 1918, s. 16 – contained two separate sections using the term 'living with' ambiguously. The Revenue was keen to avoid a construction in which all husbands serving abroad would now find that some trading income could be assessed solely to their wives, as this would open up a different avenue of avoidance (Note, 'Income Tax Liability', at 201). The Court of Appeal attempted to achieve this by focusing their attention on s. 16, cl. 2, but nonetheless produced what the author of this note described as a 'bad' decision: 'This decision opens up considerable opportunities to the taxpayer of cutting down his tax liability where he has a common home with his wife in the United Kingdom, but is temporarily separated from her from time to time' (*ibid.*, at 203).

in ancient wording to which they have got accustomed and of which they think (often rightly) they know the meaning (though the taxpayer probably does not) may lead to unnecessary disputes and therefore much public inconvenience'.[257] The case itself acknowledges the importance of what could be described as the emotional context of the family in UK tax law. As a jurisdiction which approaches international jurisdiction to tax on the basis of residence,[258] the actual, physical, geographical location of the taxpayer is important. The emotional context of the family, however, is carved out as an exception. For tax purposes, the Nugent-Head family were still living together, even if they were not.

The *Nugent-Head* court emphasised a form of emotional solidarity as underpinning the economic context of the family, in a manner which is evocative of Durkheim.[259] Schwartz suggested that Durkheim believed that the emotional construct of the family was important for the continuance of economic life and traditions – essentially, economic traditions, for example concerning child labour,[260] are borne out of family emotional ties – although, Schwartz argued, Durkheim believed that the family would diminish in importance.[261] The *Nugent-Head* case demonstrates this: the basis for taxing the family, even in an area of law which is dependent upon a cold, hard precept of physical, geographical location, is inextricably linked with the emotional ties that bind the family.

These emotional ties lead to clear economic obligations. Consider, for example, the *dicta* in *Nugent-Head* addressing the financial obligations of the husband to a wife from whom he has separated, but not yet divorced. Because the tax system encourages and supports the concept of the family, 'it is very difficult to opt out of family life'.[262] Thus, the *Nugent-Head* court held that the separated but not divorced husband would be in an analogous position to that of the taxpayers in this case, because it was clear that the separated but not divorced husband would continue to have an obligation to support his wife financially, even though he would not be living with her.[263]

257 [1947] KB 17, at 19 (*per* Scott LJ). As mentioned, the legislation in question is the Income Tax Act 1918, s.16, which at various points uses the term 'living with' ambiguously.
258 As opposed to source.
259 M. A. Lamanna, *Emile Durkheim on the Family* (London: Sage, 2002), at p. 52.
260 See E. Durkheim, 'The Conjugal Family', in *Emile Durkheim on Institutional Analysis*, pp. 229–39.
261 See discussion throughout T. P. Schwartz, 'Durkheim's Prediction about the Declining Importance of the Family and Inheritance: Evidence from the Wills of Providence, 1775–1985', *Sociological Quarterly* (1996), 503–19.
262 Weedon, *Feminist Practice*, at p. 39.
263 [1948] AC 321, at 331–2.

Of course the tax system, on its own, may not be powerful enough to persuade women to have a family, but when it is considered that taxes operate in conjunction with organised religion, cinema, education and other institutions, it becomes possible to argue that taxes at least play a role in this powerful societal push.[264] Indeed, in the early days of the modern US income tax, Seligman argued that 'it is the family income as a whole which serves as the best test of ability to pay'.[265] He also considered it to be 'very unlikely that married women will be assessed at all, even though the letter of the law calls for the taxation of "all persons of lawful age"'.[266]

The *Arctic Systems* case has implications which extend beyond the strict issues of 'entitlement to profit' for the purposes of tax. As was discussed, the taxpayers in the *Arctic Systems* case ran a family business, structured such that the husband transferred part of the wealth produced to his wife. His wife contributed to the business through the provision of administrative services. Although the Revenue ultimately did not succeed, in litigation that reached the House of Lords, in an effort to establish that the taxpayers' arrangement constituted tax avoidance, this chapter has suggested that a number of wider issues are raised by this fact pattern.

First, the debate concerning the interaction between paid and unpaid labour, and the extent to which the valuation of labour often occurs along gendered lines, is relevant. Second, the *Arctic Systems* case raises the question of whether the tax system, when it decides to allow some tax arrangements, and to deny others, contributes to the classification and valuation of labour. This is not to suggest that this analysis has queried whether the tax system contributes to the monetary value of supportive labour in family business, for, by allowing tax relief for some activities, it obviously does so. Rather, this analysis has questioned whether the tax system contributes to gendered divisions of, and assumptions concerning, the relationship between labour and gender economic equity.

It might seem odd to refer to the 'family business', certainly in the context of classic feminist analyses of labour within the home. Every family could be described as a business, and every head of a family could be described as a CEO. Additionally, putting a selection of supportive, family-based activities up for analysis, and deciding which are inherently commercial, and which are private, invokes a range of issues – largely,

264 Weedon, *Feminist Practice*.

265 Edwin R. A. Seligman, 'The Income Tax', *Political Science Quarterly*, 9 (1894), 610–48, at 630.

266 *Ibid.*

because placing chores of the private sphere into the commercialised marketplace can have a confusing impact. For example, if a price is placed on an activity (e.g., parenting or housework), has it been raised in the public estimation, or lowered? Additionally, are some activities too precious or important for cost analysis?[267]

One response to this question would be simply to look at it from the perspective of the gendered nature of economic inequality.[268] The system might be deployed to place women in stronger economic positions, by redistributing significant sums of money to them, in recognition of housework and childcare. Arguments against this approach include the allegation that it commodifies family life and disconnects women from their homes.[269] Second, that is defeatist, in that it accepts the existing foundations of the public–private divide and the marketplace and requires women's labour to be conceptualised in traditional contractual forms on which, in turn, traditional taxation arrangements can be formed, rather than going for a radical rethink of what we mean by value and how we measure and tax it.[270]

These will not necessarily be the concerns of the taxpayers enduring the scrutiny of the Revenue. Their concerns will be to achieve a lower tax burden, not to engage with vagaries of societal esteem. This may be a concern of the Revenue, however, engaged as it is – however indirectly, through administration of the benefits system – with wider questions of economic equity. When the Revenue is empowered by Parliament both to decide who must pay taxes, and who owes benefits, it could be described as a vital part of the engine powering the economy. And the economy, as fiscal sociology has long acknowledged, relies upon housework. Indeed, it could not function without it.

Schumpeter, perhaps the father of fiscal sociology, acknowledged the importance of housework, and, indeed, the housewife, in research conducted in the 1930s as part of an effort to identify and ideally cure the ills plaguing the German economy at the time. Schumpeter believed that the German housewife, more or less, controlled the German economy, as she made decisions about how best to ensure the financial survival of

267 Discussed in Mumford, 'Towards a Fiscal Sociology'.

268 Many thanks to Kate Malleson, for drawing many of these arguments to my attention.

269 This is discussed in Tony Fahey, 'The Family Economy in the Development of Welfare Regimes: A Case Study', *European Sociological Review*, 18 (2002), 51–64.

270 Heidi I. Hartmann suggests many of these issues should be addressed by viewing the family as 'a location', where 'production and redistribution take place', as opposed to an 'active agent' with 'unified interests' ('The Family as the Locus of Gender, Class, and Political Struggle: The Example of Housework', *Signs*, 6 (1981), 366–94, at 368).

her family.[271] Feminist analysis of this question has been led by Oakley's classic work, warning that employment in the paid marketplace should not be viewed as distinct from housework: 'the definition of housewifery is cast in terms of *responsibility* for the running of a home'.[272] A 'responsibility' is not constrained by tasks, in any finite sense; rather, it is drawn along lines of accountability. Borders are not easily drawn defining the obligations of a person who is accountable for the well-being of a family unit.

Such borders, however, may be drawn in tax. Relying still on the terms of Oakley's analysis, a housewife may perform a variety of activities that support her husband's business. Some of these activities may constitute sufficiently to the business for which she may be compensated with profits in the form of either income or capital, and the tax system will support this. Other activities will not be classified in this way. The tax system frequently makes choices about the classification of economic activity for tax purposes. For example, there are any number of activities strictly that a trader may need to perform (such as eating and sleeping) in order to be able to work towards a profit, but not all of the costs associated with this will be deductible. The housewife of course will share in the wealth that the husband earns. She will not, however, be compensated for it in terms that are recognised by tax.

If the housewife in the above example divorces her husband, it is possible that the divorce settlement will compensate her, in effect, for labour, unpaid at the time, which has contributed to the wealth amassed by the family unit. If her husband is highly paid, and she is not, a settlement may acknowledge some of the labour she contributed so as to enable her husband to achieve his position. Given that tax consequences will not necessarily flow from the language used in such a settlement, the Revenue could argue that this is simply a matter of expression – and that, in fact, the housewife is not being compensated. Instead, on divorce the housewife is being permitted to share in the wealth her husband has amassed.

Different systems, different aims

Family law and tax law are divergent systems, with different aims. The clashes that can occur when two systems of law use the same terms, for different purposes, is highlighted in Wikeley's work identifying the

271 He explained this in Joseph A. Schumpeter, 'The March into Socialism', *American Economic Review*, 40 (1950), 446–56.

272 Ann Oakley, *The Sociology of Housework* (London: Martin Robertson, 1974).

problems caused by the reliance upon gross income for tax purposes within the calculations for child support.[273] The challenge to protests of separateness is found in the frequent instrumentalist deployment of the tax system in support of the family as a social institution.

These criticisms have been levied at every aspect of the New Labour effort to encourage women into the marketplace. The Child Trust Fund, for example, has been criticised for denying parents the autonomy to make financial decisions on behalf of their children.[274] One advantage of the Child Trust Fund, however, is that it provides families with a higher wage that varies according to family size. The market is never going to provide this.[275] The value of the Child Trust Fund is its symbolism, and it was described as an important, if incomplete, step.[276] As Le Grand wrote, 'we are more than willing to accept half a loaf, and accept any plausible tax scheme that generates significant stakeholding for the next generation'.[277]

Following along these lines, Wikeley's work with the definitional problems of income is particularly relevant to this analysis. Wikeley has argued that problems surrounding definitions of income are linked to important

273 N. Wikeley, 'Child Support Reform – Throwing the Baby Out with the Bathwater?', *Child and Family Law Quarterly*, 19 (2007), 434.

274 H. Reece has written: '[s]pecifically, I would welcome higher wages and free (no strings attached) childcare as opposed to tax credits, which demand that families disclose financial circumstances with cap in hand, or the ludicrous Child Trust Fund, under the terms of which the Government gives every child a little bit of money to be held on trust until the child is 18, demonstrating that the State does not even trust parents with the autonomy to make financial decisions on behalf of their children' ('The Autonomy Myth: A Theory of Dependency', *Child and Family Law Quarterly*, 20(1) (2008), 109–10, at 109).

275 A problem Beveridge identified. This is discussed throughout H. Land, 'The Family Wage', *Feminist Review*, 6 (1980), 55–77 (at: http://staging-www.palgrave-journals.com/fr/journal/v6/n1/pdf/fr198019a.pdf), which provides an excellent summary of the literature and arguments surrounding the idea of a 'family wage', spanning over one hundred years. This has been an important part of socialist discourse in the UK. I am enormously grateful to Nick Wikeley for drawing this point to my attention.

276 J. Le Grand, 'Implementing Stakeholder Grants: The British Case', in Bruce Ackerman, *et al.* (eds.), *Redesigning Distribution: Basic Income And Stakeholder Grants as Alternative Cornerstones for a More Egalitarian Capitalism* (Making Social Policy Work: Essays in Honour of Howard Glennerster) (London: Verso, 2006), at p. 171. See also N. Wikeley, who points out that the value extends beyond mere symbolism, into a form of instrumentalism, such that '[i]n terms of its broader long-term objectives, the success of the Act will depend, as one Labour backbencher observed, on its ability to attract low-income families into the habit of saving for their children' ('Child Trust Funds: Asset-based Welfare or a Recipe for Increased Inequality?', 2004, at: http://eprints.soton.ac.uk/27919/).

277 Le Grand, 'Implementing Stakeholder Grants'.

questions concerning child support.[278] He explained that '[t]he adoption of the gross income test is based on the erroneous assumption that the assessment of income for one purpose (tax) is necessarily congruent with its assessment for other purposes (eg, child maintenance)'.[279] Wikeley explains that this approach is not common in other countries; and, indeed, '[e]ven the Australian child support scheme, which is much more closely integrated with the tax system, adds back in to the assessment some forms of tax-free income'.[280] The danger of this is that given a taxpayer might wish to minimize his declaration of income for tax purposes, the income relied upon for determining assessments may be too low, and unrepresentative. The child, as a result, may suffer. Wikeley warns that '[t]he argument that unreasonably low child support assessments can be challenged by way of an application for a variation from the formula carries little weight in the light of experience'.[281]

Wikeley's criticism raises a number of interesting issues. First, it is noteworthy that the trend for blending the administration of benefits with the collection of tax has extended from structure to the foundations of some aspects of law. Child support of course is not a benefit, but falls within what could be described as a concept of 'family finances' that falls within the jurisdiction of the Revenue. Second, from a tax perspective the government has little incentive for understanding, forgiving or

278 Wikeley, 'Child Support Reform', at 435. 279 *Ibid.* 280 *Ibid.*

281 *Ibid.* The classic case in this area is *Smith* v. *Smith*, [2006] UKHL 35; [2005] 1 WLR 1318; [2004] EWCA Civ 1318 which is analysed in N. Wikeley and L. Young, '*Smith* v. *Secretary of State for Work and Pensions*: Child Support, the Self-employed and the Meaning of "Total Taxable Profits" – Total Confusion Reigns', *Child and Family Law Quarterly*, 17 (2005), 267–92. The case held that capital allowances should be deducted from a father's total taxable income for the purposes of assessing his liability to pay child support. Wikeley and Young suggest 'that this apparently technical question hides some fundamental policy choices' (*ibid.*, at 267). For example: '*the court's approach may only be sustained if one takes the view that the purposes of revenue law and child support law always coincide*, and so the statutory building blocks for calculating liabilities should likewise be aligned. Yet any such assumption is clearly misplaced, for reasons both of practice and principle' (*ibid.*, at p. 268, emphasis added). Wikeley and Young demonstrate throughout their comment that different approaches to this question are found internationally. Although they lament that Parliament appears not to have considered this issue when drafting the legislation, they conclude by observing that 'discretion' should be possible in determining how income should be calculated for the purposes of child support (*ibid.*, at 292). The House of Lords agreed with Wikeley and Young's concern over the poorly drafted legislation, and began their consideration of the *Smith* appeal by observing that they were tasked with 'the interpretation of a singularly unhappy piece of drafting' (*Smith* v. *Smith* [2006] UKHL 35, at para.1). The *Smith* appeal succeeded (3:2), although Lord Walker observed that 'either interpretation is possible as a matter of language' (*ibid.*, at para. 60).

somehow accommodating the fact that a taxpayer's motivation to underestimate his or her income could have a negative impact upon his or her children. That the child is most likely to be at a financial disadvantage as a result of this makes it less easy to accommodate the government's reluctance. Adopting the approach that Wikeley describes as taken in countries like Australia, however, could be described as having the impact of permitting a rupture between individual interests (i.e., the best interest of the child) and the wider interest of the state (i.e., those who benefit from the programmes funded by taxation). There are ongoing efforts to tackle the 'dividend problem', which concerns the extent to which dividend compensation is taken into account for the purposes of child support.[282]

The blurring of boundaries in tax is not always timid. Consider the example of criminal law. Tax investigations may commence as civil investigations (with concomitantly reduced procedural protections for taxpayers), but evolve into criminal investigations at a later point. The materials, and indeed the assessments, of a civil investigation all may be used in the criminal investigation. Additionally, tax assessments may be relied upon for the purposes of determining the proceeds of crime.[283] What is the forum of criminal law? On the one hand, criminal law is a classic example of public law, and represents the regulation of the individual's behaviour by the state. On the other hand, criminal law intervenes freely, if not always easily, into the relationships of family members. As criminal law takes its start from tax, so, in the UK, may family law.

The advantage of separate boundaries in areas of law is frequently expressed in terms of values of the state, in a discourse which suggests that tax represents, not a low value, but a lower value. Wikeley's argument presents a good example of this. In his analysis, the collection of tax is a lesser value, say, than the immediate interest of a child. The argument in the criminal context would run along the lines that a taxpayer's liberty is

282 See, generally, N. Wikeley, 'Child Support, Dividend Income and the Bertie Wooster Escape Clause', *Family Law*, (2005), 707–11, explaining that there are two child support schemes in operation, the 'old' and the 'new' scheme. Under the old scheme, dividend income is always taken into account. Under the new scheme, '[t]he drive for simplification and greater efficiency resulted in a policy decision ... to exclude dividend income from the new formula and to leave awkward cases to be resolved through the variations procedure. This approach has been adopted by the Child Support Agency in practice, but has now been shown to be mistaken' (*ibid.*, at 711). Hence, 'a child support reform which was designed as a simplification has turned out to be anything but that' (*ibid.*).

283 See P. Alldridge and A. Mumford, 'Tax Evasion and the Proceeds of Crime Act 2002', *Legal Studies*, 25 (2005), 353–73.

ultimately the most important consideration, lesser even to the importance of collecting a 'just' amount of tax. Wikeley explains that 'some parents who operate through one-man companies have paid themselves largely in dividends as a means of reducing their liabilities for both income tax and child support'.[284] The problem, as Wikeley points out, when discussing the (then) Child Maintenance and Other Payments Bill,[285] is that '[t]here is nothing in the 2007 Bill to suggest that there is any prospect of restoring the broader definition of income which applies in the old scheme'.[286]

This chapter has addressed issues surrounding independent taxation within the context of the family, specifically arising from the famous *Arctic Systems* case. Questions addressed by this chapter included: (a) is it possible to reconcile tax avoidance jurisprudence with judicial support for tax policies encouraging the financial independence of women? (b) Will women's financial independence ever graduate from a secondary to a primary objective of the tax structure? These questions will be investigated further in the following chapter, addressing the contributions of the new institutionalist literature to questions concerning tax policy, women and the law.

The terms and relevance of new institutionalist literature will be addressed in the chapter which follows. This chapter, however, will draw to a close by offering observations from an article by Wax, in 1998. The impact of tax upon the institution of marriage was the subject of this chapter, which aimed to present a theoretical structure for consideration of the applications of tax policy upon the institution of the family, and its implications for women. Any aspect of law which impacts upon the family, invites analyses from a perspective drawn along the lines of gender. Wax, thus, has argued that 'the built in structural inequalities of marriage, which may once have been thought to be a source of strength for the institution, may now have come to represent a fatal weakness ...'[287] Her predictions perhaps may be linked to the observations offered by Bowler, discussed throughout this chapter, that fewer and fewer families are choosing to marry. As Wax observes (albeit in the US, but this is a trend which is echoed in the UK) that '[m]ore and more women are turning their backs on marriage, seemingly at great cost to themselves and

284 Wikeley, 'Child Support Reform'.

285 Now the Child Maintenance and Other Payments Act 2008.

286 Wikeley, 'Child Support Reform', at 436.

287 Amy L. Wax, 'Bargaining in the Shadow of the Market: Is There a Future for Egalitarian Marriage?', *Virginia Law Review*, 84 (1998), 509–672, at 672.

their children'.[288] It may well prove significant that the Cohabitation Bill, as of the conclusion of research for this book, has elected not to integrate tax issues.

Given that, generally, it makes tax sense to marry, Wax suggests that '[o]ne possible explanation for this otherwise puzzling behaviour is that women, as weak bargainers, are losing out in the marital give and take to the point where they perceive themselves as better off outside marriage than within it'.[289] Thus, even the tax system is not enough to encourage women to marry, and, Wax suggests, that the persisting economic and social inequalities of marriage are turning women away. This, she suggests, 'may represent the most potent and ominous threat to the institution of marriage so far'.[290] It may also perpetuate the economic disadvantages with which women must cope, inside and outside of the family unit. A 'perfect' response to taxation of the family unit is not possible, until wider issues concerning the institutional place of tax law within the wider market economy are addressed.

288 *Ibid.* 289 *Ibid.* 290 *Ibid.*

7

Tax policy in systems revisited

Families, tax law and the interaction of institutions

The previous chapter addressed the ways in which tax laws have been applied to the family, perhaps the central socio-economic institution. Child centricism presently defines the approach of the UK to taxation of the family, although individualism (concerning adults at least) is also an objective, pursued in part through the tax system. Historically, the idea of the family was based upon a heterosexual marriage at centre, and connections to biological children.[1] This is changing, as the analysis of the CPA 2004 demonstrated, in particular, but not in a holistic way. Historical understandings of the family did not promote gender equality; and, gradually, analysts concerned with poverty came to realise the gendered nature of poverty, and the connections to the family.[2] The idea that poverty, family and gender were connected was articulated, and 'no less than a radical restructuring of the public and the private'[3] entered the public discourse. Institutions required restructuring: families, and the marketplace.

McCaffery stresses that he is not an 'essentialist', in that he does not believe that there are any distinctly female characteristics which lead to women either being treated unfairly by tax systems, or somehow managing them less effectively than men.[4] He is, rather, what could be described as an 'institutionalist', in that he believes that the US tax system historically was set up in such a way as to place women at a disadvantage.[5] McCaffery's use

1 N. Bala and R. J. Bromwich, 'Context and Inclusivity in Canada's Evolving Definition of the Family', *International Journal of Law, Policy and the Family*, 16 (2002), 145–80, at 145 (discussing Canada).

2 As N. Rose explained, '[f]eminism exploded the boundary lines of traditional socialist politics, and re-inserted questions of family, sexuality, children and domestic life into the heart of progressive political discourse' ('Beyond the Public/Private Division: Law, Power and the Family', *Journal of Law and Society* (1987), 61–76, at 61).

3 C. McGlynn, 'Reclaiming a Feminist Vision: The Reconciliation of Paid Work and Family Life in European Union Law and Policy', *Columbia Journal of European Law*, 7 (2001), 241, at 243.

4 McCaffery, 'Last Words (?)', at 608. 5 *Ibid.*

of the word 'institutionalist' embraces political and economic elements – another way of phrasing it is as 'simply an argument that the organization of political life makes a difference'.[6] The purpose of this chapter is to explore the new institutionalist turn in writings about law and society, and to discern the place for analyses of the intersection of women, tax policy and the law.

What is the 'new institutionalism'?

New institutionalism embraces economics,[7] sociology, law and other disciplines because interdisciplinarity is in many ways the point.[8] New institutionalism provides the framework, for example, for tax lawyers who are interested in economic theory, but are uncertain about the intellectual point of entry. It has influenced economic theory, by focusing attention on the importance of transaction costs to the rejuvenation of stagnating market economies.[9] Thus, it has revealed that legislation which reduces the costs of transactions may increase the number of transactions which occur (thus stimulating economic growth) without any other changes to the detail of legislation, or indeed any other additional stimulus.[10] Reagan's tax cuts in the US in the 1980s are presented as an example of this, as is reform of the West German currency in 1948.[11]

A primary distinction between old and new institutional economics is an appreciation of the cultural context within which economic actors operate.[12] Both new and old institutionalism study institutional change. New institutionalism, however, views institutional change as just one of many variables to be studied.[13] It has been criticised for declining to address basic questions, including the definition of 'institution', and a

6 J. G. March and J. P. Olsen, 'The New Institutionalism: Organizational Factors in Political Life', *American Political Science Review* (1984), 734–49, at 747.

7 'It is commonly said, and it may be true, that the new institutional economics started with my article, "The Nature of the Firm" (1937) with its introduction of transaction costs into economic analysis' (Ronald H. Coase, 'The New Institutional Economics', *American Economic Review*, 88 (1998), 72–4, at 72).

8 Victor Nee, 'Sources of the New Institutionalism', in M. C. Brinton and V. Nee (eds.), *The New Institutionalism in Sociology* (New York, NY: Russell Sage Foundation, 1998), at p. 1.

9 E. G. Furubotn and R. Richter, *Institutions and Economic Theory: The Contribution of the New Institutional Economics* (Dearborn, MI: University of Michigan Press, 2005), at p. 69.

10 *Ibid.*, at pp. 69–70. 11 *Ibid.*, at p. 69.

12 D. Dequech, 'The Demarcation between the "Old" and the "New" Institutional Economics: Recent Complications', *Journal of Economic Issues*, 36 (2002), 565–72, at 565.

13 Hira and Hira, 'The New Institutionalism', at 269.

description of how institutions evolve.[14] The accounts that are provided have been described as 'ambiguous' and 'contradictory'.[15]

Three categories

New institutionalism emerged after the radical challenges to established, Parsonian sociological theory in the 1960s.[16] The innovation of the old institutionalism was to focus attention upon the context within which actors operate;[17] whether, for the purposes of this book, those actors are taxpayers, legislators or even an institutionalist idea of 'tax policy'. New institutionalism combines elements of the old institutionalism,[18] although Hall and Taylor have described three, identifiable schools of new institutionalist theory: historical institutionalism,[19] rational choice institutionalism[20] and sociological institutionalism.[21]

First, the historical focus of the new institutionalism allows for retrospectivity; for example, historical texts are reconsidered to see if insight on their modern impact might be afforded through this modern social science.[22] Modern institutionalist theory stressed the importance of history, and suggests that it is possible to view history in an 'evolutionary'

14 *Ibid.*; T. O'Riordan and A. Jordan, 'Institutions, Climate Change and Cultural Theory: Towards a Common Analytical Framework', *Global Environmental Change*, 9 (1999), 81–93, at 84.

15 Hira and Hira, 'The New Institutionalism', at 267ff.

16 Orville Lee explained that '[t]he radical sociology of the 1960s and Marxism ... presented both a challenge and an opportunity to institutional sociology' ('Social Theory across Disciplinary Boundaries: Cultural Studies and Sociology', *Sociological Forum*, 14 (1999), 547–81, at 574–5).

17 Ian F. Haney Lopez argued that '[i]nstitutionalism ... focuses theoretical attention not on actions in isolation, but on the organizational contexts in which interaction occurs, and on the received grammars dictating individual behavior' ('Institutional Racism: Judicial Conduct and a New Theory of Racial Discrimination', *Yale Law Journal*, 109 (2000), 1717–1884, at 1784).

18 A study by R. Greenwood and C. R. Hinings concluded that 'institutional theory does ... have a contribution to make to understanding organizational change, which goes beyond the ideas of inertia and persistence. But this can only happen when the old and the new institutionalism are combined in a neo-institutionalist framework' ('Understanding Radical Organizational Change: Bringing together the Old and the New Institutionalism', *Academy of Management Review*, 21 (1996), 1022–54, at 1047–8).

19 P. A. Hall and R. C. R. Taylor, 'Political Science and the Three New Institutionalisms', *Political Studies*, 44 (1996), 936–57, at 937.

20 *Ibid.*, at 942. 21 *Ibid.*, at 946.

22 *See*, e.g., B. Grofman and D. A. Wittman (eds.), *The Federalist Papers and the New Institutionalism* (New York, NY: Agathon Press, 1989).

way.[23] Steinmo argues that this is particularly important because '[u]nderstanding institutions and polices in this evolutionary context allows us to get beyond the quite useless debate that aims to separate ideas and interests as *independent variables*'.[24] They are rather, Steinmo suggests, interdependent.

Thus, the decision to allocate the power to tax to the federal US government (via the US Constitution) is identified as having an enormously important impact on the resulting structure of the centralised government.[25] New institutionalism also has been applied retrospectively to the post-Second World War focus on welfarism, and the post Great Depression focus on Keynesian economics,[26] to determine the institutional structures produced during those times, and to analyse whether those structures are effective today.[27] New and old institutionalism in some ways agree on the importance of historical analysis, although old institutionalism identifies the evolution of economic institutions.[28] New institutionalism views history as less planned, and is also reluctant to accept institutions as autonomous (a prerequisite to the idea of institutions that are evolutionary).[29] Thus, while stressing the value of historical institutionalism to advancing understanding of European governance, Bulmer reminds us that '[h]istorical institutionalism cannot get to the very mainsprings of integration. It offers an explanation based on intermediating factors rather than going to the underlying sources of macro-social change'.[30]

The boundaries between historical institutionalism, and the second category, rational choice institutionalism, have lessened in recent years; both, for example, have begun to acknowledge the importance of context to the question of why political actors behave in a certain

23 S. Steinmo, 'The Evolution of Policy Ideas: Tax Policy in the 20th Century', *British Journal of Politics and International Relations*, 5(2003), 206–36, at 207.

24 *Ibid.*

25 H. W. Chappell and W. R. Keeck, 'Electoral Institutions in the Federalist Papers: A Contemporary Perspective', in Grofman and Wittman, *Federalist Papers*, pp. 39–53, at p. 46.

26 Picciotto explained that '[t]he problem of legitimacy of income taxation has been a key factor in the crisis of the Keynesian fiscal state since the mid-1970s' ('Constructing Compliance', at 13).

27 See T. Eggertsson, 'Rethinking the Theory of Economic Policy: Some Implications of the New Institutionalism', in J. M. Nelson, C. Tilly and L. Walker (eds.), *Transforming Post-communist Political Economies* (Washington, DC: National Academies Press, 1997), at pp. 61–2ff.

28 Hira and Hira, 'The New Institutionalism', at 268.

29 *Ibid.*

30 S. J. Bulmer, 'New Institutionalism and the Governance of the Single European Market', *Journal of European Public Policy*, 5 (1998), 365–86, at 382.

way.[31] Thus, if the question is what an actor is trying to achieve, both schools of analysis will delay consideration until the issue of what power means, in which context, has been addressed.[32] New institutionalism attempts to preserve what is useful about rational choice theory.[33] This includes the development of legal norms and practices.[34] Within rational choice theory, institutions actually embody rules, and actors are external to institutions.[35] Actors therefore have clear roles, and power to change laws.[36]

The third category, sociological institutionalism, has variations along geographical lines. New institutionalism acknowledges that rules travel globally, but does not always acknowledge that these rules may be translated in different ways in different legal cultures.[37] This has produced different patterns. Teubner has suggested that '[t]he more sober Anglo-American New Institutionalism distinguishes a plurality of governance regimes that produce specific routines, normative patterns, and institutional requirements, and analyzes the resulting politics of inter-institutional conflicts'.[38] French theorists, Teubner suggests, by contrast, focus on discourse theory, and the importance of language to cultural difference.[39] Finally, autopoiesis, and its concern for the many different ways in which a legal system reproduces itself, dominates what Teubner describes as Germanic theory.[40]

31 This is explained by K. Thelen, 'Historical Institutionalism in Comparative Politics', *Annual Review of Political Science*, 2 (1999), 369–404, at 376.

32 *Ibid.*, explaining that '[t]he point is that the move from general propositions about what political actors are seeking to maximize inevitably brings the theorist face to face with the question of what it means to, say, maximize power within a given context. Until this step is complete, the analysis cannot begin.'

33 Described as 'New Institutionalism's Attempt to Save Rational Choice', in Hira and Hira, 'The New Institutionalism', at p. 268.

34 'Of all the branches of New Institutionalism, rational choice institutionalism is the one that has placed the problem of norm genesis and evolution most prominently on its research agenda' (Marc Amstutz, 'Global (Non-)Law: The Perspective of Evolutionary Jurisprudence', *German Law Journal*, 13(9) (2008), 465–76, at 467).

35 *Ibid.* 36 *Ibid.*

37 Peter Walgenbach and Anne Tempel, 'Global Standardization of Organizational Forms and Management Practices? What New Institutionalism and the Business-Systems Approach Can Learn from Each Other', *Journal of Management Studies*, 44(1) (2007), 1–24, at 2.

38 Gunther Teubner, 'Beyond the State: Rethinking Private Law – State Policies in Private Law?', *American Journal of Comparative Law*, 56 (2008), 835–43, at 839.

39 'Theories of discourse plurality à la francaise [sic] celebrate le différend between conflicting genres of hermetically closed language games based on different grammars and life practices' (*ibid.*).

40 'German neo-romantic autopoiesis imagines a rich plurality of self-producing contextures in which specific operations, codes, and programs emerge and shape the rich tapestry of the many social worlds, but wholly without a prestabilized harmony' (*ibid.*).

Sociological institutionalism moves beyond the tangible rules and measures that defines institutions, and into analyses of their impact upon culture. Indeed it breaks down the boundaries between institutions and culture.[41] Within this varied category, two points of reference emerge. The first, the 'ecological perspective' is based on the 'mimetic principle', which analyses 'not the origin but the rates at which new organizational forms emerge and cease to exist'.[42] It is less concerned with the details of institutions in action (not just at their births and deaths) than the second, more popular point of reference: isomorphism. Isomorphism, effectively, 'suggests that social action is a product of ideology and conceptions that define the reality (culture) of managers and create similarities among organizations as they adopt the prevailing conception of the legitimate corporate form'.[43] Zey and Swenson note the links between the ecological perspective, and isomorphism, and indeed suggest that isomorphism essentially has been extracted from the ecological analyses of similarities between different types of organisations.[44]

Inertia and change

This chapter endeavours to use new institutionalist analysis to discern patterns in tax policy. Subject matter in such an analysis could include what is new, but also could consider what has not changed. There can be many reasons that explain inertia, from a positive choice to maintain what is in place (i.e. the second category of new institutionalism, the revival of rational choice theory), to inability to effect change, to stasis. Any of these reasons can be significant, but what is more important is the fact that, for one reason or another, an aspect of governance has been protected.

41 See chapter by S. Baden and A. M. Goetz, in C. Jackson and R. Pearson (eds.), *Feminist Visions of Development* (London: Routledge, 1998), pp. 19–36.

42 Zey and Swenson, 'Corporate Tax Laws', at 558.

43 *Ibid.* As Zey and Swanson explain: '[t]hree perspectives have tended to dominate the debate on corporate strategy and form ... [These include] managerialism, institutionalism, and agency theory' (*ibid.*, at 557). Thus, '[c]hanges in corporate form through M&As are variously defined by each perspective as mechanisms to promote one of the following corporate outcomes: (1) efficiency, (2) growth, or (3) return to shareholders' (*ibid.*).

44 *Ibid.*, at 558: Institutional theory, 'widely accepted in the sociological literature', is defined as an 'adapt[ation] of the isomorphism principle from ecological theories of organizations that hold similar organizational environments produce similar organizations due to similar organizational constraints'.

Clemens argued that:

> for students of legal conflict and political interpretation, the inability of most citizens to assess their 'interest' in tax provisions suggests that this is a particularly promising field for tracing processes of the construction of identities and interests, the *operation of institutions*, and the role of ideologies and intentions. Cloaked in an appearance of technical rationality, the politics of taxation are deeply structured by imperfect information, institutional embeddedness, and ideological commitments.[45]

An example of this in fiscal legislation, with relevance for the scope of this project, is provided by the rules governing residence (of which domicile is an element) for tax purposes in the UK. There are three different types of domicile: domicile by dependency, domicile by choice and domicile of origin. Taxpayers may acquire a domicile through origin only from their father, and not from their mother. The reasons for this distinction are rooted in history, and have little practical relevance. A domicile of origin can be acquired even if a taxpayer is not born in the UK; for example, if a taxpayer's father is born while his mother is accompanying his father, who is working in another country.

This might be viewed as somewhat antediluvian; a hangover, with little modern relevance. It is still an operational principle, in place – indeed, the rules governing domicile were amended in the Finance Act 2008, ss. 24–25, but this particular principle was not addressed. Rather, the amendments concerned both strengthening of the 183-day rule for individuals residing temporarily in the UK, and revision of the remittance basis for earnings abroad of ordinary UK residents. The easiest explanation for the persistence of this principle in UK tax law – which, interestingly, is unsupported by any direct legislation, but is a summary of practice and custom – is that the Revenue did not perceive any need to change it. It may not be popular, but it is also uncontroversial. By contrast, the 183-day rule has been the subject of recent, controversial case law.[46]

Not all countries take this approach. By way of comparison, the US exerts the jurisdiction to tax solely on the basis of citizenship, and is the only country in the world to take this approach. Most other countries approach the issue either from the perspective of the residence of the taxpayer, or the source of the income. The UK is a residence-based jurisdiction, and domicile of the father is one of the characteristics selected

45 Clemens, 'Good Reasons', at 518.

46 See *Robert Gaines-Cooper* v. *HMRC*, Case No: CH/2007/APP/0894 [2007] EWHC 2617 (Ch) Ch D.

for consideration of what, ultimately, is always going to be a question of fact, with attendant, subjective analyses. The US and the UK differ on this point, but not on every point in their tax systems.[47]

This principle in UK tax law that domicile may be acquired through one's father (but not one's mother) is more of interest these days, because of the major changes to legislation governing residence in 2008 (which did not reconsider this principle. Other things were changed; why not this?). One reason for sacrificing a rule such as the domicile through father principle would concern arguments of gender equality. Tax law does claim to address gender equity, but gender *fiscal* equity – for example, through child tax credits, which target families who live in poverty (which, statistically, largely will include single mothers and their children).

Tax law frequently is described by courts as different from other areas of law, or as special, because it has a fiscal bottom line.[48] The justification is that, because the administration of tax law must make a profit for it to be effective, resources should not be exhausted on ensuring that every taxpayer is treated equally. A principle which gives precedence to the nationality of fathers in determining jurisdiction for tax purposes does not prima facie appear to ensure gender equity, but, as the principle extends the jurisdiction to tax, it may lead to the collection of more tax revenue, which the government then may spend to assist those living in poverty (overwhelmingly, women).

The domicile principle even privileges women, if indirectly, over men. The children of fathers will be required to pay tax under this principle, whereas the children of mothers will not. This distinguishes this discussion from, by way of example, earlier analyses of the division between paid labour in the marketplace, and unpaid labour in the private sphere of the family, which patently does not benefit women.

Simply because the UK includes a focus upon the domicile of the father in questions of international tax jurisdiction – a new institutionalist approach would argue – and, simply because this focus is different from the factors considered by other countries, it does not necessarily follow that this difference is significant. A new institutionalist approach would

47 Indeed, there is a history of sharing between the UK and the US on difficult questions of tax law. Bennett provides compelling evidence that the first US income tax was effectively copied from a model of the British income tax. Colin J. Bennett, 'What Is Policy Convergence and What Causes It?', *British Journal of Political Science*, 21 (1991), 215–33, at 222.

48 See, e.g., *IRC* v. *Mead* [1993] 1 All ER 772; [1992] STC 482; [1992] COD 361.

not seek to explain the reason why the Revenue has left the domicile of the father principle in place. Rather, it would consider this difference, among others, as signifiers of patterns of governance and historical evolution.

There are elements of circularity and repetitiveness to institutionalist analyses, which may be explained by reference to 'time and change' – in essence, a call to identify cycles.[49] As Parsons explained, it is important to remember that '[t]he goal toward which behavior is directed while institutionally prescribed roles are being acquired is not necessarily "to acquire the prescribed role"'.[50] It is less deliberate than that. Rather, '[r]oles are also acquired while behaviour is directed toward food, fun, relaxation, or almost anything else'.[51] The new institutionalist analysis acknowledges the tendency of actors to favour maintaining the status quo.[52] Some institutions are more effective than others in controlling the behaviour of individuals.[53] New institutionalist theory encourages legal analysis to move away from what is typically the end of the story; for example, the enactment of a law, or the handing down of a legal decision.[54] The daily interaction of actors within a legal culture can highlight law's limits and produce confusion, the reaction against which, itself, can act as a catalyst for legal change.[55] Institutions also contribute to the incentives that influence an actor's behaviour.[56] The point is that laws and cases are

49 B. Guy Peters and Jon Pierre, 'Institutions and Time: Problems of Conceptualization and Explanation', 8(4) (1998), *Journal of Public Administration Research and Theory*, 565–84, at 568.

50 Talcott Parsons, 'The Position of Sociological Theory', *American Sociological Review*, 13(2) (1948), 156–71, at 169.

51 *Ibid.*

52 'People are afraid of changing the rules because it is difficult to know what will happen after the rules are changed' (Sven Steinmo, 'The New Institutionalism', in B. Clark and J. Fowerarker (eds.), *The Encyclopaedia of Democratic Thought*, London: Routledge, 2001, at 3; posted online at: https://docs.google.com/viewer?url=http://stripe.colorado.edu/~steinmo/foweracker.pdf).

53 This is a particularly sensitive point in tax law, for different reasons, given that some citizens who would not dream of breaking other laws apparently feel comfortable avoiding tax: 'even normally law-abiding citizens tend to avoid many aspects of tax law when given the opportunity' (Peters, B. G., *Institutional Theory in Political Science: The 'New Institutionalism'* (London: Continuum International Publishing Group, 2005, at p. 64).

54 Still, at p. 1513. 55 *Ibid.*

56 James M. Ferris and Shui-Yan Tang, 'A Series on the New Institutionalism and Public Administration: The New Institutionalism and Public Administration: An Overview', *Journal of Public Administration Research and Theory*, 3(1) (1993), 4–10, at 7.

not the end of the story; rather, they are 'just the beginning'.[57] Indeed, laws and cases need not be more important than mere 'accidents of history'.[58]

New institutionalist analysis helps to address the question of masculinity in the jurisdiction to tax principle. Connell explains that '[f]or too long the discussion of masculinity has been bogged down in psychological readings of the issue, most often in an ego-psychology based on an extreme individualism'.[59] He suggests that '[w]e need to let the breezes of politics, economics, *institutional sociology*, and history blow through the psychology'.[60] The reason for this is that '[t]hey may puff strategies of reform away from an individualized masculinity – therapy towards a collective politics of gender equality'.[61] It can begin with questions as simple as: 'Why do some countries tax and spend more than others?'[62] Or, in this instance, why do some countries focus upon fathers in exerting the jurisdiction to tax, and not mothers?

A benefit of the jurisdiction to tax principle, focusing on fathers, is the certainty that results from lack of change.[63] Institutionalist analysis reveals that lack of change can benefit a tax system. First, maintaining certainty in the tax system is one way the state can reduce transaction costs.[64] Second, once taxes have been deployed to fund social programmes, it is difficult politically to 'claim back',[65] because the beneficiaries of the social programmes are far more likely to vote for the politicians who will cut specific programmes out of office, than the taxpayers who may receive the money 'back' are to vote to keep the politicians in office.[66] For this

57 Marcy C. Still, 'Family Responsibilities Discrimination and the New Institutionalism: The Interactive Process through which Legal and Social Factors Produce Institutional Change', *Hastings Law Journal*, 59 (2007–8), 1491–1516.

58 Edward L. Rubin, 'The New Legal Process, the Synthesis of Discourse, and the Microanalysis of Institutions', *Harvard Law Review*, 109 (1995), 1393, at 1424.

59 R. W. Connell, 'The Big Picture: Masculinities in Recent World History', *Theory and Society*, 22 (1993), 597–623, at 619.

60 *Ibid.*, at 619 (emphasis added). 61 *Ibid.* (emphasis added).

62 Thelen, 'Historical Institutionalism', at 369–70 (emphasis added).

63 Nonetheless, change is a constant of political decision-making, and in any case the objective should be 'intersubjective agreement reached by free citizens under political conditions most conducive to the plasticity and mutuality of individual interests' (Fagan, 'Recent and Contemporary Theories', at 497).

64 Eggertsson, 'The Old Theory', at 1197.

65 P. Pierson explains that '[a] simple "redistributive" transfer of resources from program beneficiaries to taxpayers, engineered through cuts in social programs, is generally a losing proposition' ('The New Politics of the Welfare State', *World Politics*, 48 (1996), 143–79, at 145).

66 *Ibid.*, observing: '[t]he concentrated beneficiary groups are more likely to be cognizant of the change, are easier to mobilize, and because they are experiencing losses rather than

reason, institutionalist analysis stresses the importance of focusing upon how the economy should be organised, rather than how comparatively smaller issues, such as tax policy, should be addressed.

New institutionalist approaches to organising economies, and tax law

Institutionalists believe that decisions about the organisation of the economy are at least as important for raising revenue as decisions about tax law.[67] Revenue is an important focus of what could be described as institutionalist economists, as maximising revenue is identified as a motivating factor in the organisation of several different kinds of states.[68]

Tax law does not necessarily understand the nuances of relationships in the family any better than, say, economics, but it is to economists that lawyers turn when fashioning policy for the taxation of the family.[69] The search for efficiency, however, is not the reason why economic analyses are consulted. Rather, tax collection strategies which are low cost are preferred, even if they are inefficient.[70]

Although institutionalism has been criticised for lacking a clear focus,[71] uncertain of the actors that should be considered (taxpayers, the state, both?), the importance of all forms of institutionalist theory to tax law is that it takes account of the significance of the political process to the production of fiscal legislation, an aspect which is too frequently ignored.[72] Institutionalist theory also addresses the resolution of conflicts that occur between actors both within and across institutions.[73] The decision of

gains are more likely to incorporate the change in their voting calculations. Retrenchment advocates thus confront a clash between their policy preferences and their electoral ambitions'.

67 'the ruler's choice of the organization of the economy is as important as his choice of tax law' (Furubotn and Richter, *Institutions and Economic Theory*, at p. 99).

68 *Ibid.*, at p. 476.

69 Philipps, 'Tax Law', in Cossman and Fudge (eds.), *Privatization*, at p. 43.

70 Furubotn and Richter, *Institutions and Economic Theory.*

71 'There is very little consensus on the definition of key concepts, measures or methods within this theoretic tradition' (P. S. Tolbert and L. G. Zucker, 'The Institutionalization of Institutional Theory', in S. R. Clegg and C. Hardy (eds.), *Studying Organization: Theory and Method*, London: Sage, 1999, at p. 169).

72 'Despite the fact that the tax structure is a product of the political process, rarely does an economic analysis of tax policy take account of the political environment within which the tax structure is designed' (R. G. Holcombe, 'Tax Policy from Public Choice Perspective', *National Tax Journal*, 5 (1999), 359–71, at 359).

73 Blom-Hansen, '"New Institutional" Perspective', at 681.

whether or not to pay taxes (perhaps in particular, taxes that might easily be avoided) presents a good example of this.[74] Institutionalist theory has suggested that, while challenging, it can be possible to resolve such a conflict within the 'common interest'.[75] Such arguments complement Schumpeter's fiscal sociology, which stressed the historical moment when states moved to a modern system of tax collection as pivotal to the understanding of a modern state.[76]

Institutions themselves contribute to the formulation of identifiable interests. The collapse of the real estate market in the US presents a good example of this.[77] Once the federal government decided to become involved in the housing market, the decision ceased to involve just the government and taxpayers, but then included other actors (for example, banks) who benefited from this support, and thus worked to prolong the government's support, perhaps after this intervention had ceased to be in the taxpayers' best interests.[78]

Steinmo has applied new institutionalist theory to tax policy, explaining, for example 'cross-national differences in tax policy largely by reference to the way in which political institutions structure the kinds of social interests most likely to be represented in the policy process'.[79] Steinmo explains that taxes introduced early in the industrial age could be described as 'class taxes', because they largely were targeted only at the richest taxpayers.[80] The start of the First World War had an important impact on societal view of such taxes, because 'the fiscal needs of the state expanded enormously just as the new tax ideas had been institutionalized'.[81] The outcome of this was that, by the end of the First World War, '[t]axes, it was now clear, *could and should* be used as an instrument of economic redistributive policy'.[82]

The early operation of the income tax laws in the US, at the start of the twentieth century, provides a good example of the institutionalisation of a tax system.[83] Steinmo has produced some striking research which suggests

74 *Ibid.* 75 *Ibid.*

76 This is discussed in Mumford, 'Towards a Fiscal Sociology'.

77 E. S. Clemens and J. M. Cook, 'Politics and Institutionalism: Explaining Durability and Change', *Annual Reviews in Sociology*, 25 (1999), 441–66, at 456.

78 As explained (*ibid.*).

79 Hall and Taylor, 'Political Science', at 941.

80 Steinmo, 'Evolution of Policy Ideas', at 210, citing J. L. Waltman, *Political Origins of the US Income Tax* (Jackson, MS: University Press of Mississippi, 1985).

81 *Ibid.* 82 *Ibid.*

83 Sheldon Pollack, 'Tax Complexity, Reform, and the Illusions of Tax Simplification', *George Mason Independent Law Review*, 2 (1994), 319–59.

that, between roughly 1993 and 2003, middle-class families in the UK, Sweden, Germany, Japan and the US did not experience increased rates of taxation, although the amount of taxes paid by poor families did increase (and the amount of tax paid by the wealthy decreased).[84] As Clemens observed, '[t]ax systems, like modes of economic production, have the potential to generate class identities and patterns of conflict'.[85] It has also been suggested that the new institutionalist theory represents a 'convergence' between the sociology of law, and the sociology of organisations.[86]

The EU has been described as 'an alternative venue' for gender equality.[87] It is unclear whether what is now studied as 'European policy making' ultimately will constitute an entirely separate body of governance theory.[88] If it does, the focus will be the consequences of loss of control by national states over processes such as the formulation of tax policy.[89] In this context, Armstrong has argued that 'law as a medium must confront law as an institution which shapes external attempts at steering but also structures the element of agency possessed by legal actors, including the ECJ'.[90] It is important to appreciate the different levels of institutionalism, especially when discussing tax policy.[91] By way of example, Armstrong has emphasised the importance of the UK's movement away from the McClement's equivalence scale, in favour of the OECD's modified scale of indication of poverty.[92] The reason behind this shift was to enable EU comparative analysis of practice of different states, and its immediate impact was twofold: first, an increased number of children were classified as living in poverty; and, second, the new scale was more 'sensitive' to the

84 Steinmo, 'Evolution of Policy Ideas', at 232, fn. 23.

85 Clemens, 'Good Reasons', at 522.

86 Suchman, M. C. and L. B. Edelman, 'Legal Rational Myths: The New Institutionalism and the Law and Society Tradition', *Law and Social Inquiry*, 21 (1996), 903–41, at 903.

87 S. Mazey, 'The European Union and Women's Rights', in D. Hine and H. Kassim (eds.), *Beyond the Market: The EU and National Social Policy* (London: Routledge, 1998), at p. 140.

88 R. Mayntz, 'New Challenges to Governance Theory', in Henrik Paul Bang (ed.), *Governance as Social and Political Communication* (Manchester University Press, 2009), at p. 33.

89 *Ibid.*

90 K. A. Armstrong, 'Legal Integration: Theorizing the Legal Dimension of European Integration', *Journal of Common Market Studies – Annual Review*, 36 (1998), 155–74, at 155ff.

91 As Armstrong explains, '[r]esponsibilities for European policy-making, employment policy and for tax and benefits policies remain "reserved" to Westminster, while responsibility for social inclusion strategies has been devolved to the sub-state level' (K. A. Armstrong, 'The "Europeanisation" of Social Exclusion: British Adaptation to EU Co-ordination', *British Journal of Politics and International Relations*, 8 (2006), 79–100, at 91).

92 *Ibid.*, at 95.

effect of tax credits on a family's economic status.[93] The new institutionalism avoids the dangers of broad generalisations across states, in favour of what could be described as an educative, comparative approach.[94] As neo-functionalism is very broadly defined as a study of regional integration, it is unsurprising that its strongest resurgence would appear to be occurring within European legal theory, particularly addressing the subject of European legal integration.[95]

There has been a growing acceptance among socio-legal theorists that, if one is interested in the operation of law, then one must consider what could be described as the sociology of bureaucracy.[96] If one is interested in UK tax law, changes to the bureaucracy of the Revenue are enormously significant. The incorporation of the benefit structure within HMRC indicated an effort to achieve harmonisation of home life (the personal sphere) with the marketplace. In this context, the rule pertaining to domicile of origin acquired through one's father is simply one aspect of a pattern of governance, largely enforced through HMRC. One reason for preserving the domicile-through-father rule is that, in an area of law which frequently suffers from lack of clarity – from broadly construed terms without clear definitions, multiplied over literally thousands of lines – is that this is a simple rule. Simple rules are not uncommon in legislation offering tax relief; but, in principles extending the jurisdiction or the right to tax, they are relatively uncommon. Such a rule would not be sacrificed easily.

93 *Ibid.*

94 B. Grofman, 'Arend Lijphart and the New Institutionalism', in Markus M. L. Crepaz, Thomas A. Koelble and David Wilsford (eds.), *Democracy and Institutions: The Life Work of Arend Lijphart* (Ann Arbor , MI: University of Michigan Press, 2000), at pp. 44–5.

95 See, among others: P. C. Schmitter, 'Neo-Neofunctionalism' (posted at: https://docs.google.com/viewer?url=http://www.eui.eu/Documents/DepartmentsCentres/SPS/Profiles/Schmitter/NeoNeoFunctionalismRev.pdf); Lisbet Hooghe and Gary Marks, 'The Neofunctionalists Were (almost) Right: Politicization and European Integration' (posted at: http://ideas.repec.org/p/erp/conweb/p0024.html); T. Risse, 'Neofunctionalism, European Identity, and the Puzzles of European Integration', *Journal of European Public Policy*, 12(2) (2005), 291–309; A. Moravcsik, 'The European Constitutional Compromise and the Neofunctionalist Legacy', *Journal of European Public Policy*, 12(2) (2005), 49–86.

96 M. C. Suchman, L. B. Edelman: 'Contemporary sociolegal scholarship increasingly recognizes that important aspects of legal life occur within bureaucratic settings, such as law firms, regulatory agencies and corporations' ('Legal Rational Myths: The New Institutionalism and the Law and Society Tradition', *Law and Social Inquiry*, 21 (1996), 903–966, at 903).

8

Putting into the system

Gender, markets and tax policy

This penultimate chapter has three purposes. First, the project of this book will be reassessed, in light of the analyses in the preceding chapters. After this review, the chapter will reformulate the questions that should be asked, so as to be able articulate the place of gender in contextual analyses of tax policy and the law. The second aim of this chapter is to clarify (again in an informed way, based on the analyses which precede) why gender is a problem in tax policy; or, put differently, why tax policy has failed effectively to connect with the gendered economy. Finally, this chapter will re-engage with the literature. It will identify and summarise how it has theorised the failure of tax policy in this regard, and to suggest next steps.

This book asked, first: is gender ignored in the functioning of the market, as currently formed? Or, second, does the paid marketplace, and the tax system which both contributes to and draws from it, need to be restructured so as to incorporate the goal of gender equality? The overall aim of this chapter is, within this review of the literature, to identify common ground. The nature of the relationship between gender and markets, and by extension the tax system, is inherently contradictory.

This book has identified three, key problems. First, expectations are unclear when women are considered as market workers. Additionally, literature considering the core value of even identifying gender as a factor within the working of the marketplace is divided. The only time gender appears to become an issue is when caregiving activities that might be performed by government on behalf of citizens, are considered. At that point, there arises an assumption that, if the government chooses not to act, then women will perform these activities. There are six basic approaches to this problems in the literature, each of which will be discussed in turn: the equality presumption argument; allocation; tax as a forum; economic foundations of the family; what could be described as a 'return to bias'; and, finally, the intersection of clarity, spheres and states.

The aim of this chapter is to identify key, theoretical aspects of socio-legal analysis concerning the taxation of women. The chapter is constructed with broad strokes. For example, the analysis commences with consideration of the extent to which unpaid work is valued, or should be valued, by the paid marketplace. The chapter then proceeds to address the impact of commodification of caring activities on assumptions in law underpinning the taxing of women. These sections are constructed broadly, as the intention of this chapter largely is to present a review. This review is focused, however, to identify arguments that consider the extent to which gender is a formative factor in the structure of the paid marketplace. This process of identification serves foundational questions of this project. Is gender ignored in the functioning of the market, as currently formed?

The market and equality

The nature of the relationship between gender and markets, and by extension the tax system, is inherently contradictory. As Philipps explains, '[w]hile it is still in the process of congealing, a salient feature of this gender order appears to be its contradictory construction of women as both gender-neutral market workers and primary caregivers who can take up the slack for degraded public services'.[1] There can be difficulties when market workers generally are not addressed by tax systems on the terms of gender; and, are perceived as gender neutral, especially insofar as neutrality is perceived as an indicator of equality. The only time gender appears to become an issue is when caregiving activities, that might be performed by government on behalf of citizens, are considered. At that point, there arises an assumption that, if the government chooses not to act, then women will perform these activates.[2]

The emergence of gender as a problem perhaps only when unpaid care giving (the activities upon which a paid marketplace depends to function) is at question, but otherwise as an issue at few other times in a tax system, contributes directly to the presumption that there is equality of opportunity. To explain, the assumption that, if one wants more resources, then one should work harder, supports the perception that, among other things, income tax is a fair tax, taxing both ability

1 Philipps, 'Tax Law', in Cossman and Fudge (eds.), *Privatization*, at p. 83.

2 Consideration of tax-based initiatives targeted at single mothers, in particular, would tend to support this suggestion.

and effort. The problems with this assumption have been addressed by, among others, Hurley.[3] Hurley engaged with what could be described as the 'equality presumption argument' in a response to Cohen's suggestion that the wealthy are responsible for their fortune, because they have the choice to work harder, and that this is desirable because the wealthy then produce more resources for the poor (through taxation).[4] Hurley argued that production is an important part of redistribution; and thus any adjustment of production through taxation could interfere with redistribution.[5] More generally, she expressed concern with the impact that redistributive taxation of natural 'luck' can have on considerations of economic efficiency.[6]

There is a need to unpack differences between redistribution because of general income inequality and because of gender inequalities.[7] Positively, focusing on poverty may be one of the most important and achievable ways to address many of the worst forms of gender inequality. Negatively, this highlights potential conflicts of interests between different kinds of women (for example, where tax measures to secure gender equality for middle-class or highly paid men and women conflict with the interests of poorer women).[8] There are also international dimensions to some of these issues; for example, the international

3 S. L. Hurley, 'Replies', *Philosophy and Phenomenological Research*, 72 (2006), 447–65.

4 *Ibid.*

5 *Ibid.* See also Chris William Sanrichio, 'Progressivity and Potential Income: Measuring the Effect of Changing Work Patterns on Income Tax Progressivity', *Columbia Law Review*, 108 (2008), 1151–1609, addressing the impact upon redistribution of 'implicitly' excluding non-market labour activity from taxation. Additionally, Kaplow and Shavell demonstrated that the tax system is a more efficient choice than the legal system for distributing income; and have argued that it makes sense for those working with legal rules to focus on other objectives, and (more or less) to leave the job of redistributing income to the poor to income tax. L. Kaplow and S. Shavell, 'Why the Legal System is Less Efficient than the Income Tax in Redistributing Income', *Journal of Legal Studies*, 23 (1994), 667–81.

6 See discussion of Hurley's work throughout P. Vallentyne, 'Hurley on Justice and Responsibility', *Philosophy and Phenomenological Research*, 72 (2006), 433–8, and esp. at 437.

7 I am enormously grateful to Lizzie Barmes for drawing this distinction to my attention, and for introducing me to much of the rich literature which follows.

8 This issue comes to the fore in literature such as: K. Rittich: 'Feminization and Contingency: Regulating the Stakes of Work for Women', in J . Conaghan, R. M. Fischl and K. Klare (eds.), *Labour Law in an Era of Globalization: Transformative Practices and Possibilities* (Oxford University Press, 2002); *Recharacterizing Restructuring: Law, Distribution and Gender in Market Reform* (The Hague and London: Kluwer Law International, 2002); R. M. Fischl, 'A Woman's World', *Buffalo Law Review*, 52 (2004), 659–78. It is also important to note sociological work addressing lower-paid women, for example, Ehrenreich and Hochschild, *Global Woman.*

chains of care that sociologists, among others, have been discovering and analysing.[9]

The identification of a clash between economic efficiency and redistribution of wealth (depending on the kind of redistribution) has important consequences for a tax system. This is particularly evident in consideration of the question of whether or not housework should be taxed. A number of years ago, the taxation of housework was a standard facet of discussion in conferences and other academic fora.[10] The argument essentially was that housework was not appreciated in the paid marketplace, and this leads to the devaluing of women. The market is structured to compensate men for much of the labour they perform, and they receive the benefit of housework for free. If they have to pay for housework through the tax system, at the least, attention will be drawn to it.

In critical tax theory, the debate concerning the taxation of housework has been led by Staudt.[11] Her work demonstrated that, while the execution of the taxation of housework would be difficult, it was nonetheless a theoretical possibility. One of the difficulties, as Staudt acknowledged, it that '[a]lthough tax theorists have rejected the bulk of Simons' work, nearly every theorist examining the value of women's nonmarket labor has agreed with Simons that housework does not produce taxable income'.[12] Instituting a system which taxed housework thus would face a significant uphill battle. Simons' influence was, perhaps, stronger in the middle part of the twentieth century, when Americans were exhorted to pay attention to his writings for the sake of their tax laws.[13] Instituting tax laws which did not take heed of, for example, Simons' definition of income, was thought to be bad for the economy. Thus, pursuing an equality-based goal in opposition to one of Simons' precepts was thought to

9 I am grateful to Lizzie Barmes for the following example: thus, a northern family contracts out their home and care work to a poorer southern mother who must relocate to do it, hence leaving her children with a family member or a poorer-paid mother in the south, in the latter case with a further link in the chain as that mother leaves her children with other family members. See Ehrenreich and Hochschild, *Global Woman*.

10 I am again grateful to Kate Malleson for reminding me of this, and for the points which follow.

11 See Staudt: 'Taxing Housework' and 'The Political Economy of Taxation: A Critical Review of a Classic', *Law and Society Review*, 30 (1996), 651–66.

12 Staudt, 'Political Economy', at 662. Staudt proceeded to criticise this reliance on Simons. She has written extensively on the question of household labour. See also Staudt, 'Taxing Housework'.

13 K. L. M. Carter, 'Canadian Tax Reform and Henry Simons', *Journal of Law and Economics*, 11 (1968), 231–42, at 231.

come at a very high price,[14] in particular, relative to the allocation of resources.

Would taxing housework, thus, help in 'fixing' the problem of gender economic inequality? Would it help to allocate, through the market, more economic resources to women? 'Allocation', as an idea, is different from redistribution. Would women benefit economically if unpaid labour were identified, say, as a benefit in kind, ascribable to their husbands' income? If the husband is the sole source of income, then, no. If a woman's source of income is provided solely by her husband, then assessing her labour as a benefit in kind ascribable to her husband's income would increase her husband's tax obligations, and lower the amount of money available to the family.

From this point alone, however, it does not necessarily follow that taxing housework is a bad idea. Of course, negative economic outcomes for women should be avoided, but they should also be analysed, in perspective, and in the context of a market which may demand, as McGlynn described, fundamental restructuring.[15] It may be, for example, that the fact that quantifying the economic contribution of unpaid labour in the family unit would decrease the amount of money available to the family, itself has served as a reason to stop closer consideration of the relationship between paid and unpaid labour altogether.[16] The 'economic belief' that unpaid labour cannot be taken into consideration by the tax system without harming women economically may have contributed to the arrangement under which women continue to do it, continue not to be paid for it and continue also to occupy positions below the poverty line in far greater quantities than men. Women's economic inequality, thus, is naturalised.

Tax as a forum

Acknowledgement of this does not make the problem of how the market might be reorganised any easier. If unpaid labour performed by women within the home is connected with economic inequality – and, given

14 In the twenty-first century, perhaps in particular during a period when the tax system is being relied upon to address problems associated with the economic recession, there may be more comfort in the idea of using the tax system to fix something, even if it contradicts Simons' economic analyses.

15 McGlynn, 'Reclaiming a Feminist Vision', at 243.

16 As Fellow argues, '[s]ocial and economic beliefs and practices frequently naturalise subordination' ('Rocking the Tax Code', at 393).

that housework deprives women of time and energy to work in the paid marketplace, why would it not? The tax system could be explored as a forum within which to address this. This would not be without precedent, as using the tax system to address problems of gender is common.[17] It may well be that the tax system could be explored as a forum for addressing the restriction that housework exerts over women's earning capacity, and not simply as a means of encouraging women to enter the paid marketplace.

This sort of exploration could be important, as encouraging or assisting women to enter the paid marketplace is not a complete response to the problem of economic inequality for women. Simply because a tax incentive may have succeeded, and a woman may have acquired paid work as a result, it does not follow that she will be able to leave the demands of unpaid labour behind. Among other issues, care workers may watch children while women work, but other forms of labour await parents when they return, and women continue to perform this labour disproportionately.[18] As this factor alone may restrict women's ability to earn as much as men in the paid marketplace, it would not be surprising if women did not have as much time and enthusiasm for paid labour as men.[19]

Picking apart the economic foundations of the family, which is in effect what this book has encouraged at several points, is notoriously difficult. Problems with the Haig–Simons definition of income are often at the core of this. For example, as Jones argued, the Haig–Simons definition of income has been relied upon, essentially, to assume that 'income-splitting is largely a technical, economic, or tax-system decision'.[20] This simplified approach, which views such changes as technical, or relatively unimportant, can have unintended consequences. Indeed, given that markets pay

17 For example, the Family Policy Studies Centre has suggested that the tax and benefits system should be used to help some men who may find fatherhood 'difficult'. L. Burghes, *et al.*, *Fathers and Fatherhood in Britain* (London: Family Policy Studies Centre, 1997), at p. 8.

18 See, among others: A. R. Hochschild and A. Machung, *The Second Shift: Working Parents and the Revolution at Home* (New York, NY: Viking, 1989); Thompson and Walker, 'Gender in Families', at 858–9; and, generally, Nancy Rollins Ahlander and Kathleen Slaugh Bahr, 'Beyond Drudgery, Power, and Equity: Toward an Expanded Discourse on the Moral Dimensions of Housework in Families', *Journal of Marriage and the Family*, 57 (1995), 54–68.

19 But cf. Jennifer Glass and Tetsushi Fujimoto, 'Housework, Paid Work, and Depression Among Husbands and Wives', *Journal of Health and Social Behavior*, 35 (1994), 179–91, concluding that an increase in paid work is associated with less depression for women, whereas an increase in housework is associated with more.

20 Jones, 'Split Income', at 261

attention to labour which is paid, and have a tendency to pay less attention to unpaid labour, an unintended consequence of a superficially technical point may be more likely to be visited upon women.[21]

This is a point which Fontana has emphasised. She explains that:

> [p]ossible shifts in government spending and taxes resulting from trade liberalisation, as well as changes in risk and vulnerability of households, should ... be given attention, as these are likely to have gender-differentiated outcomes (for example when a reduction in tariff revenue affects the public provision of infrastructure and social services that are more frequently used by women).[22]

It is a short step from unintended consequence to bias. Fontana's choice of trade liberalisation is particularly apt, because it is the sort of choice which might be perceived to have gender-neutral outcomes. Whether or not trade is liberalised is the sort of choice made with an eye upon the impact on the economy. If trade liberalisation would be good for the economy, then the assumption would be that it is a good thing. The benefits of a strong economy would be viewed as beneficial for both men and women. More resources will be available for everybody, both within and without the paid marketplace. Fontana emphasises that trade liberalisation may happen through the cost of a shift in government spending away from the household (where more women labour, unpaid), and towards industry (where more men labour, and are paid for it).

McCaffery has argued that, in the US, '[t]he time is right – indeed, it is long overdue – to fix the tax system's biases against two-worker families, which fall so often on the working mothers within them'.[23] There would be little support for a suggestion that tax bias against two-worker families in the US would be intentional. Indeed, earned income tax credits are designed to encourage two-worker families, so to target such an outcome would be illogical. That it is an unintended consequence can be one of the only explanations for a system structured both to encourage women into work, and yet also penalise two-worker families. That the problem proved so difficult in the US that McCaffery was prompted to call its eradication

21 But cf. Donald B. Marsh, 'The Taxation of Imputed Income', *Political Science Quarterly*, 58 (1943), 514–36, at 519: 'This is not to argue that the definition of income in terms of a flow of satisfaction is philosophically sound'. Marsh does proceed to defend this, however.

22 M. Fontana, 'Modelling the Effects of Trade on Women, at Work and at Home: Comparative Perspectives', *Economie Internationale*, 99 (2004), 49–80.

23 McCaffery, 'Women and Taxes', at 22.

'long overdue' indicates that there is something about the taxation of two incomes, within the private context of the family, that is uniquely challenging.

The challenge may arise from the fact that the taxation of two-worker families involves the exposure of private economic decisions to the scrutiny of a public marketplace. Two workers may be considered individually by the marketplace, but McCaffery called for consideration of how their incomes function within a private, family context. How this mingling of separate spheres should be treated by the government will involve a number of difficult choices, including the fundamental decision as to what kind of government taxpayers want to support.[24]

Schumpeter explained that '[a]ll that we mean by the "march into socialism" is ... the migration of people's economic affairs from the private into the public sphere'.[25] The tax treatment of two-worker families is an important part of this migration, yet whether it forms a part of a 'march into socialism' may be controversial. Decisions about the taxation of two-worker families could provide a forum for a government to articulate ideas about the operation of economies and markets that could not have been articulated within the election process without political cost. From this perspective, women's economic inequality could be an unintended consequence of elections in which candidates do not fully engage with voters about the nature of economic choice.

Economic choice involves making value judgements. Whether housework is a valuable activity which supports the paid economy, or a leisure activity which improves one's quality of life in a way that loosely equates with a hobby, is an example of the sort of value judgement that economic choice can involve. As Folbre explains:

> [o]bviously, taxing one person's paid employment income to support another person's leisure creates perverse incentives. But if we consider the possibility that much of what has traditionally been called leisure is actually unpaid work, including the work of caring for family members, the picture becomes considerably more complex.[26]

24 For example: I am grateful to Kate Malleson for her insight as to the difficulties that arise from taxing housework, not just from the perspective of the work itself, but from the perspective of who is performing the work. On these points, see Hartmann, 'The Family', at 368ff.

25 Schumpeter, 'The March Into Socialism', at 446. Interestingly, Schumpeter also argued that there is a general tendency in the organisation of the English fiscal state 'towards socialism'. Schumpeter, 'English Economists', at 373–4.

26 N. Folbre, 'Blowing the Whistle on Poverty Policy', *Review of Social Economy*, 61 (2003), 479–85, at 482.

Using the tax system as a forum for considering the impact of housework could force these sorts of value judgements, or choices. A clean and organised home offers pleasure, in addition to other things. Is it valuable enough for the tax system to support it, or should limits on the amount of time someone spends working within the home that should receive support be specified? By way of contrast, consider the tax relief offered in the UK for work-related travel. Some work-related travel is given tax relief, but not all. Travel from home to the office generally is not offered relief, presumably on the basis that travel from the private sphere of the home is not wholly, exclusively (and necessarily, for employees) connected to the effort to earn profits/employment income. Similar classifications could be imposed upon housework (washing dishes, or colour coordinating dishes – is it comparable activity?).

The nature of the classifications made with housework could extend to the challenge of taxing two-worker families. In such a family, each worker has acquired payment and tax obligations within the paid marketplace, but it is their interaction within the private context of the family that causes a problem. And, again, it is the inconsistency of encouraging two-worker families in some parts of the tax system, but not others, that attracts the attention of scholars such as McCaffery. The fact that every US government insists that it is pro-family is another inconsistency that problematises the 'marriage penalty' there.[27] Thus, the movement of women into the paid marketplace actually inspired a movement to join the finances of men and women. But what is it about the context of the family that makes it difficult for a tax system to ensure that two workers will be taxed more or less the same within a family, as without?

Clarity, spheres and states

The locus of the family is frequently the target of government activity. While tax and other forms of commercial law engage with the paid marketplace, the family is targeted by all of these things, in addition to the attention of benefits and welfare regimes. Given this amount of attention, the lack of clarity concerning terms and activities within the private sphere of the family was bound to cause problems. But this lack of clarity is not necessarily always a bad thing. The concept of the private sphere

27 Jones has suggested that, in the US, something did change about the way women and the workplace were viewed after the Second World War ('Split Income', at 261). Importantly, there was now an assumption that women would be involved in paid work, and, as a result, the joint income tax return was introduced in 1948 (*ibid.*).

originated from individualist assumptions that individuals owe accountability to government in some areas (public), but not all (private). The change happened when the tax system started to be used (earned income tax credits are the classic example) to target choices (is it financially viable for a mother to work outside of the home?) with important consequences in the private sphere.

In the UK, this change can be linked to changes in the concepts underlying the welfare state. Atlee's format for a 'cradle to grave' welfare state[28] did not begin with the concept of influencing behaviour, but, by the time of New Labour, Giddens and others argued that 'cradle to grave' support would not continue to be affordable without the participation of benefit recipients in the market. Giddens suggested that the state must step back in some areas of increasing expense, and acknowledge that the crisis of the welfare state was in many ways based in a failure to manage market risk properly.[29] This did not involve an abrogation of responsibility from one set of shoulders to another, but rather a new partnership and intermingling of the public–private sphere.[30]

This growing partnership in the New Labour era occurred during a period of developing feminist criticism for the forms of gender inequality sustained within the family.[31] Labour would have wished to align itself with feminist analysis, and, thus, the family was often discussed in confusing ways. As Driver and Martell explain:

> [a]s the feminist critique of gender inequalities in the family grew in influence, Labour neutrality on the structure of the family often turned to hostility towards arguments for its traditional form.[32]

28 See Krishan Kumar, 'Sociology and the Englishness of English Social Theory', *Sociological Theory*, 19 (2001), 41–64, at 47 and 49, for an interesting discussion of how sociologists in the UK at this time felt compelled to support the welfare state, to help the government to achieve its admirable goals.

29 Giddens, 'Risk and Responsibility', at 7, 9 and 10.

30 As J. Lewis argued, 'any further development of the concept of "welfare regime" must incorporate the relationship between unpaid as well as paid work and welfare' ('Gender and the Development of Welfare Regimes', *Journal of European Social Policy*, 2 (1992), 159–73, at 159).

31 Among this wide literature, see, among others: Fox Greer Litton and Velma McBride Murry, 'Gender and Families: Feminist Perspectives and Family Research', *Journal of Marriage and the Family*, 62 (2000), 1160–72; Lori A. McGraw, *et al.*, 'Studying Postmodern Families: A Feminist Analysis of Ethical Tensions in Work and Family Research', *Journal of Marriage and the Family*, 62 (2000), 68–77; Nancy E. Riley, 'Challenging Demography: Contributions from Feminist Theory', *Sociological Forum*, 14 (1999), 369–7.

32 S. Driver and L. Martell, 'New Labour, Work and the Family', *Social Policy and Administration*, 36 (2002), 46–61, at 49.

This hostility needed to be packaged in a way that suggested that Labour supported the institution of the family, for purposes of re-election. Thus, tax initiatives introduced during this era were promoted as pro-family, even as the conventional strictures of the family were challenged in other fora.[33] In some ways this contradiction was addressed through efforts to resolve criticism of the family by focusing on its exclusiveness. Thus, the campaign for the CPA 2004 was both supportive of the family, as it increased the number of people recognised by the state as part of a family, and subversive, as it inherently criticised the (largely, tax-based) privileges enjoyed exclusively by those in state-recognised families before the Act.

Gender is a formative factor in the structure of the paid marketplace in ways that extend beyond unpaid labour. Differential pricing of services on the basis of gender is another common form of economic inequality. The US state of California enacted the Gender Tax Repeal Act of 1995[34] to remedy the fact that, to take one example, it frequently costs more for a woman to have her hair cut than it would for a man.[35] Although described as 'laudable' in the *Harvard Law Review*, it ultimately predicted that the protections that the legislation would provide would be 'feeble', given the exemptions provided for 'amount of time, difficulty, or cost of providing the services'.[36] The Gender Tax Repeal Act presents an interesting example of an attempt to direct the public discourse of tax and gender.

The term 'gender tax' in fact was used by a Californian legislator to describe the extra costs, or 'tax', that women faced because of their gender.[37] The ethos of the tax emphasised the fact that every aspect of a woman's participation in the marketplace that differs from that of a man attracts an extra cost. If the male experience is the norm, then men occupy a privileged position within the marketplace from a number of different perspectives, including the bare cost of services. The Californian gender tax emphasises the tension in the relationship between the state and the tax system on the question of gender equity. While the state has a positive obligation to tackle and to redress obvious inequality within the tax system, gender inequality may assume subtle forms. Redressing this form of inequality may involve disruption of market practices with

33 See the discussion of strategies developed in L. Glennon, 'Strategizing for the Future through the Civil Partnership Act', *Journal of Law and Society*, 33 (2006), 244.

34 Gender Tax Repeal Act 1995 (California Civil Code) (US).

35 See Note, 'California Prohibits Gender-Based Pricing', *Harvard Law Review*, 109 (1996), 1839–44.

36 *Ibid.*, at 1839, citing Cal. Civ. Code s. 51.6(c). 37 *Ibid.*, at 1840.

which a government otherwise may not seek to interfere; for example, the question of setting prices for services.

As Staudt explained, '[i]n addition to income inequality, feminist tax scholars have argued that the federal government has a role to play in promoting gender equality and have devised a number of methods that [the US] Congress could use to redistribute income to women'.[38] She continues, however, '[t]he feminist arguments ... are also often grounded in an efficiency analysis'.[39] This is not to suggest that relying upon economic market efficiency as a standard of gender equality analysis is without merit; indeed, forging such a link can have wider benefits, throughout the economy, for both men and women. For example, research by Besley confirms that there is a clear link between turmoil in financial markets and spending patterns in the family home.[40] If the family is identified as a locus of gender inequality, spending patterns will flow from this. Whether the disruption in spending patterns contributes to or detracts from greater gender equality could be determined through efficiency-based analyses. A Schumpeterian approach also would consider the extent to which spending decisions taken within the home are linked with and contribute to economic stability.[41] Thus, this sort of interactive, efficiency-based analysis has a broader promise.

Despite the potential merit of such an approach, there are some difficulties. First, determining household 'wealth' is notoriously difficult.[42] Few figures exist, except for inheritance and capital gains tax collected by HMRC.[43] Yet the figures for inheritance and capital gains taxes are of limited use, given that the wealth a person has at the end of a lifetime may have little connection with the amount received, earned or spent during a lifetime.[44] There is little promise in such material for a thorough, efficiency-based analysis of the pursuit of feminist objectives in tax law. Second, and more importantly, feminist objectives must not depend on economic efficiency as a justification for their pursuit. It is a basic principle of this book that they do not demand justification, and simply require pursuit and instantiation.

38 Staudt, 'Political Economy', at 661. 39 *Ibid.*

40 Timothy Besley, 'Financial Markets and Household Consumption' (Institute for Fiscal Studies, 18 February 2008).

41 See discussion at p. 00–0.

42 Mike Brewer, *et al.*, 'Racing away? Income Inequality and the Evolution of High Incomes', in Institute for Fiscal Studies (ed.), IFS Briefing Notes, BN76 (January 2008), at pp. 31–2.

43 *Ibid.* 44 *Ibid.*

9

Conclusion

The aim of this conclusion is to return to the some of the themes that have been addressed in previous chapters. Its purpose is to summarise, whereas the penultimate chapter had a more practical aim – to identify the most important arguments covered in this book, and from this to articulate a theoretical basis for consideration of the intersections between women, tax policy and the law. Three themes emerged: the uncomfortable relationship between the paid market, and equality; the usefulness of tax as a forum for analysing the place of women in the paid market economy; and the difficulty of achieving clarity in the distinctions between the different spheres (public–private), and indeed states (one's country; the international, economic order; the 'tax state') within which women work, interact with their governments and pay taxes. This book concludes that a woman-focused analysis of the relationship between tax policy and the law will need to engage with each of these themes.

This book has constructed arguments on several platforms, with differing degrees of specificity, and focus. In some places – for example, Chapter 6, 'Tax Policy Applied' – the focus quite directly was upon the UK. The reason for this focus in some ways simply was to acknowledge the enormous interest in recent developments in UK tax law. Those concerned about tax policy and women are likely to want to know more about the well-publicised child-centric vision of the Blair–Brown welfare state; and, perhaps even more so, would wish to read about the *Arctic Systems* case. The enormous curiosity about this case, and in the developments in the UK tax and benefits system, derives quite patently from their universality. Simply, other countries around the world are dealing with similar problems.

In other places, this book developed a broader, international focus. Gender budgeting is an international movement, embraced on an EU-wide platform, that now has come to the UK. Thus Chapter 3 considered perhaps the most interesting international development in the relationship between women, tax policy and the law in a tracing fashion; i.e. this chapter traced an international path, focused on the EU, and then left for other chapters the predictions as to the importance of some of the information that gender budgeting will produce. Gender budgeting will reveal that budgeting decisions have negative consequences for women, even if these consequences were the result of unintentional, implicit bias. The question is: how does implicit bias become embedded in government fiscal processes?

A response to this question was considered in a number of different ways. Chapter 5 considered whether implicit bias derives as a reaction to complexity in tax systems; or, from a persistent belief that tax and spending decisions are 'neutral'. Alternatively, Chapter 4 considered the role of business in structuring unequal economies, and queried whether the tax element of the corporate social responsibility literature might speak to this question. The interactive nature of the relationship between businesses, government and all participants in the 'tax state' led to Chapter 7's analysis of the new institutionalist turn in socio-legal theory, and its investigation of the potential contribution of this literature to a common understanding of what 'tax policy' means.

An understanding or definition of tax policy is indeed a difficult task; so much so that the book began, in Chapter 2, by asking, exactly what is tax policy for women? This is a question which has persisted throughout this book. As the penultimate chapter crafted a tripartite platform for analysis of 'women's tax policy' – the uncomfortable relationship between the paid market, and equality; the usefulness of tax as a forum for analysing the market status of women; and the difficulty of achieving clarity in the distinctions between the different spheres (public–private), and states – this final chapter now will draw to a close with a brief review of some of the conclusions reached above, and suggest how these conclusions fit within these themes.

The market and equality revisited

The book at various points considered the problematic relationship between unpaid labour and the paid marketplace. The market relies on women's work, both paid and unpaid, but it is at a loss as to how to deal with it. The book also considered the significance of tax incentives which encourage women to work, and argued that gauging the success of such provisions often involves picking apart the economic foundations of the family. This point was illustrated through consideration of the problems that taxation of two-worker families has caused, and the suggestion was made that problems surrounding this centre upon the exposure of private economic decisions to the scrutiny of a public marketplace.

Tax as a tool to combat 'feminised' poverty appears to confront almost insurmountable odds. Among other problems, not much is known about the potential for tax on the question of gender equality, and further empirical research on this subject would be very useful. Additionally, the sociological literature engaging with tax policy, from a pragmatic perspective – i.e., what is a normative tax policy for women; or, what is wanted from tax on behalf of gender economic equality – could be developed.[1] Studies considering the interaction of tax policy and women typically address, by way of example, the differing responses of women (as compared to men) to tax compliance.[2] The goal of this sort of research is to determine whether a gendered, 'tax morality' exists, and if tax laws should be structured accordingly;[3] and, additionally, if knowledge, or comprehension, of tax rules is connected to this sense of 'tax morality'.[4] It would be useful to move beyond this, into poverty. Thus, in some ways this book presented a call for research, but it did so while acknowledging that the collection of more data on the interaction between income tax systems and gender would only start to present a fuller picture, not least because the tax system always involves an element of guesswork; and, indeed, is founded upon it.[5]

Consideration of the textual progression of tax legislation in the UK, for example, from enforced joint taxation of a family to provisions permitting independent taxation of wives reveals much about the history of gender inequity.[6] This book's analysis of whether the tax system should be used

1 R. M. Alvarez and E. J. McCaffery, 'Gender and Tax', 91–113 (California Institute of Technology 1998, at: www.hss.caltech.edu/SSPapers/wp1046.pdf, at 22).

2 Orviska and Hudson, 'Tax Evasion', at 96.

3 Chung and Trivedi, 'Effect of Friendly Persuasion'.

4 Lars Fallan, 'Gender, Exposure', at 182–3. See also discussion of the literature in this area at J. Hasseldine and P. A. Hite, 'Framing, Gender and Tax Compliance', *Journal of Economic Psychology*, 24 (2003), 517–33, s. 2.3.

5 As Joseph E. Stiglitz argued, '[i]f the government knew everyone's ability, it should simply levy lump sum taxes on everyone' ('The Contributions of the Economics of Information to Twentieth Century Economics', *Quarterly Journal of Economics*, 115(2000), 1441–78, at 1450). But of course it does not, and so the question is not capable of being fully pursued. It is not necessarily, however, a non-starter, as the government does know something about the ability of women, and, that is, that through the demands of unpaid labour it is curtailed.

6 This sort of approach was developed in McCaffery, 'Women and Taxes'.

to encourage marriage included reference to the CPA 2004, which has had an important impact upon analyses of heteronormativity in the tax system.

Legal scholarship which engages with the impact of law on identifiable groups/subjects (outsider scholarship) provides a useful structure for a project which considers the impact of law (and tax policy) on a group (in this instance, women). Outsider scholarship often engages with evolved, sophisticated 'non-law' literature. Feminist institutional philosophy presents a good example of this, and may be helpful towards identifying a comparative, cultural grounding for tax law.

The locus of the family is frequently the target of government activity. While tax and other forms of commercial law engage with the paid marketplace, the family is targeted by all of these things, in addition to the attention of benefits and welfare regimes. An important change occurred when the tax system started to be used (earned income tax credits are the classic example) to target choices (is it financially viable for a mother to work outside of the home?). In the UK, this change can be linked to changes in the concepts underlying the welfare state. It is interesting that developments during the New Labour era occurred during a period of developing feminist criticism for the forms of gender inequality sustained within the family.

Tax as a forum, employed

Tax law often involves decisions by government as to whether it should intervene in choices that otherwise might be left to the individual. This is why tax is an important gender issue. As Brush argued, '[t]he state is an area of women's mobilization too important to abandon simply because when we *use* state power, we may *build* state power'.[7] The building process may occur with the deployment of the results of gender budgeting, in service to uncovering entrenched (or embedded) biases, perhaps in some sense attributable to the budgeting process itself.

Political strategy will play an important part in the success of gender budgeting. Gender economic inequality has always existed; thus, how will its redress be 'sold'? With gender budgeting, the government has an opportunity for redressing gender economic inequality, but it does not necessarily possess all of the necessary power to do so. Polanyi's analyses

7 L. D. Brush, 'The Curious Courtship of Feminist Jurisprudence and Feminist State Theory: Smart on the Power of Law', *Law and Social Inquiry*, 19 (1994), 1059–77, at 1076.

are useful to these considerations, as they demonstrate that the institutions which support a market stretch far beyond government and its agencies, and include, essentially, all of wider society. It is a difficult problem, but the process and aura of expertise surrounding gender budgeting may assist.[8] Economic governance will increase in transparency.[9] When the impact of spending initiatives are analysed post-Budget, change will be sought for forthcoming budgets.[10] That a disproportionate impact will be identified is inevitable, as even if domestic, national budgets start from a premise of fiscal neutrality and dispassionate revenue allocation, the combination of women's disproportionate share of unpaid work, inferior levels of pay to men, and reduced political voice all result in inequity.[11]

Poverty is not something that is inflicted on women through tax systems. The tax system however does contribute to its 'bleak'[12] fact, but it need not necessarily follow that tax law should be used as a tool of redress. Rather, consideration of the *interaction* of tax law, women and poverty may commence what are perhaps now described as comparative, legal discussions.

Issues of tax, law and gender may find a receptive forum within some of the 'new' approaches to comparative law, if premised upon the acknowledgement of global, economic gender inequality. The combination of the complexity of tax law, however, with the aim of avoiding essentialism in its analysis, can hinder understanding of the importance of this subject for women. Although taxes affect every aspect of women's economic lives,[13]

8 Walby has explained that 'the representation of the intervention as one that is based on expertise may itself be a political strategy' ('Gender Mainstreaming', at 333).

9 The significance is that '[g]ender budgeting helps to monitor the achievement of policy goals and to hold governments accountable in this regard. By tracking how money is spent, gender budgeting helps to increase accountability and transparency and, thus, good economic governance in a country' (OECD Department for International Development, 'Evaluation of DFID's Policy and Practice in Support of Gender Equality and Women's Empowerment', August 2006, at: www.oecd.org/dataoecd/52/38/37390142.pdf, at slide 5). D. Budlender has written that two of the main benefits of gender budgeting are 'increased transparency' and 'accountability' ('The Political Economy of Women's Budgets in the South', *World Development*, 28 (2000), 1365–78, at 1377).

10 Yet '[g]ender budgeting initiatives traditionally analyse budgets ex-post and then use that analysis to advocate for change in the subsequent budget' (OECD, 'Evaluation', at 34). Perhaps most importantly, they are also a 'tool for change' (Budlender, 'The Political Economy', at 1376).

11 Ruth Pearson, 'Feminist Responses to Economic Globalisation: Some Examples of Past and Future Practice', *Gender and Development*, 11 (2003), 25–34, at 32.

12 McCaffery, 'Women and Taxes'.

13 E. J. McCaffery, 'Women and Taxes' (National Center for Policy Analysis 2002, at: www.ncpa.org/pub/st/st250/st250.pdf).

it also impacts upon many aspects of (not just) economic life. It is in this context that this book has aimed to demonstrate that tax law has contributed to a gendered socio-economy, in an institutionalist sense.

Institutionalist theory is particularly useful in attempts to establish what exactly should be the role of perspectives in the study of tax. While it goes without saying that there are a variety of examples of jurisprudence which may enhance tax legal research (far too many to be considered within a project of this size), institutionalist, as well as critical cultural studies (including, but not limited to, the discussion of comparative law earlier in this book) seems particularly full of promise for the questions posed by the intersection of tax policy, women and the law. The aim is not to deny the relevance of interpretative scholarship (i.e. formalism) to women and tax policy. Rather, it is to take the analysis further, beyond the boundaries of explicit bias.

Implicit inequities along lines of gender in the values at the basis of the tax system benefit neither women nor men. Tax policy and the law in many ways represent an excellent example of what has been put in place. An analysis of 'individuals in relation' to tax law inevitably raises the question of the topic of study itself, and how it should be approached. While the 'cultural focus' has enormously enriched legal scholarship, a cost of this development is a lack of engagement with explicitly economic law; and, in particular, with tax law. It is for this reason that one purpose of this book has been to argue for the development of a specifically feminist, materialist analysis of UK tax law and policy. This project was undertaken with the hope that such a call also may serve to reinvigorate the 'tax project' of fiscal sociology.[14]

Clarity in spheres and states, considered

This book has considered the extent to which a 'tax policy', and, in particular, a feminist tax policy may be international; and, the project of this book has included consideration of both international and comparative elements. On one level, an international tax policy could be approached from the perspective of targeted international agreement, especially if the consequence of these agreements include gendered impact. A different approach could include what has been described as the 'family of nations'

14 On this point, see generally E. J. McCaffery, 'Where's the Sex in Fiscal Sociology? Taxation and Gender in Comparative Perspective', *University of Southern California Working Series*, paper 70 (2008) (at: http://law.bepress.com/cgi/viewcontent.cgi?article=1072&context=usclwps).

approach in sociology, which takes a shared language, or historical background, very seriously in the effort to 'comprehend the variety of policy outcomes to be found in modern states'.[15] Both of these approaches, however, would focus more on explicit than implicit bias.

This book builds upon a generation of endeavour in this field, all demonstrating that paying attention to women and tax law is important and necessary. The prolonged, lingering delays that have beset each UK legislative step in the direction of gender tax equality serve to underscore, among other things, that there is little that is simple about the place of the household in the economy. A switch to independent taxation could not be expected to address fully such a complicated subject, and indeed might have been expected to reproduce and to reflect some of the confusion surrounding the economic model of the family.[16] Tax policies designed to challenge gendered models only have any hope of succeeding if reductionist models are fully abandoned.[17]

Nelson's concept of 'engulfment' is useful here, and has implications for both men and women.[18] It is through 'engulfment' that the individual is lost in the notion of the 'household' unit, and it is important 'to be wary of the extremes of isolation and engulfment'.[19] From a feminist perspective, it is particularly important, given that a model under which a *family* unit, *together*, has responsibility for the well-being of children may be unrecognisable to many women.[20]

It is interesting to note that antipathy towards taxation does seem to be the one common factor among all modern democracies.[21] It is thus striking that a form of government which is so disliked, is being relied upon to assist a social institution – the family – which most governments

15 F. G. Castles and M. Flood, 'Divorce, the Law and Social Context: Families of Nations and the Legal Dissolution of Marriage', *Acta Sociologica*, 34 (1991), 279–97, at 279.

16 J. Wheelock, *et al.* have suggested that the complicated nature of household economics are frequently treated in a reductionist way by policy makers, and this is part of the problem. They argue that 'UK policy-makers [should] ... jettison the simplistic and reductionist economic model of the household, and pay serious attention to the ways in which household decision-making reproduces gendered and traditional behaviour' ('Getting by with a Little Help from Your Family: Toward a Policy-relevant Model of the Household', *Feminist Economics*, 9 (2003), 19–45, at 38).

17 *Ibid.*

18 J. Nelson, *Feminism, Objectivity, and Economics* (London: Routledge, 1996), at p. 27.

19 *Ibid.*

20 McIntosh, 'Feminism', in Pierson and Castles (eds.), *Welfare State Reader*, at p. 120.

21 As Steinmo memorably has written, 'it is interesting to note that there does seem to be a rather remarkable consistency in public attitudes toward taxation in all advanced democracies: People hate taxes' (S. Steinmo and C. J. Tolbert, 'Do Institutions Really Matter?', *Comparative Political Studies*, 31 (1998), 165–88, at 167).

are so keen to support. This book acknowledged that not all of the issues arising from the clashes that can occur when private activities – for example, parenting – encounter commercial values are drawn along lines of gender, although many of them are. Even research considering the role of gender solely in public contexts (for example, sexist discrimination in the workplace), frequently finds that discussions stray back to the realm of the private. Indeed, if it were possible to identify a factor which most frequently straddles the public–private divide, it would be gender.

Why use taxes to bridge this divide? Clemens wrote that '[t]axes, as Lévi-Strauss said of "savages", are good to think with'.[22] The reason for this is that '[t]axes discourage some behaviors, encourage others, and demarcate the "normal" from the deviant or illicit'.[23] Thus this book has considered instances in which the tax system has changed to reflect evolving social patterns. It has queried whether tax law has evolved enough to reflect these changes, and suggested that there is potential for the tax system in some cases to actually lead a call for change. One of the more intriguing proposals along these lines is Pearson's 'Maria Tax'.[24]

This book also has suggested that it may be instructive to return to some of the conclusions of the consideration of the value of diversity in (international) tax law. The OECD has assumed a pivotal role in 'addressing' diversity; in particular, through the promulgation of tax treaties. There may well be a strong argument for forging a global tax policy. The revenue rule may no longer be as strong as perhaps it once was, but there are still many aspects of the relationship between taxpayer and the state that render tax law, as a subject, domestic. In some ways, tax could be described as an intensely personal relationship, insofar as the relationship between taxpayer and the state is concerned. If the taxpayer is voluntarily to permit the government to extract money which otherwise would belong to the taxpayer, then the terms of this consent will be constructed delicately, and, as between different states, differently.

Consider, for example, that the annual production of the Finance Acts in the UK is the result of the execution of a monarch (over a tax issue). The pact between government and governed was redefined dramatically with the execution of Charles I. Indeed, it is worth noting in closing that Harris' important work with tax in common law jurisdictions confirmed what had long been expected: i.e., that a wide-reaching survey of tax practices around the world would reveal that many common law jurisdictions have

22 Clemens, 'Good Reasons', at 518. 23 *Ibid.*
24 Pearson, 'Feminist Responses', at 31–5.

inherited UK tax rules.[25] Some of these rules still exist in UK tax law, and many others do not – producing an interesting alternative universe of what might have, or could have, happened had the UK decided to hold on to an aspect of tax law, rather than discard it. While it is not always possible to identify why some tax choices were made in these common law jurisdictions, what is intriguing about Harris' research is that he demonstrates that it may be possible to make predictions about future developments in tax law around the world, based upon comparative analysis of the past.

Additionally, the future of tax, globally, has been targeted by the corporate social responsibility movement. The integration of gender with corporation social responsibility objectives, through tax, would not be without cost.[26] Yet simply because gender equality may affect other aspects of the economy is not sufficient reason to fail to pursue its objectives.

The tax system is often deployed as an agent of redistribution. But it struggles with the question whether, and if so how, the tax system should recognise family structures per se. This book has not sought to prescribe solutions, merely to point out some of the inconsistencies and difficulties that arise from the present state. It also has attempted to place them in theoretical context, to identify those platforms which appear ready to receive the difficult and rewarding (in their analyses) issues arising from the intersection of women, tax policy and the law. If dynamic systems theory is about the general, and if feminist legal theory is moving beyond the oppression of the general, it does not necessarily follow that feminist legal theory is about the specific, and the details. Indeed, it is much bigger than that. It is bigger than the general. It is about 'questioning everything, inserting women everywhere'.[27] Whitman has worried that 'there is a sense in which much of current feminist jurisprudence seems unmoored,

25 P. Harris, *Income Tax in Common Law Jurisdictions: From the Origins* to 1820 (Cambridge University Press, 2006).

26 As H. Gordon Fitch explains, '[a]chievement of desired levels of corporate social responsibility will, in many instances, add to the cost of production of many of these goods and services, and these costs ultimately will be borne by society in the form of higher taxes ...' ('Achieving Corporate Social Responsibility', *Academy of Management Review*, 1(1) (1976), 38–46, at 38). Yet, as Fitch also explains by way of example, 'the corporation which emits pollution imposes a neighborhood cost upon all of those who must breathe the air in its vicinity and should, if it were striving to achieve corporate social responsibility, be willing to try to eliminate the pollution or pay the costs of doing so through heavier taxes which, in turn, are used to provide pollution control equipment' (*ibid.*, at 40).

27 Dalton, 'Where We Stand', at 11.

directionless'[28] – perhaps this is because feminist legal theorists have been so busy, or, at least, so ambitious. Feminist theory is always about women, however, and in this sense it is more grounded than dynamic systems theory, which, other than anti-reductionism, would purport to have no agenda.[29]

Finally, in tax law, history is often important, as is considering how we may have reached a particular point. The CPA 2004 was not accompanied by any initiative to reconsider the taxation of couples, largely because that was not the issue. One aim of the CPA 2004 was to strengthen support for marriage, by increasing the number of people who now would have access to it. Additionally, this book suggested that the UK tax system is not entirely consistent in its support for marriage and civil partnerships, and possesses its version of the much discussed (in the US) 'marriage penalty'. For example, when two people marry, their two private residence exemptions for capital gains tax purposes merges into one. And yet, the settlor legislation anticipated from the Revenue, in response to the *Arctic Systems* case, presumably will target couples especially. This inconsistency would appear to reverberate at many levels, throughout the socio-economy.

In closing, this book began by stating that the problem of women's economic inequality is universal, and cannot be solved by tax law, in any state, or through any tax-based international agreement. It stated that, simply, tax law is not a capable forum for redressing gender equality. And it is difficult to identify which provisions of tax law, exactly, benefit women, because every aspect of a tax system has the potential to affect women. This book, ultimately, suggests that the tax system puts women on the margin. The challenge of a coherent, revised tax policy, informed by the important development of gender budgeting, would be to move women from the margin, to the economic mainstream.

28 Christina Brooks Whitman, 'Review Essay: Feminist Jurisprudence', *Feminist Studies*, 17 (1991), 493–507, at 505.

29 Nozickian 'filter devices' are more appropriate for feminist legal theories, than for dynamic system theories, because the need to acknowledge that 'people are complex' is more of an issue in the face of agendas. R. Nozick, *Anarchy, State, and Utopia* (Oxford: Basil Blackwell, 1974), at pp. 312, 313–34.

BIBLIOGRAPHY

'Developments in the Law: Corporations and Society'. *Harvard Law Review*, 117(7) (2004), 2169–2295.

'The Myth of Context in Politics and Law'. *Harvard Law Review*, 110(6) (1997), 1292–1309.

Abramovitz, M. *Taxes Are a Woman's Issue: Reframing the Debate.* (New York, NY: Feminist Press at the City University of New York, 2007).

Abreu, A. 'Tax Counts: Bringing Money-Law to LatCrit'. *Denver University Law Review*, 78 (2000), 575–93.

Ahlander, N. R. and K. S. Bahr. 'Beyond Drudgery, Power, and Equity: Toward an Expanded Discourse on the Moral Dimensions of Housework in Families'. *Journal of Marriage and the Family*, 57(1) (1995), 54–68.

Alba, R. M. *Offshore Centres of Latin America and the Caribbean: The Need for a Level Playing Field in the Search for Integrity.* Twenty First International Symposium on Economic Crime, Jesus College, University of Cambridge, vol. 11 (2003) (at: www.freedomandprosperity.org/alba.pdf).

Alldridge, P. and A. Mumford. 'Tax Evasion and the Proceeds of Crime Act 2002'. *Legal Studies*, 25 (2005), 353–73.

Alm, J., S. Dickert-Conlin and L. A. Whittington. 'Policy Watch: The Marriage Penalty'. *Journal of Economic Perspectives*, 13(3) (1999), 193–204.

Alstott, A. L. 'Tax Policy and Feminism: Competing Goals and Institutional Choices'. *Columbia Law Review*, 96(8) (1996), 2001–82.

Alstott, A. L. *No Exit: What Parents Owe Their Children and What Society Owes Parents.* (New York, NY: Oxford University Press, 2004).

Alvarez, R. M. and E. J. McCaffery. 'Gender and Tax'. Gender and American Politics: Women, Men, and the Political Process; Social Science Working Paper 1046: California Institute of Technology, 1998 (at: www.hss.caltech.edu/SSPapers/wp1046.pdf).

Alvarez, R. M. and E. I. McCaffery. 'Gender and Tax', in S. Tolleson-Rinehart and J. J. Josephson (eds.), *Gender and American Politics: Women, Men, and the Political Process* (Armonk, NY: M. E. Sharpe, 2000), pp. 91–114.

Amenta, E., C. Bonastia and N. Caren. 'US Social Policy in Comparative and Historical Perspective: Concepts, Images, Arguments, and Research Strategies'. *Annual Review of Sociology*, 27(1) (2001), 213–34.

Anne Tempel, P. W. 'Global Standardization of Organizational Forms and Management Practices? What New Institutionalism and the Business-systems Approach Can Learn from Each Other'. *Journal of Management Studies*, 44(1) (2007), 1–24.

Armstrong, K. A. 'Legal Integration: Theorizing the Legal Dimension of European Integration'. *Journal of Common Market Studies – Annual Review*, 36(2) (1998), 155–74.

Armstrong, K. A. 'The "Europeanisation" of Social Exclusion: British Adaptation to EU Co-ordination'. *British Journal of Politics and International Relations*, 8(1) (2006), 79–100.

Aspers, P., S. Kohl, J. Roine and P. Wichardt. 'An Economic Sociological Look at Economics'. *Economic Sociology: The European Electronic Newsletter*, 9(2) (March 2008).

Atkins, S. 'The Sex Discrimination Act 1975: The End of a Decade'. *Feminist Review*, (24) (1986), 57–70.

Auchmuty, R. 'Same-sex Marriage Revived: Feminist Critique and Legal Strategy'. *Feminism and Psychology*, 14(1) (2004), 101–26.

Avery Jones, J. 'Are Tax Treaties Necessary?' *Tax Law Review*, 53 (1999), 1–38.

Avi-Yonah, R. S. 'Corporations, Society, and the State: A Defense of the Corporate Tax'. *Virginia Law Review*, 90(5) (2004), 1193–1255.

Avi-Yonah, R. S. *Corporate Social Responsibility and Strategic Tax Behavior*. SSRN, 2006 (at: http://ssrn.com/paper=944793).

Baber, K. and K. Allen. *Women and Families: Feminist Reconstructions*. (New York, NY: Guilford Press, 1992).

Baden, S. and A. M. Goetz. 'Who Needs [Sex] When You Can Have [Gender]? Conflicting Discourses on Gender at Beijing'. *Feminist Review*, 56 (1997), 3–25.

Bakker, I. C. and Alternatives Canadian Centre for Policy, 'Gender Budget Initiatives: Why They Matter in Canada', Technical Paper 1, Canadian Centre for Policy Alternatives, 2006.

Bala, N. and R. Bromwich. 'Context and Inclusivity in Canada's Evolving Definition of the Family'. *International Journal of Law, Policy and the Family*, 16(2) (2002), 145–80.

Banerjee, S. 'Corporate Social Responsibility: The Good, the Bad and the Ugly'. *Critical Sociology*, 34(1) (2008), 51–79.

Bank, T. W. *Gender Equality as Smart Economics*. (January 2002) (at: http://web.worldbank.org/WBSITE/EXTERNAL/TOPICS/EXTGENDER/0,,menuPK:336874~pagePK:149018~piPK:149093~theSitePK:336868,00.html).

Bankman, J. and T. Griffith. 'Social Welfare and the Rate Structure: A New Look At Progressive Taxation'. *California Law Review*, 75(6) (1987), 1905–67.

Barker, N. 'Sex and the Civil Partnership Act: The Future of (Non) Conjugality?' *Feminist Legal Studies*, 14(2) (2006), 241–59.

Barmes, L. and W. S. Ashtiany. 'The Diversity Approach to Achieving Equality: Potential and Pitfalls'. *Industrial Law Journal*, 32(4) (2003), 274–96.

Barnett, K. and C. Grown. *Gender Impacts of Government Revenue Collection: The Case of Taxation.* (Commonwealth Secretariat, 2004).

Bashevkin, S. 'From Tough Times to Better Times: Feminism, Public Policy, and New Labour Politics in Britain'. *International Political Science Review/Revue internationale de science politique*, 21(4) (2000), 407–24.

Beatson, J. 'Has the Common Law a Future?' *Cambridge Law Journal*, 56(02) (2009), 291–314.

Beckert, J. 'The great transformation of embeddedness: Karl Polanyi and the new economic sociology'. Manuscript. (2006) (at: www.mpifg.de/pu/mpifg_dp/dp07–1.pdf).

Beneria, L. 'Globalization, Gender, and the Davos Man', in E. Mutari and D. M. Figart (eds.), *Women and the Economy: A Reader* (Armonk, NY: M.E. Sharpe, 2003), pp. 312–25.

Bennett, C. J. 'What Is Policy Convergence and What Causes It?' *British Journal of Political Science*, 21(2) (1991), 215–33.

Bennett, F. 'Policy Implications of Tax Credits' (at: www.genet.ac.uk/workpapers/GeNet 2005 p8.pdf).

Bergmann, B. R. 'What Policies Toward Lone Mothers Should We Aim For?' *Feminist Economics*, 10(2) (2004), 240–6.

Berland, J. 'On Reading "the Weather"'. *Cultural Studies*, 8(1) (1994), 99–114.

Bernburg, J. G. 'Anomie, Social Change and Crime: A Theoretical Examination of Institutional–Anomie Theory'. *British Journal of Criminology*, 42 (2002), 729–39.

Beveridge, F. 'Building against the Past: The Impact of Mainstreaming on EU Gender Law and Policy'. *European Law Review*, 32(2) (2007), 193–212.

Bevir, M. 'Narrating the British State: An Interpretive Critique of New Labour's Institutionalism'. *Review of International Political Economy*, 10(3) (2003), 455–80.

Biswas, R. *International Tax Competition: Globalisation and Fiscal Sovereignty.* (Commonwealth Secretariat, 2002).

Bittker, B. I. 'Federal Income Taxation and the Family'. *Stanford Law Review*, 27 (1975), 1389–1463.

Bittker, B. I. 'Dedication: Charles Stuart Lyon – Being an Epitome of His Letters, Marginalia, Graffiti, and Other Fugitive Scribblings'. *Tax Law Review*, 37 (1981), 159–92.

Black, A. and S. Brooke. 'The Labour Party, Women, and the Problem of Gender, 1951–1966'. *Journal of British Studies*, 36(4) (1997), 419–52.

Block, F. 'Karl Polanyi and the Writing of the Great Transformation'. *Theory and Society*, 32(3) (2003), 275–306.

Blom-Hansen, J. 'A "New Institutional" Perspective on Policy Networks'. *Public Administration*, 75(4) (1997), 669–93.

Blumberg, R. L. 'A General Theory of Gender Stratification'. *Sociological Theory*, 2 (1984), 23–101.

Blundell, R. and C. Meghir. 'Active Labour Market Policy vs Employment Tax Credits: Lessons from Recent UK Reforms'. Institute for Labour Market Policy Evaluation Working Paper No. 1. (2002).

Blundell, R., A. Duncan, J. McCrae and C. Meghir. 'The Labour Market Impact of the Working Families' Tax Credit'. *Fiscal Studies*, 21(1) (2000), 75–104.

Borison, J. 'Alice through a Very Dark and Confusing Looking Glass: Getting Equity from the Tax Court in Innocent Spouse Cases'. *Family Law Quarterly*, 30 (1996), 123–72.

Boschken, H. L. 'Institutionalism: Intergovernmental Exchange, Administration-centered Behavior, and Policy Outcomes in Urban Agencies'. *Journal of Public Administration Research and Theory*, 8(4) (1998), 585–614.

Boskin, M. J. and E. Sheshinski. Optimal Tax Treatment of the Family: Married Couples. *NBER Working Paper No.* 368, 1984 (also Reprint No. r0468) (at: www.nber.org/papers/W0368.pdf).

Bossons, J. 'The Value of a Comprehensive Tax Base as a Tax Reform Goal'. *Journal of Law and Economics*, 13(2) (1970), 327–63.

Bowler, T. Taxation of the Family. Tax Law Review Committee Discussion Paper No. 6 (April 2007).

Boyd, S. B. *Challenging the Public/Private Divide: Feminism, Law, and Public Policy* (University of Toronto Press, 1997).

Boyd, S. B. 'Family, Law and Sexuality: Feminist Engagements'. *Social and Legal Studies*, 8(3) (1999), 369–90.

Boyd, S. B. and C. F. L. Young. 'Feminism, Law, and Public Policy: Family Feuds and Taxing Times'. *Osgoode Hall Law Journal*, 42(4) (2004), 545–82.

Bradford, D. *et al.* 'The Incidence and Allocation Effects of a Tax on Corporate Distributions' (NBER Working Paper, 1981).

Bradley, M., C. A. Schipani, A. K. Sundaram and J. P. Walsh. 'The Purposes and Accountability of the Corporation in Contemporary Society: Corporate Governance at a Crossroads'. *Law and Contemporary Problems*, 62(3) (1999), 9–86.

Braithwaite, J. *Markets in Vice,* Markets in Virtue (Oxford University Press, 2005).

Brazer, H. E. 'The Report of the Royal Commission on Taxation'. *Journal of Finance*, 22(4) (1967), 671–83.

Brazier, A. 'The Fiscal Maze: Parliament, Government and Public Money'. *Parliamentary Affairs (Hansard Society)*, 60(2) (16 March 2007), 346–55.

Brewer, M., A. Duncan, A. Shephard and M. Suarez. 'Did Working Families' Tax Credit Work? The Impact of In-work Support on Labour Supply in Great Britain'. *Labour Economics*, 13(6) (2006), 699–720.

Brooks, K. and D. Parkes. 'Queering Legal Education: A Project of Theoretical Discovery'. *Harvard Women's Law Journal*, 27 (2004), 89–136.

Brooks, N. 'The Irrelevance of Conjugal Relationships in Assessing Tax Liability' Tax Units and the Tax Rate Scale (1996) (at: http://law.harvard.edu. http://law.harvard.edu).

Brudney, V. 'The Independent Director – Heavenly City or Potemkin Village?' *Harvard Law Review*, 95 (1982), 597–660.

Brush, L. D. 'The Curious Courtship of Feminist Jurisprudence and Feminist State Theory: Smart on the Power of Law'. *Law and Social Inquiry*, 19(4) (1994), 1059–77.

Budlender, D. *The South African Women's Budget Initiative*. Meeting on Women and Political Participation: 21st Century Challenges, United Nations Development Programme, New Delhi, India. Edn. BPN 2.166166 (24–26 March 1999) (at: http://iggi.unesco.or.kr/web/iggi_docs/02/952310746.pdf).

Budlender, D. 'The Political Economy of Women's Budgets in the South'. *World Development*, 28(7) (2000), 1365–78.

Budlender, D., D. Elson, G. Hewitt and T. Mukhopadhyay. *Gender Budgets Make Cents: Understanding Gender Responsive Budgets*. Gender Responsive Budget Initiatives (Commonwealth Secretariat, 2002).

Budlender, D., R. Sharp and K. Allen. *How to Do a Gender-sensitive Budget Analysis: Contemporary Research and Practice* (Commonwealth Secretariat, 1998).

Bulmer, S. J. 'New Institutionalism and the Governance of the Single European Market'. *Journal of European Public Policy*, 5(3) (1998), 365–86.

Burghes, L., L. Clarke and N. Cronin. *Fathers and Fatherhood in Britain*. (London: Family Policy Studies Centre, 1997).

Burk, M. 'A Feminist Tea Party?: Time to Start Righting the Tax System's Wrongs'. *Ms Magazine*, 17 (2007) (at: www.msmagazine.com/spring2007/afeministteaparty.asp).

Burns, N. 'Finding Gender'. *Politics and Gender*, 1(01) (2005), 137–41.

Burton, M. 'Responsive Regulation and the Uncertainty of Tax Law'. *eJournal of Tax Research*, 5(1) (July 2007), 71–104.

Butler, J. 'Merely Cultural'. *Social Text*, 52/53 (1997), 265–77.

Byrne, D. M. 'Progressive Taxation Revisited'. *Arizona Law Review*, 37 (1995), 739–89.

Cain, P. A. 'Heterosexual Privilege and the Internal Revenue Code'. *University of San Francisco Law Review*, 34 (2000), 465–94.

Cain, P. A. 'Federal Tax Consequences of Civil Unions'. *Capital University Law Review*, 30 (2002), 387–408.

Cain, P. M. 'Taxing Lesbians'. *Southern California Review of Law and Women's Studies*, 6 (1996–7), 471.

Campbell, J. L. 'The State and Fiscal Sociology'. *Annual Review of Sociology* 19 (1993), 163–85.

Carroll, A. 'Corporate Social Responsibility: Evolution of a Definitional Construct'. *Business and Society*, 38(3) (1999), 268–95.

Carter, A. M. 'Income-tax Allowances and the Family in Great Britain'. *Population Studies*, 6(3) (1953), 218–32.

Carter, K. L. M. 'Canadian Tax Reform and Henry Simons'. *Journal of Law and Economics*, 11(2) (1968), 231–42.

Castles, F. G. and M. Flood. 'Divorce, the Law and Social Context: Families of Nations and the Legal Dissolution of Marriage'. *Acta Sociologica*, 34(4) (1991), 279–97.

Çeagatay, N. 'Gender Budgets and Beyond: Feminist Fiscal Policy in the Context of Globalisation'. *Gender and Development*, 11(1) (2003), 15–24.

Chan, W. 'Women, Childcare and Taxation'. *Kings' College Law Journal*, 10 (1999), 71–92.

Cherry, R. 'Rational Choice and the Price of Marriage', in K. S. Moe (ed.), *Women, Family, and Work: Writings on the Economics of Gender* (London: Blackwell, 2003).

Chow, E. N. L. and C. W. Berheide. 'The Interdependence of Family and Work: A Framework for Family Life Education, Policy, and Practice'. *Family Relations*, 37(1) (1988), 23–8.

Chung, J. and V. U. Trivedi. 'The Effect of Friendly Persuasion and Gender on Tax Compliance Behavior'. *Journal of Business Ethics*, 47(2) (2003), 133–45.

Clarkson, M. B. E. 'A Stakeholder Framework for Analyzing and Evaluating Corporate Social Performance'. *Academy of Management Review*, 20(1) (1995), 92–117.

Clemens, E. S. 'Good Reasons to Stop Avoiding Taxes'. *Law and Social Inquiry*, 24(2) (1999), 517–31.

Clemens, E. S. and J. Cook. 'Politics and Institutionalism: Explaining Durability and Change'. *Annual Reviews in Sociology*, 25(1) (1999), 441–66.

Clement, K. 'Environmental Auditing for Industry: A European Perspective'. *European Environment*, 1(3) (1991), 1–4.

Coase, R. H. 'The New Institutional Economics'. *American Economic Review*, 88 (1998), 72–4.

Cohen, G. A. 'Where the Action is: On the Site of Distributive Justice'. *Philosophy and Public Affairs*, 26(1) (1997), 3–30.

Colinvaux, R. P. 'Income Tax Liability of Married Women'. *Modern Law Review*, 11(3) (1948), 346–7.

Collins, P. 'It's All in the Family: Intersections of Gender, Race, and Nation'. *Hypatia* (1998), 62–82.

Conaghan, J. 'Reassessing the Feminist Theoretical Project in Law'. *Journal of Law and Society*, 27(3) (2000), 351–85.

Connell, R. W. 'The Big Picture: Masculinities in Recent World History'. *Theory and Society*, 22(5) (1993), 597–623.

Cook, K. 'The Power of Sociological Ideas'. *Sociological Perspectives*, 34(2) (1991), 115–26.

Copelon, R. 'International Human Rights Dimensions of Intimate Violence: Another Strand in the Dialectic of Feminist Lawmaking'. *American University Journal of Gender, Social Policy and the Law*, 11 (2003), 865–76.

Cornell, D. 'Review: Sexual Difference, the Feminine, and Equivalency: A Critique of MacKinnon's Toward a Feminist Theory of the State'. *Yale Law Journal*, 100(7) (1991), 2247–75.

Cornwall, A. 'Whose Voices? Whose Choices? Reflections on Gender and Participatory Development'. *World Development*, 31(8) (2003), 1325–42.

Cotterrell, R. *Seeking Similarity, Appreciating Difference: Comparative Law and Communities.* Comparative Law in the Twenty-First Century. E. Örücü and A. Harding, (eds.), vol. 4. (The Hague: Kluwer, 2002).

Cotterrell, R. *Law, Culture and Society: Legal Ideas in the Mirror of Social Theory* (Aldershot: Ashgate, 2006).

Coutts, J. A. 'Income Tax Liability of Married Women'. *Modern Law Review*, 12(1) (1949), 110–12.

Crawford, B. J. 'Outsourcing Intimacy: The Taxation of Powers of Attorney' (2007) (at: http://digitalcommons.pace.edu/cgi/viewcontent.cgi?article=1397&context=lawfaculty).

Crawford, B. J. 'Tax Avatars'. *Utah Law Review* (2008), 793–833 (at: http://digitalcommons.pace.edu/cgi/viewcontent.cgi?article=1549&context=lawfaculty).

Crawford, C. and J. Freedman. 'Small Business Taxation: A Special Study of the Structural Issues Surrounding the Taxation of Business Profits of Owner Managed Firms'. Prepared for the Report of a Commission on Reforming the Tax System for the 21st Century, Chaired by Sir James Mirrlees (21 April 2008) (at: www.competition-law.ox.ac.uk/tax/documents/Dimensions_Tax_Design_MR2008.pdf, or www.ifs.org.uk/mirrleesreview/press_docs/small_businesses.pdf, at 22–3, on the IFS website).

Creedy, J. and N. Gemmell. 'Corporation Tax Buoyancy and Revenue Elasticity In the UK'. *Economic Modelling*, 25(1) (2008), 24–37.

Cretney, S. M. *Family Law in the Twentieth Century* (Oxford University Press, 2003).

Crowther, B. 'Viewing What Comes Naturally: A Feminist Approach to Television Natural History'. *Women's Studies International Forum*, 20(2) (1997), 289–300.

Daly, M. 'Gender Mainstreaming in Theory and Practice'. *Social Politics*, 12 (2005), 433–50.

Daly, M. and S. Clavero. *Contemporary Family Policy: A Comparative Review of Ireland, France, Germany, Sweden and the UK* (London: Institute of Public Administration, 2002).

Daunton, M. *What Is Income?* Studies in the History of Tax Law, J. Tiley (ed.) (Oxford: Hart Publishing, 2004), pp. 3–14.

Davies, H., H. Joshi and R. Peronaci. 'Forgone Income and Motherhood: What Do Recent British Data Tell U?' *Population Studies*, 54(3) (2000), 293–305.

Dearden, L. 'PBR Analysis: Childcare Strategy' (December 2004) (at: www.ifs.org.uk/publications/3196).

Deech, R. 'The Case against Legal Recognition of Cohabitation'. *International and Comparative Law Quarterly*, 29(2–3) (2008), 480–97.

Delphy, C. and D. Leonard. 'A Materialist Feminism Is Possible'. *Feminist Review*, (4) (1980), 79–105.

Demleitner, N. V. 'A Response to Mathias Reimann: More, More, More But Real Comparative Law'. *Tulane European and Civil Law Forum*, 11 (1996), 73–83.

Dennis, J. M. 'The Lessons of Comparable Worth: A Feminist Vision of Law and Economic Theory'. *UCLA Women's Law Journal*, 4 (1993), 1–36.

Dequech, D. 'The Demarcation between the "Old" and the "New" Institutional Economics: Recent Complications'. *Journal of Economic Issues*, 36(2) (2002), 565–72.

Devereux, M., R. Griffith, A. Klemm, M. Thum and M. Ottaviani. 'Corporate Income Tax Reforms and International Tax Competition'. *Economic Policy* (2002), 449–95.

Dingeldey, I. 'European Tax Systems and their Impact on Family Employment Patterns'. *Journal of Social Policy*, 30(04) (2001), 653–72.

Dodd, Jr., E. M. 'For Whom Are Corporate Managers Trustees?' *Harvard Law Review*, 45(7) (1932), 1145–63.

Dolan, J. 'In Defense of the Discourse: Materialist Feminism, Postmodernism, Poststructuralism ... And Theory'. *TDR (1988–)* 33(3) (1989), 58–71.

Drenth, A. van, T. Knijn and J. Lewis. 'Sources of Income for Lone Mother Families: Policy Changes in Britain and the Netherlands and the Experiences of Divorced Women'. *Journal of Social Policy*, 28(04) (2000), 619–41.

Driver, S. and L. Martell. 'New Labour, Work and the Family'. *Social Policy and Administration*, 36(1) (2002), 46–61.

DTI. 'Gender Analysis of Expenditure Project' (Final Report) (July 2004) (at: www.womenandequalityunit.gov.uk/research/gender_analysis.pdf).

Duncan, S. and R. Edwards. 'Lone Mothers and Paid Work – Rational Economic Man or Gendered Moral Rationalities?' *Feminist Economics*, 3(2) (1997), 29–61.

Durkheim, E. 'The Conjugal Family', in *Emile Durkheim on Institutional Analysis*, ed. and trans. M. Traugott (Chicago, IL and London: University of Chicago Press, 1978), pp. 229–39.

Dworkin, R. *Liberalism* (orig. pub.), *Public and Private Morality*, Stuart Hampshire (ed.) (Cambridge University Press, 1978), in J. Nida-Rumelin and W. Vossenkuhl (eds.), *Ethische und Politische* (Cambridge, MA: Walter de Gruyter, 1998).

Eggertsson, T. 'The Old Theory of Economic Policy and the New Institutionalism'. *World Development*, 25(8) (1997), 1187–1203.

Eggertsson, T. 'Rethinking the Theory of Economic Policy: Some Implications of the New Institutionalism', in J. M. Nelson, C. Tilly and L. Walker (eds.), *Transforming Post-communist Political Economies* (Washington, DC: National Academies Press, 1997), pp. 61–79.

Ehrenreich, B. and A. Hochschild. *Global Woman: Nannies, Maids, and Sex Workers in the New Economy* (New York, NY: Metropolitan Books, 2003).

Eisenhardt, K. 'Agency Theory: An Assessment and Review'. *Academy of Management Review* (1989) 57–74.

Eissa, N. and J. B. Liebman. *Labor Supply Response to the Earned Income Tax Credit* (Cambridge, MA: National Bureau of Economic Research, 1995).

Ellwood, D. T. 'The Impact of the Earned Income Tax Credit and Social Policy Reforms on Work, Marriage, and Living Arrangements'. *National Tax Journal*, 53(4) (2000), 1063–1105.

Ellwood, D. T. and J. B. Liebman. 'The Middle-class Parent Penalty: Child Benefits in the US Tax Code', in James M. Poterba (ed.),*Tax Policy and the Economy* (Boston, MA: MIT Press, 2001).

England, K. *Who Will Mind the Baby?: Geographies of Childcare and Working Mothers* (London: Routledge, 1996).

Epstein, R. *Simple Rules for a Complex World* (Cambridge, MA: Harvard University Press, 1995).

Ergas, Y. *Child-care Policies in Comparative Perspective an Introductory Discussion. Lone-Parent Families: The Economic Challenge* (Paris: OECD, 1990).

Erhel, C. and H. Zajdela. 'The Dynamics of Social and Labour Market Policies in France and the United Kingdom: Between Path Dependence and Convergence'. *Journal of European Social Policy*, 14(2) (2004), 125–42.

Erturk, Y. 'Considering the Role of Men in Gender Agenda Setting: Conceptual and Policy Issues'. *Feminist Review*, 78 (2004), 3–21.

Espeland, W. N. and M. L. Stevens. 'Commensuration as a Social Process'. *Annual Review of Sociology*, 24 (1998), 313–43.

Fagan, E. D. 'Recent and Contemporary Theories of Progressive Taxation'. *Journal of Political Economy*, 46(4) (1938), 457–98.

Fahey, T. 'The Family Economy in the Development of Welfare Regimes: A Case Study'. *European Sociological Review*, 18(1) (2002), 51–64.

Fallan, L. 'Gender, Exposure to Tax Knowledge, and Attitudes Towards Taxation; An Experimental Approach'. *Journal of Business Ethics*, 18(2) (1999), 173–84.

Farmer, P. and R. Lyal. *EC Tax Law* (New York, NY: Oxford University Press, 1994).

Fedeli, S. and F. Forte. 'Joint Income-tax and VAT-chain Evasion'. *European Journal of Political Economy*, 15(3) (1999), 391–415.

Feenberg, D. R. *The Tax Treatment of Married Couples and the 1981 Tax Law*. Working Paper No. 872 (Cambridge, MA, USA: National Bureau of Economic Research, 1983) (at: www.nber.org/papers/w0872.pdf).

Fellows, M. L. 'Rocking the Tax Code: A Case Study of Employment-related Child-care Expenditures'. *Yale Journal of Law and Feminism*, 10 (1998), 307–95.

Fischl, R. 'A Woman's World'. *Buffalo Law Review*, 52 (2004), 659–78.

Fitch, H. G. 'Achieving Corporate Social Responsibility'. *Academy of Management Review*, 1(1) (1976), 38–46.

Folbre, N. 'Blowing the Whistle on Poverty Policy'. *Review of Social Economy*, 61(4) (2003), 479–85.

Fontana, M. 'Modelling the Effects of Trade on Women, at Work and at Home: Comparative Perspectives'. *Economie international*, 99(2004), 49–80.

Franke, J. 'Political Evolution of EMAS: Perspectives from the EU, National Governments and Industrial Groups'. *European Environment*, 5(6) (1995), 155–9.

Frankel, J. and NBOER. *How Well Do Foreign Exchange Markets Function: Might a Tobin Tax Help?* (Cambridge, MA: National Bureau of Economic Research, 1996).

Frankenberg, G. 'Stranger than Paradise: Identity and Politics in Comparative Law'. *Utah Law Review*, (1997), 259–74.

Fredman, S. and S. Spencer. 'Beyond Discrimination: It's Time for Enforceable Duties on Public Bodies to Promote Equality Outcomes'. *European Human Rights Law Review*, 6 (2006), 598–606.

Freedman, J. 'Why Taxing the Micro-business Is Not Simple – A Cautionary Tale from the "Old World"'. *Journal of the Australasian Tax Teachers Association* (2006) (at: http://search.austlii.edu.au/au/journals/JATTA/2006/5.html).

Freedman, J. 'Interpreting Tax Statutes: Tax Avoidance and the Intention of Parliament'. *Law Quarterly Review*, 123 (2007), 53–90.

Fried, B. *The Progressive Assault on Laissez Faire: Robert Hale and the First Law and Economics Movement* (Cambridge, MA: Harvard University Press, 1998).

Friedman, L. 'Is there a Modern Legal Culture?' *Ratio Juris*, 7(2) (1994), 117–31.

Friese, A., S. P. Link and S. Mayer. 'Taxation and Corporate Governance'. SSRN (2006) (at: http://ssrn.com/paper=877900).

Fuchs, V. R. 'Women's Quest for Economic Equality'. *Journal of Economic Perspectives*, 3(1) (1989), 25–41.

Furubotn, E. G. and R. Richter. *Institutions and Economic Theory: The Contribution of the New Institutional Economics* (Dearborn, MI: University of Michigan Press, 2005).

Gammie, M. 'Taxing Capital Gains –Thoughts from the UK'. *University of New South Wales Law Journal*, 23(2) (2000), 309.

Ganghof, S. 'Globalization, Tax Reform Ideals and Social Policy Financing'. *Global Social Policy*, 5(1) (2005), 77–95.

Garrett, G. and D. Mitchell. 'Globalization, Government Spending and Taxation in the OECD'. *European Journal of Political Research*, 39(2) (2001), 145–77.

Gelardi, A. M. G. 'The Influence of Tax Law Changes on the Timing of Marriages: A Two-country Analysis'. *National Tax Journal*, 49(1) (1996), 17–30.

Gemici, K. 'Karl Polanyi and the Antinomies of Embeddedness'. *Socio-Economic Review*, 6 (2008), 5–33.

George, S. 'Globalizing Rights?', in *Globalizing Rights: The Oxford Amnesty Lectures 1999* (Oxford University Press, 2003).

Giddens, A. 'Living in a Post-traditionalist Society', in U. Beck (ed.), *Reflexive Modernisation: Politics, Tradition, and Aesthetics in Modern Social Order* (Cambridge: Polity Press, 1995).

Giddens, A. 'Risk and Responsibility'. *Modern Law Review*, 62(1) (1999), 1–10.

Ginn, J., D. Street and S. Arber. *Women, Work, and Pensions* (Buckingham: Open University Press, 2001).

Ginsburg, N. *Divisions of Welfare: A Critical Introduction to Comparative Social Policy* (London: Sage, 1992).

Glass, J. and T. Fujimoto. 'Housework, Paid Work, and Depression among Husbands and Wives'. *Journal of Health and Social Behavior*, 35(2) (1994), 179–91.

Glennon, L. 'Strategizing for the Future through the Civil Partnership Act'. *Journal of Law and Society*, 33(2) (2006), 244–76.

Gornick, J. C. 'Gender Equality in the Labour Market: Women's Employment and Earnings'. *Gender and Welfare State Regimes*, (1999) 210–42.

Gottfried, H. 'Beyond Patriarchy? Theorising Gender and Class'. *Sociology*, 32(03) (2000), 451–68.

Graetz, M. J. 'Implementing a Progressive Consumption Tax'. *Harvard Law Review*, 92(8) (1979), 1575–1661.

Grbich, J. 'Taxation Narratives of Economic Gain: Reading Bodies Transgressively'. *Feminist Legal Studies*, 5 (1997) 131–68.

Green, D. and M. Griffith. 'Globalization and Its discontents'. *International Affairs (Royal Institute of International Affairs 1944–)* (2002), 49–68.

Greenwood, R. and C. R. Hinings. 'Understanding Radical Organizational Change: Bringing together the Old and the New Institutionalism'. *Academy of Management Review*, 21(4) (1996), 1022–54.

Greer Litton, F. and V. M. Murry. 'Gender and Families: Feminist Perspectives and Family Research'. *Journal of Marriage and the Family*, 62(4) (2000), 1160–72.

Grofman, B. 'Arend Lijphart and the New Institutionalism', in Markus M. L. Crepaz, Thomas A. Koelble and David Wilsford (eds.), *Democracy and Institutions:*

The Life Work of Arend Lijphart (Ann Arbor, MI: University of Michigan Press, 2000).

Grofman, B. and D. Wittman. *The Federalist Papers and the New Institutionalism* (New York, NY: Agathon Press, 1989).

Grosser, K. and J. Moon. 'Gender Mainstreaming and Corporate Social Responsibility: Reporting Workplace Issues'. *Journal of Business Ethics*, 62(4) (2005), 327–40.

Group, C. P. A. *Welfare Benefits and Tax Credits Handbook*, 9th edn (London: Child Poverty Action Group, 2007/2008).

Gunnarsson, Å., M. Davies and E. M. Svensson. *Exploiting the Limits of Law: Swedish Feminism and the Challenge to Pessimism* (Aldershot: Ashgate, 2007).

Hakim, C. 'Five Feminist Myths about Women's Employment'. *British Journal of Sociology*, 46(3) (1995), 429–55.

Hall, P. A. and R. C. R. Taylor. 'Political Science and the Three New Institutionalisms'. *Political Studies*, 44(5) (1996), 936–57.

Hall, P. A. and R. C. R. Taylor. 'Political Science and the Three New Institutionalisms', in Karol Soltan *et al.* (eds.), *Institutions and Social Order* (Dearborn, MI: University of Michigan Press, 1998).

Harberger, A. 'The Incidence of the Corporation Income Tax'. *Journal of Political Economy*, 70(3) (1962), 215–40.

Harbury, C. D. and D. Hitchens. 'Women, Wealth and Inheritance'. *Economic Journal*, 87(345) (1977), 124–31.

Harris, A. P. 'Race and Essentialism in Feminist Legal Theory'. *Stanford Law Review*, 42(3) (1990), 581–616.

Harris, P. *Income Tax in Common Law Jurisdictions: From the Origins to 1820.* (Cambridge University Press, 2006).

Hart, H. L. A. *The Ascription of Responsibility and Rights* (London: Harrison & Sons Ltd, 1948).

Hart, H. L. A. 'Positivism and the Separation of Law and Morals'. *Harvard Law Review*, 71 (1957), 593–629.

Hart, H. L. A. *The Concept of Law*, 2nd edn (Oxford University Press, 1994).

Hartmann, H. I. 'The Family as the Locus of Gender, Class, and Political Struggle: The Example of Housework'. *Signs*, 6(3) (1981), 366–94.

Haslanger, S. 'Feminism in Metaphysics: Negotiating the Natural', in M. Fricker and J. Hornsby (eds.), *The Cambridge Companion to Feminism in Philosophy* (Cambridge University Press, 2000).

Hasseldine, J. and P. A. Hite. 'Framing, Gender and Tax Compliance'. *Journal of Economic Psychology*, 24(4) (2003), 517–33.

Hausman, J. and P. Ruud. 'Family Labor Supply with Taxes'. *American Economic Review*, 74(2) (1984), 242–8.

Hennessy, R. *Materialist Feminism and the Politics of Discourse* (New York, NY: Routledge, 1993).

Hennessy, R. and C. Ingraham. *Materialist Feminism: A Reader in Class, Difference, and Women's Lives* (London: Routledge, 1997).

Herz, M. 'Judicial Textualism Meets Congressional Micromanagement: A Potential Collision in Clean Air Act Interpretation'. *Harvard Environmental Law Review*, 16 (1992), 175–82.

Hewitson, G. J. *Feminist Economics: Interrogating the Masculinity of Rational Economic Man* (Cheltenham: Edward Elgar, 1999).

Himmelweit, S. 'The Experience of the UK Women's Budget Group'. Contribution to International Workshop on Gender Auditing of Government Budgets (2000) (at: www.e-quality.nl/assets/e-quality/publicaties/2004/presentatiesGBA/slides%20for%20FENN_Susan%20Himmelweit.pdf).

Himmelweit, S. 'Making Visible the Hidden Economy: The Case for Gender-impact Analysis of Economic Policy'. *Feminist Economics*, 8(1) (2002), 49–70.

Hira, A. and R. Hira. 'The New Institutionalism Contradictory Notions of Change'. *American Journal of Economics and Sociology*, 59(2) (2000), 267–82.

Hirsch, P. M. 'Sociology without Social Structure: Neoinstitutional Theory Meets Brave New World'. *American Journal of Sociology*, 102(6) (1997), 1702–23.

Hochschild, A. and A. Machung. *The Second Shift: Working Parents and the Revolution at Home* (New York, NY: Viking, 1989).

Holcombe, R. G. 'Tax Policy from Public Choice Perspective'. *National Tax Journal*, 51(2) (1999), 359–71.

Hollingsworth, J. R. and R. Boyer. *Contemporary Capitalism: The Embeddedness of Institutions* (Cambridge University Press, 1997).

Hollingsworth, K., F. White and I. Harden. 'Audit, Accountability and Independence: The Role of the Audit Commission'. *Legal Studies*, 18(1) (1998), 78–99.

Hood, C. 'Privatizing UK Tax Law Enforcement?' *Public Administration*, 64(3) (1986), 319–33.

Hovenkamp, H. 'First Great Law and Economics Movement'. *Stanford Law Review*, 42 (1990), 993–1058.

Humphreys, S. C. 'History, Economics, and Anthropology: The Work of Karl Polanyi'. *History and Theory*, 8(2) (1969), 165–212.

Hunt, J. C., C. D. DeLorme, Jr. and R. C. Hill. 'Taxation and the Wife's Use of Time'. *Industrial and Labor Relations Review*, 34(3) (1981), 426–32.

Hurley, S. L. 'The Unit of Taxation Under an Ideal Progressive Income Tax'. *Oxford Journal of Legal Studies*, 4(2) (2002), 157–97.

Hurley, S. L. 'Replies'. *Philosophy and Phenomenological Research*, 72(2) (2006), 447–65.

Infanti, A. C. 'The Internal Revenue Code as Sodomy Statute'. *Santa Clara Law Review*, 44 (2004), 763–804.

Infanti, A. C. 'A Tax Crit Identity Crisis? Or Tax Expenditure Analysis, Deconstruction, and the Rethinking of a Collective Identity'. *Whittier Law Review*, 26 (2005), 707–821.

Infanti, A. C. and B. J. Crawford. *Critical Tax Theory – An Introduction*. (Cambridge University Press, 2009).

Infanti, A. C. and B. Crawford. 'Critical Tax Theory: An Introduction'. University of Pittsburgh Legal Studies Research Paper No. 2009–04690690 (2009) (at: http://papers.ssrn.com/sol3/papers.cfm?abstract_id=1333799).

Jackson, S. 'Why a Materialist Feminism Is (Still) Possible – and Necessary'. *Women's Studies International Forum*, 24(3–4) (2001), 283–93.

James, S. and I. Wallschutzky. 'Tax Law Improvement In Australia and the UK: The Need for a Strategy for Simplification'. *Fiscal Studies*, 18(4) (1997), 445–60.

Johnson, R. 'Law and the Leaky Woman: The Saloon, the Liquor Licence, and Narratives of Containment'. *Continuum: Journal of Media and Cultural Studies*, 19(2) (2005), 181–99.

Jones, C. C. 'Split Income and Separate Spheres: Tax Law and Gender Roles in the 1940s'. *Law and History Review*, 6(2) (1988), 259–310.

Jordan, A. and A. Lenschow. '"Greening" the European Union: What Can Be Learned from the "Leaders" of EU Environmental Policy?' *European Environment*, 10(3) (2000), 109–20.

Kahn, V. 'Rhetoric and the Law'. *Diacritics*, 19(2) (1989), 21–34.

Kahne, H. and A. I. Kohen. 'Economic Perspectives on the Roles of Women in the American Economy'. *Journal of Economic Literature*, 13(4) (1975), 1249–92.

Kantowicz, E. R. 'The Limits of Incrementalism: Carter's Efforts at Tax Reform'. *Journal of Policy Analysis and Management*, 4(2) (1985), 217–33.

Kaplow, L. 'How Tax Complexity and Enforcement Affect the Equity and Efficiency of the Income Tax', in J. Slemrod (ed.), *Tax Policy in the Real World* (Cambridge University Press, 1999).

Kaplow, L. and S. Shavell. 'Why the Legal System Is Less Efficient than the Income Tax in Redistributing Income'. *Journal of Legal Studies*, 23 (1994), 667–81.

Karran, T. 'The Determinants of Taxation in Britain: An Empirical Test'. *Journal of Public Policy*, 5(3) (1985), 365–86.

Kaye, T. A. 'Sheltering Social Policy in The Tax Code: The Low-Income Housing Credit'. *Villanova Law Review*, 38 (1993), 871–931.

Kaye, T. A. 'Show Me the Money: Congressional Limitations on State Tax Sovereignty'. *Harvard Journal on Legislation*, 35 (1998), 149–88.

Kendall, G. and G. Wickham. *Understanding Culture: Cultural Studies, Order, Ordering* (London: Sage, 2001).

Kennedy, D. 'New Approaches to Comparative Law: Comparativism and International Governance'. *Utah Law Review*, (1997), 545–637.

Kerridge, R. '*Jones* v. *Garnett* (*Arctic Systems*): Another Way of Getting to the Same Result'. *British Tax Review*, 5 (2007), 591–6.

Kershnar, S. 'For discrimination against women'. *Law and Philosophy*, 26(6) (2007), 589–625.

Kingson, C. I. 'The Coherence of International Taxation'. *Columbia Law Review*, (1981), 1151–1229.

Knauer, N. 'Heteronormativity and Federal Tax Policy'. *West Virginia Law Review*, 101 (1998), 129–234.

Kordana, K. A. and D. H. Tabachnik. 'Tax and the Philosopher's Stone'. *Virginia Law Review*, 89(3) (2003), 647–78.

Kornhauser, M. E. 'The Rhetoric of the Anti-Progressive Income Tax Movement: A Typical Male Reaction'. *Michigan Law Review*, 86(3) (1987), 465–523.

Kornhauser, M. E. 'A Taxing Woman: The Relationship of Feminist Scholarship to Tax'. *Southern California Review of Law and Women's Studies*, 6 (1996–7), 301–22.

Krause, K. 'Tax Complexity: Problem or Opportunity?' *Public Finance Review*, 28(5) (2000), 395–414.

Kudrle, R. T. 'The OECD's Harmful Tax Competition Initiative and the Tax Havens: From Bombshell to Damp Squib'. *Global Economy Journal*, 8(1) (2008), 1–23.

Kumar, K. 'Sociology and the Englishness of English Social Theory'. *Sociological Theory*, 19(1) (2001), 41–64.

Lahey, K. A. *Are We 'Persons' Yet?: Law and Sexuality in Canada* (University of Toronto Press, 1999).

Lahey, K. A. *The Benefit/Penalty Unit in Income Tax Policy Diversity and Reform* (Law Commission of Canada, 2000).

LaLumia, S. 'The Effects of Joint Taxation of Married Couples on Labor Supply and Non-wage Income'. *Journal of Public Economics*, 92(7) (July 2008), 1698–1719.

Lamanna, M. *Emile Durkheim on the Family* (London: Sage, 2002).

Land, H. 'The Family Wage', *Feminist Review*, 6 (1980), 55–77 (at: http://staging-www.palgrave-journals.com/fr/journal/v6/n1/pdf/fr198019a.pdf).

Land, H. 'Spheres of Care in the UK: Separate and Unequal'. *Critical Social Policy*, 22(1) (2002), 13–32.

Lazar, L. 'Finance Act 1965: The Capital Gains Tax'. *Modern Law Review*, 29(2) (1966), 181–4.

Lazar, L. 'Finance Act 1965: The Corporation Tax'. *Modern Law Review*, 29(1) (1966), 50–3.

Leadbetter, H. 'Gender Budgeting' (at: www.dfid.gov.uk/aboutdfid/organisation/pfma/pfma-gender-budget.pdf).

Lee, N. 'The New Tax Credits'. *Journal of Social Security Law*, 10(1) (2003), 7–52.

Lee, N. 'The Effect of the Human Rights Act 1998 on Taxation Policy and Administration'. *eJournal of Tax Research*, 2(2) (2004), 155–82.

Lee, O. 'Social Theory Across Disciplinary Boundaries: Cultural Studies and Sociology'. *Sociological Forum*, 14(4) (1999), 547–81.

Le Grand, J. 'Implementing Stakeholder Grants: The British Case', in Bruce Ackerman, *et al.* (eds.), *Redesigning Distribution: Basic Income and Stakeholder Grants as Alternative Cornerstones for a More Egalitarian Capitalism* (Making Social Policy Work: Essays in Honour of Howard Glennerster) (London: Verso, 2006) (at: www.ssc.wisc.edu/~wright/Redesigning%20Distribution%20v1.pdf#page=100).

Lewis, J. 'Gender and the Development of Welfare Regimes'. *Journal of European Social Policy*, 2(3) (1992), 159–73.

Lewis, J. 'The "Problem" of Lone Motherhood in Comparative Perspective', in J. Clasen (ed.), *Comparative Social Policy: Concepts, Theories, and Methods* (London: Blackwell Publishing, 1999).

Lewis, J. 'Gender and Welfare Regimes: Further Thoughts'. *Social Politics: International Studies in Gender, State and Society* 4(2) (2002), 160–77.

Lewis, J. 'Gender and Welfare State Change'. *European Societies*, 4(4) (2002), 331–57.

Lie, J. 'Embedding Polanyi's Market Society'. *Sociological Perspectives*, 34(2) (1991), 219–35.

Liebert, U. 'Europeanising Gender Mainstreaming: Constraints and Opportunities in the Multilevel Euro-polity'. *Feminist Legal Studies*, 10(3) (2002), 241–56.

Lippe, T. Van Der and L. van Dijk. 'Comparative Research on Women's Employment'. *Annual Review of Sociology*, 28(1) (2002), 221–41.

Lister, R. 'Future Insecure: Women and Income Maintenance under a Third Tory Term'. *Feminist Review*, (27) (1987), 9–16.

Littlewood, M. 'Tax Competition: Harmful To Whom'. *Michigan Journal of International Law*, 26 (2004), 411–87.

Livingston, M. A. 'Radical Scholars, Conservative Field: Putting Critical Tax Scholarship in Perspective'. *North Carolina Law Review*, 76 (1997), 1791.

Livingston, M. A. 'Reinventing Tax Scholarship: Lawyers Economists and the Role of the Legal Academy'. *Cornell Law Review*, 83 (1997), 365.

Livingston, M. A. 'Blum and Kalven at 50: Progressive Taxation, "Globalization", and the New Millennium'. *Florida Tax Review*, 4 (2000), 731–68.

Lloyd, G. *The Man of Reason: Male and Female in Western Philosophy* (London: Routledge, 1993).

Lombardo, E. 'Integrating or Setting the Agenda? Gender Mainstreaming in the European Constitution-Making Process'. *Social Politics*, 12(3) (2005), 412–32.

Lopez, I. F. H. 'Institutional Racism: Judicial Conduct and a New Theory of Racial Discrimination'. *Yale Law Journal*, 109(8) (2000), 1717–1884.

LoPucki, L. 'The Systems Approach to Law'. *Cornell Law Review*, 82 (1997), 479–521.

Loutzenheiser, G. '*Jones* v. *Garnett*: High Court Gives Taxpayer the Cold Shoulder'. *British Tax Review*, 4 (2005), 401–11.

Loutzenheiser, G. 'Income Splitting and Settlements: Further Observations on *Jones* v. *Garnett*'. *British Tax Review*, 6 (2007), 693–716.

Lovenduski, J. 'Women and Politics: Minority Representation or Critical Mass?' *Parliamentary Affairs*, 54(4) (2001), 743–58.

Lucia, C. 'Women on Trial: The Female Lawyer in the Hollywood Courtroom', in M. Fineman and M. T. McCluskey (eds.), *Feminism, Media, and the Law* (Oxford University Press, 1997).

Luenberger, D. G. *Introduction to Dynamic Systems: Theory, Models, and Applications* (New York, NY: Wiley, 1979).

Luhmann, N. 'Law as a Social System'. *Northwestern University Law Review*, 83 (1988), 136–50.

McBarnet, D. 'After Enron Will "Whiter than White Collar Crime" Still Wash?' *British Journal of Criminology*, 46(6) (2006), 1091–1109.

McBarnet, D. *Corporate Social Responsibility Beyond Law, Through Law, for Law.* SSRN (2009) (at: http://ssrn.com/paper=1369305).

McBarnet, D. and C. Whelan. 'The Elusive Spirit of the Law: Formalism and the Struggle for Legal Control'. *Modern Law Review*, 54 (1991), 848–73.

McCaffery, E. J. 'Last Words (?): Towards a Feminization of Wealth'. *Southern California Review of Law and Women's Studies* (1996–7), 605–10.

McCaffery, E. J. *Taxing Women* (University of Chicago Press, 1997).

McCaffery, E. J. *Women and Taxes.* NCPA Policy Report No. 250. (Dallas, TX: National Center for Policy Analysis, 2002) (at: www.ncpa.org/pub/st/st250/st250.pdf).

McCaffery, E. J. 'Where's the Sex in Fiscal Sociology? Taxation and Gender in Comparative Perspective'. University of Southern California Law and Economics Working Paper Series (2008) (at: http://law.bepress.com/cgi/viewcontent.cgi?article=1072&context=usclwps).

McCrudden, C. 'Mainstreaming Equality in the Governance of Northern Ireland'. *Fordham International Law Journal*, 22 (1998), 1696–1775.

MacDonald, M. 'Gender and Social Security Policy: Pitfalls and Possibilities'. *Feminist Economics*, 4(1) (1998), 1–25.

McGlynn, C. 'Reclaiming a feminist vision: the reconciliation of paid work and family life in European Union law and policy'. *Columbia Journal of European Law*, 7 (2001), 241–72.

McGraw, L. A., A. M. Zvonkovic and A. J. Walker. 'Studying Postmodern Families: A Feminist Analysis of Ethical Tensions in Work and Family Research'. *Journal of Marriage and the Family*, 62(1) (2000), 68–77.

McIntosh, M. 'Feminism and Social Policy', in Christopher Pierson and Francis G. Castles (eds.), *The Welfare State Reader* (Cambridge: Polity Press, 2006).

MacKinnon, C. A. 'Feminism, Marxism, Method, and the State: An Agenda for Theory'. *Signs*, 7(3) (1982), 515–44.

March, J. G. and J. P. Olsen. 'The New Institutionalism: Organizational Factors in Political Life'. *American Political Science Review*, 78(3) (1984), 734–49.

Margolis, J. D. and J. P. Walsh. 'Misery Loves Companies: Rethinking Social Initiatives by Business'. *Administrative Science Quarterly*, 48(2) (2003), 268–305.

Marks Rubin, M. and J. R. Bartle. 'Integrating Gender into Government Budgets: A New Perspective'. *Public Administration Review*, 65(3) (2005), 259–72.

Marsh, D. B. 'The Taxation of Imputed Income'. *Political Science Quarterly*, 58(4) (1943), 514–36.

Mason, R. and L. D. Calvin. 'A Study of Admitted Income Tax Evasion'. *Law and Society Review*, 13(1) (1978), 73–89.

Mattei, U. 'Some Realism About Comparativism: Comparative Law Teaching in the Hegemonic Jurisdiction'. *American Journal of Comparative Law*, 50 (2002), 87–99.

Mayntz, R. Mayntz, 'New Challenges to Governance Theory', in Henrik Paul Bang (ed.), Governance as Social and Political Communication (Manchester University Press, 2009).

Mazey, S. 'The European Union and Women's Rights', in D. Hine and H. Kassim (eds.), *Beyond the Market: The EU and National Social Policy* (London: Routledge, 1998).

Meehan, E. and E. Collins. 'Women, the European Union and Britain'. *Parliamentary Affairs*, 49(1) (2001), 221–34.

Menell, P. and R. Stewart. *Environmental Law and Policy* (Boston, MA: Little, Brown, 1994).

Menkel-Meadow, C. 'Exploring a Research Agenda of the Feminization of the Legal Profession: Theories of Gender and Social Change'. *Law and Social Inquiry*, 14(2) (1989), 289–319.

Merton, R. 'In Honor of Nobel Laureate, Franco Modigliani'. *Journal of Economic Perspectives* (1987), 145–55.

Mieszkowski, P. 'Tax Incidence Theory: The Effects of Taxes on the Distribution of Income'. *Journal of Economic Literature* (1969), 1103–24.

Millar, J. 'From Wage Replacement to Wage Supplementation: Benefits and Tax Credits', in J. Millar (ed.), *Understanding Social Security* (Bristol: Policy Press, 2003).

Mintz, J. 'The Corporation Tax: A Survey'. *Fiscal Studies*, 16(4) (1995), 23–68.

Monroe, H. *Intolerable Inquisition?: Reflections on the Law of Tax* (London: Stevens, published under the auspices of Hamlyn Trust, 1981).

Montanari, I. 'From Family Wage to Marriage Subsidy and Child Benefits: Controversy and Consensus in the Development of Family Support'. *Journal of European Social Policy*, 10(4) (2000), 307–33.

Moran, B. 'Setting an Agenda for the Study of Tax and Black Culture'. *University of Arkansas at Little Rock Law Review*, 21 (1999), 779–94.

Morck, R. 'Why Some Double Taxation Might Make Sense: The Special Case of Inter-corporate Dividends'. NBER Working Paper (2003).

Morck, R. 'How to Eliminate Pyramidal Business Groups – The Double Taxation of Inter-corporate Dividends and Other Incisive Uses of Tax Policy'. NBER Working Paper (2004).

Morgan, K. J. 'The Politics of Mothers' Employment: France in Comparative Perspective'. *World Politics*, 55(2) (2003), 259–89.

Mumford, A. 'Marketing Working Mothers: Contextualizing Earned Income Tax Credits within Feminist Cultural Theory'. *Journal of Social Welfare and Family Law*, 23(4) (2001), 411–26.

Mumford, A. 'Inheritance in Socio-political Context: The Case for Reviving the Sociological Discourse of Inheritance Tax Law'. *Journal of Law and Society*, 34(4) (2007), 567–93.

Mumford, A. 'Towards a Fiscal Sociology of Tax Credits and the Fathers' Rights Movement', *Social and Legal Studies*, 17(2) (2008), 217–35.

Murphy, L. and T. Nagel. *The Myth of Ownership* (New York, NY: Oxford University Press, 2002).

Musgrave, R. 'Theories of Fiscal Crises: An Essay in Fiscal Sociology', in H. J. Aaron and M. J. Boskins (eds.), *The Economics of Taxation* (Washington, DC: Brookings Institution, 1980), pp. 316–90.

Nagel, T. 'Rawls on Justice'. *Philosophical Review* (1973), 220–34.

Naumann, I. K. 'Childcare and Feminism in West Germany and Sweden in the 1960s and 1970s'. *Journal of European Social Policy*, 15(1) (2005), 47–64.

Nee, V. 'Sources of the New Institutionalism', in M. C. Brinton and V. Nee (eds.), *The New Institutionalism in Sociology* (New York, NY: Russell Sage Foundation, 1998).

Neff, D. K. 'Married Women's Labor Supply and the Marriage Penalty'. *Public Finance Review*, 18(4) (1990), 420–32.

Nelken, D. 'Disclosing/Invoking Legal Culture: An Introduction'. *Social and Legal Studies*, 4(4) (1995), 435–52.

Nelken, D. 'Comparing Legal Cultures', in A. Sarat (ed.), *The Blackwell Companion to Law and Society* (Oxford: Blackwell, 2004).

Nelson, J. A. 'Tax Reform and Feminist Theory in the United States: Incorporating Human Connection'. *Journal of Economic Studies*, 18(5–6) (1991), 11–29.

Nelson, J. A. *Feminism, Objectivity, and Economics* (London: Routledge, 1996).

Newth, J. T. 'Divorce and Separation'. *Simon's Tax Briefing* (12 June 2006), 5–6.

Ngugi, J. M. 'Forgetting Lochner in the Journey from Plan to Market: The Framing Effect of the Market Rhetoric in Market-oriented Reforms', *Buffalo Law Review*, 56 (2008), 1–97.

Nicholson, L. 'Feminism and Marx: Integrating Kinship with the Economic'. *Praxis International*, 4 (1985), 367–80 (at: www.ceeol.com).

Nolan, B. and T. M. Smeeding. 'Ireland's Income Distribution in Comparative Perspective'. Paper Prepared for the 28th General Conference of the International Association for Research in Income and Wealth. Cork, Ireland: Maxwell

School of Citizenship and Public Affairs, Syracuse University (2004) (at: www.iariw.org/papers/2004/smeeding.pdf).

Note. 'Income Tax Liability of Married Women'. *Modern Law Review*, 10(2) (1947), 198–203.

Note. 'California Prohibits Gender-based Pricing'. *Harvard Law Review*, 109(7) (1996), 1839–44.

O'Connor, J. S., A. S. Orloff and S. Shaver. *States, Markets, Families: Gender, Liberalism and Social Policy in Australia, Canada, Great Britain and the United States* (Cambridge University Press, 1999).

OECD. 'Evaluation of DFID's Policy and Practice in Support of Gender Equality and Women's Empowerment', August 2006 (at: www.oecd.org/dataoecd/52/38/37390142.pdf).

OECD. 'European Community (2007), DAC Peer Review: Main Findings and Recommendations', 2007) (at: www.oecd.org/document/0/0,3343,en_2649_34603_38897408_1_1_1_1,00.html).

Okin, S. 'Justice and Gender: An Unfinished Debate'. *Fordham Law Review*, 72 (2003), 1537–67.

Oldman, O. and R. Temple. 'Comparative Analysis of the Taxation of Married Persons'. *Stanford Law Review*, 12(3) (1960), 585–605.

O'Riordan, T. and A. Jordan. 'Institutions, Climate Change and Cultural Theory: Towards a Common Analytical Framework'. *Global Environmental Change*, 9(2) (1999), 81–93.

Orloff, A. 'Gender in the Welfare State'. *Annual Review of Sociology*, 22(1) (1996), 51–78.

Orviska, M. and J. Hudson. 'Tax Evasion, Civic Duty and the Law Abiding Citizen'. *European Journal of Political Economy*, 19(1) (2003), 83–102.

Pahl, J. 'Personal Taxation, Social Security and Financial Arrangements within Marriage'. *Journal of Law and Society*, 13(2) (1986), 241–50.

Pascall, G. *Social Policy: A Feminist Analysis* (London: Tavistock Publications, 1986).

Pearson, R. 'Feminist Responses to Economic Globalisation: Some Examples of Past and Future Practice'. *Gender and Development*, 11(1) (2003), 25–34.

Pemberton, H. 'Taxation and Labour's Modernisation Programme'. *Contemporary British History*, 20(3) (2006), 423–40.

Peters, B. G. *Institutional Theory in Political Science: The 'New Institutionalism'* (London: Continuum, 2005).

Pettit, B. and J. Hook. 'The Structure of Women's Employment in Comparative Perspective'. *Social Forces*, 84(2) (2005), 779–801.

Philipps, L. 'Taxing the Market Citizen: Fiscal Policy and Inequality in an Age of Privatization'. *Law and Contemporary Problems*, 63(4) (2000), 111–132.

Philipps, L. 'Tax Law and Social Reproduction: The Gender of Fiscal Policy in an Age of Privatization', in Brenda Cossman and Judy Fudge (eds.), *Privatization, Law, and the Challenge to Feminism* (University of Toronto Press, 2002).

Philipps, L. and M. Condon. 'Transnational Market Governance and Economic Citizenship: New Frontiers for Feminist Legal Theory'. *Thomas Jefferson Law Review* 28 (2005), 105–50.

Phillips, M. 'Reappraising the Real Entity Theory of the Corporation'. *Florida State University Law Review*, 21 (1994), 1061–1123.

Picciotto, S. *International Business Taxation* (London: Weidenfeld & Nicolson, 1992).

Picciotto, S. 'Constructing Compliance: Game Playing, Tax Law, and the Regulatory State'. *Law and Policy*, 29(1) (2007), 11–30.

Pierson, P. 'The New Politics of the Welfare State'. *World Politics*, 48 (1996), 143–79.

Pigou, A. 'The Report of the Royal Commission on the British Income Tax'. *Quarterly Journal of Economics* (1920), 607–25.

Plantenga, J. and J. Hansen. 'Assessing Equal Opportunities in the European Union'. *International Labour Review*, 138(4) (1999), 351–80.

Polanyi, K. *The Great Transformation: The Political and Economic Origins of Our Time*. (London: Beacon Press, 2001).

Polanyi, K. and H. W. Pearson. *The Livelihood of Man* (New York, NY: Academic Press, 1977).

Polikoff, N. D. 'Ending Marriage as We Know It'. *Hofstra Law Review*, 32(1) (2003), 201–32.

Pollack, M. A. 'The New Institutionalism and EC Governance: The Promise and Limits of Institutional Analysis'. *Governance*, 9(4) (1996), 429–58.

Pollack, S. D. 'Tax Complexity, Reform, and the Illusions of Tax Simplification'. *George Mason Independent Law Review*, 2 (1994), 319–58.

Power, M. 'Auditing and Environmental Expertise: Between Protest and Professionalisation'. *Accounting, Auditing and Accountability Journal*, 4(3) (1991), 30–42.

Power, M. *The Audit Society: Rituals of Verification* (Oxford University Press, 1997).

Pudrovska, T. and M. M. Ferree. 'Global Activism in "Virtual Space": The European Women's Lobby in the Network of Transnational Women's NGOs on the Web'. *Social Politics*, 11(1) (2004), 117–43.

Radaelli, C. 'Harmful Tax Competition in the EU: Policy Narratives and Advocacy Coalitions'. *Journal of Common Market Studies*, 37(4) (1999), 661–82.

Raes, F. 'What Can We Expect from Gender Sensitive Budgets? Strategies in Brazil and in Chile in a Comparative Perspective'. Network Women in Development Europe (WIDE) (2006) (at: www.eurosur.org/wide/home.htm).

Rai, S. *Mainstreaming Gender, Democratizing The State?: Institutional Mechanisms for the Advancement of Women* (Manchester University Press, 2003).

Rake, K. 'Gender Budgets. The Experience of the UK's Women's Budget Group', in paper prepared for conference Gender Balance – Equal Finance (2002).

Rawlings, G. 'Taxes and Transnational Treaties: Responsive Regulation and the Reassertion of Offshore Sovereignty'. *Law and Policy*, 29(1) (2007), 51–66.

Rawls, J. *A Theory of Justice* (orig. pub. Cambridge, MA: Harvard University Press, 1971) (Oxford University Press, 1999).

Redston, A. 'Small Business in the Eye of the Storm'. *British Tax Review*, 5 (2004), 566–81.

Redston, A. 'Income Sharing: The Nelsonian Option'. *British Tax Review*, 6 (2007), 680–6.

Reece, H. 'The Autonomy Myth: A Theory of Dependency', *Child and Family Law Quarterly*, 20(1) (2008), 109–10.

Rees, T. 'Reflections on the Uneven Development of Gender Mainstreaming in Europe'. *International Feminist Journal of Politics*, 7(4) (2005), 555–74.

Rice, R. S. 'Tax Reform and Tax Incentives'. *Law and Contemporary Problems*, 34(4) (1969), 782–804.

Riley, N. E. 'Challenging Demography: Contributions from Feminist Theory'. *Sociological Forum*, 14(3) (1999), 369–97.

Ring, D. M. 'One Nation among Many: Policy Implications of Cross-border Tax Arbitrage'. *Boston College Law Review*, 44 (2002), 79–175.

Rittich, K. 'Feminization and Contingency: Regulating the Stakes of Work for Women', in J . Conaghan, R. M. Fischl and K. Klare (eds.), *Labour Law in an Era of Globalization: Transformative Practices and Possibilities* (Oxford University Press, 2002).

Roberts, R. 'Determinants of corporate social responsibility disclosure: an application of stakeholder theory'. *Accounting, Organizations and Society*, 17(6) (1992), 595–612.

Rose, N. 'Beyond the Public/Private Division: Law, Power and the Family'. *Journal of Law and Society* (1987), 61–76.

Rosenfeld, R. A. and G. E. Birkelund. 'Women's Part-time Work: A Cross-national Comparison'. *European Sociological Review*, 11(2) (2002), 111–34.

Rubery, J. 'Gender Mainstreaming and Gender Equality in the EU: The Impact of the EU Employment Strategy'. *Industrial Relations Journal*, 33(5) (2002), 500–22.

Rubery, J., D. Grimshaw, C. Fagan, H. Figueiredo and M. Smith. 'Gender Equality Still on the European Agenda – But for How Long?' *Industrial Relations Journal*, 34(5) (2003), 477–97.

Rudd, J. 'J. B. Ruhl's Law-and-Society System: Burying Norms and Democracy under Complexity Theory's Foundation'. *William and Mary Environmental Law and Policy Review*, 29 (2004), 551–632.

Ruhl, J. B. 'Complexity Theory as a Paradigm for the Dynamical Law-and-Society System: A Wake-Up Call for Legal Reductionism and the Modern Administrative State'. *Duke Law Journal*, 45 (1996), 849–927.

Ruhl, J. B. 'Fitness of Law: Using Complexity Theory to Describe the Evolution of Law and Society and Its Practical Meaning for Democracy'. *Vanderbilt Law Review*, 49 (1996), 1406.

Ruhl, J. B. 'Thinking of Environmental Law as a Complex Adaptive System: How to Clean Up the Environment by Making a Mess of Environmental Law'. *Houston Law Review*, 34 (1997), 933–1002.

Ruhl, J. B. 'Law's Complexity: A Primer'. *Georgia State University Law Review*, 24 (2008), 885–911.

Ruhl, J. B. and H. J. Ruhl, 'The Arrow of the Law in Modern Administrative States: Using Complexity Theory to Reveal the Diminishing Returns and Increasing Risks the Burgeoning of Law Poses to Society', *UC Davis Law Review*, 30 (1997), 405–82.

J. B. Ruhl and J. Salzman, 'Mozart and the Red Queen: The Problem of Regulatory Accretion in the Administrative State', *Georgetown Law Journal*, 91 (2002), 757–850.

Runyan, S. 'Women in the Neoliberal Frame', in Mary K. Meyer and Elisabeth Prügl (eds.), *Gender Politics in Global Governance* (Lanham, MD: Rowman & Littlefield, 1999).

Sainsbury, D. *Gender and Welfare State Regimes* (Oxford University Press, 1999).

Salinas, J. G. 'The OECD Tax Competition Initiative: A Critique of Its Merits in the Global Marketplace'. *Houston Journal of International Law*, 25(3) (2003), 531–61.

Sanders, R. *The Future of Financial Services in the Caribbean*. International Tax Competition: Globalisation and Fiscal Sovereignty, London: Commonwealth Secretariat, (2002) (at: www.itio.org/documents/Speech-RonaldSanders.pdf).

Sanrichio, C. W. 'Progressivity and Potential Income: Measuring the Effect of Changing Work Patterns on Income Tax Progressivity'. *Columbia Law Review*, 108 (2008), 1151–1609.

Sargent, L. *Women and Revolution: A Discussion of the Unhappy Marriage of Marxism and Feminism* (London: South End Press, 1981).

Savage, J. D. *Making the EMU: The Politics of Budgetary Surveillance and the Enforcement of Maastricht* (Oxford University Press, 2005).

Sawer, M. 'Women's Ministries: An Australian Perspective'. *Feminist Review*, (63) (1999), 91–4.

Schauer, F. *Playing by the Rules: A Philosophical Examination of Rule-based Decision-making in Law and in Life* (New York, NY: Oxford University Press, 1991).

Scholz, J. K. 'The Earned Income Tax Credit: Participation, Compliance, and Antipoverty'. *National Tax Journal*, 47(1) (1994), 63–87.

Schumpeter, J. A. 'English Economists and the State-managed Economy'. *Journal of Political Economy*, 57(5) (1949), 371–82.

Schumpeter, J. A. 'The March Into Socialism'. *American Economic Review*, 40(2) (1950), 446–56.

Schumpeter, J. A. *Capitalism, Socialism and Democracy* (London: Routledge, 1994).

Schwartz, A. and R. E. Scott. 'Contract Theory and the Limits of Contract Law'. *Yale Law Journal*, 113 (2003), 541–620.

Schwartz, T. P. 'Durkheim's Prediction about the Declining Importance of the Family and Inheritance: Evidence from the Wills of Providence, 1775–1985', *Sociological Quarterly* (1996), 503–19.

Seligman, E. R. A. 'The Theory of Progressive Taxation'. *Publications of the American Economic Association*, 8(1) (1893), 52–5.

Seligman, E. R. A. 'The Income Tax'. *Political Science Quarterly*, 9(4) (1894), 610–48.

Servet, J.-M. 'L'institution monétaire de la société selon Karl Polanyi'. *Revue économique*, 44(6) (1993), 1127–49.

Sharman, J. C. 'Norms, Coercion and Contracting in the Struggle against "Harmful" Tax Competition', *Australian Journal of International Affairs*, 60 (2006), 143–69.

Sharp, R. 'Budgeting for Equality: The Australian Experience'. *Feminist Economics*, 8(1) (2002), 25–47.

Shaw, J. 'Process and Constitutional Discourse in the European Union'. *Journal of Law and Society*, 27(1) (2000), 4–37.

Shaw, J. 'The European Union and Gender Mainstreaming: Constitutionally Embedded or Comprehensively Marginalised?' *Feminist Legal Studies*, 10(3–4) (2002), 213–26.

Shurtz, N. E. 'A Critical View of Traditional Tax Policy Theory: A Pragmatic Alternative'. *Villanova Law Review*, 31 (1986), 1665–1701.

Silver, B. A. 'Modernizing the Revenue Rule: The Enforcement of Foreign Tax Judgments'. *Georgia Journal of International and Comparative Law*, 22 (1992), 609–33.

Simester, A. P. and W. Chan. 'On Tax and Justice'. *Oxford Journal of Legal Studies*, 23(4) (2003), 711–26.

Simon, J. B. 'The Governance of the European Union: A New Institutionalist Approach'. *Journal of Public Policy*, 13(4) (1993), 351–80.

Slemrod, J. 'Which is the Simplest Tax System of Them All', in H. J. Aaron and W. G. Gale (eds.), *Economic Effects of Fundamental Tax Reform* (Washington, DC: Brookings Institution Press, 1996).

Smeeding, T. M. 'Poor People in Rich Nations: The United States in Comparative Perspective'. *Journal of Economic Perspectives*, 20(1) (2006), 69–90.

Smith, D. K. 'Superannuating the Second Sex: Law, Privatisation and Retirement Income'. *Modern Law Review*, 64(4) (2001), 519–42.

Sperber, I. 'Sperber's Fashions in Science'. *Social Epistemology*, 6(1) (1992), 91–105.

Squires, J. 'Equality and diversity: a new equality framework for Britain?' Unpublished paper presented at School of Public Policy, University College, London University, December (2003) (at: www.bath.ac.uk/esml/Library/pdf-files/squires.pdf).

Squires, J. and M. Wickham-Jones. 'New Labour, Gender Mainstreaming and the Women and Equality Unit'. *British Journal of Politics and International Relations*, 6(1) (2004), 81–98.

Staudt, N. C. 'Taxing Housework'. *Georgetown Law Journal*, 84 (1995), 1571–1645.

Staudt, N. C. 'The Political Economy of Taxation: A Critical Review of a Classic'. *Law and Society Review*, 30(3) (1996), 651–66.

Staveley, B. 'The Quest for the Allowable Loss: Reflections on Lord Hoffmann's Approach to Ramsay'. *British Tax Review*, 6 (2005), 609–19.

Steinmo, S. 'Political institutions and tax policy in the United States, Sweden, and Britain'. *World Politics: A Quarterly Journal of International Relations*, 41(4) (1989), 500–35.

Steinmo, S. 'Globalization and Taxation: Challenges to the Swedish Welfare State'. *Comparative Political Studies*, 35(7) (2002), 839–62.

Steinmo, S. 'The Evolution of Policy Ideas: Tax Policy in the 20th Century'. *British Journal of Politics and International Relations*, 5(2) (2003), 206–36.

Steinmo, S., K. Thelen and F. Longstreth. *Structuring Politics: Historical Institutionalism in Comparative Analysis* (Cambridge University Press, 1992).

Steinmo, S. and C. J. Tolbert. 'Do Institutions Really Matter?' *Comparative Political Studies*, 31(2) (1998), 165–88.

Stiglitz, J. E. 'The Contributions of the Economics of Information to Twentieth Century Economics'. *Quarterly Journal of Economics*, 115(4) (2000), 1441–78.

Stotsky, J. G. 'How Tax Systems Treat Men and Women Differently'. *Finance and Development* (1997) (at: www.worldbank.org/fandd/english/pdfs/0397/070397.pdf).

Stretton, T. *Women Waging Law in Elizabethan England* (Cambridge University Press, 1998).

Stychin, C. 'Not (Quite) a Horse and Carriage: The Civil Partnership Act 2004', *Feminist Legal Studies*, 14 (2006), 79–86.

Suchman, M. C. and L. B. Edelman. 'Legal Rational Myths: The New Institutionalism and the Law and Society Tradition'. *Law and Social Inquiry*, 21 (1996), 903–41.

Sundstrom, M. 'The Growth in Full-time Work among Swedish Women in the 1980s'. *Acta Sociologica*, 36(2) (1993), 139–50.

Swanson, D. L. 'Addressing a Theoretical Problem by Reorienting the Corporate Social Performance Model'. *Academy of Management Review*, 20(1) (1995), 43–64.

Taylor, V. and L. Rupp. 'Women's Culture and Lesbian Feminist Activism: A Reconsideration of Cultural Feminism'. *Signs*, 19(1) (1993), 32–61.

Teubner, G. 'Substantive and Reflexive Elements in Modern Law'. *Law and Society Review*, 17(2) (1983), 239–86.

Thelen, K. 'Historical Institutionalism in Comparative Politics'. *Annual Review of Political Science*, 2(1) (1999), 369–404.

Thompson, L. and A. Walker. 'Gender in Families: Women and Men in Marriage, Work, and Parenthood'. *Journal of Marriage and the Family* (1989), 845–71.

Thuronyi, V. 'International Tax Cooperation and a Multilateral Treaty'. *Brooklyn Journal of International Law*, 26 (2001), 1641–81.

Tiley, J. 'Aspects of Schedule A', in J. Tiley (ed.), *Studies in the History of Tax Law*, vol. 1 (Oxford: Hart Publishing, 2004), pp. 81–100.

Tolbert, P. S. and L. G. Zucker. 'The Institutionalization of Institutional Theory', in S. R. Clegg and C. Hardy (eds.), *Studying Organization: Theory and Method*, London: Sage, 1999.

Townsend, Jr., A. 'Global Schoolyard Bully: The Organisation for Economic Co-Operation and Development's Coercive Efforts to Control Tax Competition'. *Fordham International Law Journal*, 25 (2001), 215–58.

Trifiletti, R. 'Southern European Welfare Regimes and the Worsening Position of Women'. *Journal of European Social Policy*, 9(1) (1999), 49–64.

True, J. 'Mainstreaming Gender in Global Public Policy'. *International Feminist Journal of Politics*, 5(3) (2003), 368–96.

True, J. and M. Mintrom. 'Transnational Networks and Policy Diffusion: The Case of Gender Mainstreaming'. *International Studies Quarterly*, 45(1) (2001), 27–57.

Urry, J. 'The Complexity Turn'. *Theory, Culture and Society*, 22(5) (2005), 1–14.

Uy, M. 'Tax and Race: The Impact on Asian Americans'. *Asian American Law Journal*, 11 (2004), 7–143.

Valentine, S. and G. Fleischman. 'Ethical Reasoning in an Equitable Relief Innocent Spouse Context'. *Journal of Business Ethics*, 45(4) (2003), 325–39.

Vallentyne, P. 'Hurley on Justice and Responsibility'. *Philosophy and Phenomenological Research*, 72(2) (2006), 433–8.

Ventry, D. J., Jr. 'Saving Seaborn: Ownership as the Basis of Family Taxation'. (2009), SSRN eLibrary.

Verbeke, A. and C. Coeck. 'Environmental Taxation: A Green Stick or a Green Carrot for Corporate Social Performance?' *Managerial and Decision Economics*, 18(6) (1997), 507–16.

Villagomez, E. 'Gender Responsive Budgets: Issues, Good Practices and Policy Options', at the conference Regional Symposium on Mainstreaming Gender into Economic Policies (NNUU Comisión Económica para Europa, 2004) (at: www.infopolis.es/web/GenderBudgets/pdf/Gender_budgets_draft.pdf).

Vogel, J. 'European Welfare Regimes and the Transition to Adulthood: A Comparative and Longitudinal Perspective'. *Social Indicators Research*, 59(3) (2002), 275–99.

Vogel, L. *Woman Questions: Essays for a Materialist Feminism* (London: Routledge, 1995).

Waite, L. 'Does Marriage Matter?' *Demography* (1995), 483–507.

Walby, S. 'Gender Mainstreaming: Productive Tensions in Theory and Practice'. *Social Politics: International Studies in Gender, State and Society*, 12(3) (2005), 321–43.

Warskett, G., S. Winer and W. Hettich. 'The Complexity of Tax Structure in Competitive Political Systems'. *International Tax and Public Finance*, 5(2) (1998), 123–51.

Wartick, S. L. and P. L. Cochran. 'The Evolution of the Corporate Social Performance Model'. *The Academy of Management Review*, 10(4) (1985), 758–69.

Watson, S. *Playing the State: Australian Feminist Interventions* (Melbourne: Verso, 1990).

Wax, A. L. 'Bargaining in the Shadow of the Market: Is There a Future for Egalitarian Marriage?' *Virginia Law Review*, 84(4) (1998), 509–672.

Webb, M. 'Defining the Boundaries of Legitimate State Practice: Norms, Transnational Actors and the OECD's Project on Harmful Tax Competition 1'. *Review of International Political Economy*, 11(4) (2004), 787–827.

Weedon, C. *Feminist Practice and Poststructuralist Theory* (London: Blackwell, 1997).

Weisbach, D. A. 'Formalism in the Tax Law'. *University of Chicago Law Review*, 66 (1999), 860–86.

Weisbach, D. A. and J. Nussim. 'The Integration of Tax and Spending Programs'. *Yale Law Journal*, 113(5) (2004), 955–1028.

West, E. G. 'Adam Smith's Public Economics: A Re-Evaluation'. *Canadian Journal of Economics/Revue canadienne d'économique*, 10(1) (1977), 1–18.

Whalen, C. J., K. P. Schumpeter, K. W. Kapp, O. E. Williamson and D. C. North. 'Post-Keynesian Institutionalism and the Anxious Society: Assessing the Evolution and Impact of Alternative Institutional Structures', in Sandra S. Batie and Nicholas Mercuro (eds.), *Alternative Economic Structures: Evolution and Impact* (London: Routledge, 2008), pp. 273–99.

Wheelock, J., E. Oughton and S. Baines. (2003) 'Getting by with a Little Help from Your Family: Toward a Policy-relevant Model of the Household'. *Feminist Economics*, 9(1), 19–45.

Whittington, L. 'Taxes and the Family: The Impact of the Tax Exemption for Dependents on Marital Fertility'. *Demography* (1992), 215–26.

Wikeley, N. 'Child Trust Funds: Asset-based Welfare or a Recipe for Increased Inequality?' *Journal of Social Security Law*, 11(4) (2004) (at: http://eprints.soton.ac.uk/27919/).

Wikeley, N. 'Child Support, Dividend Income and the Bertie Wooster Escape Clause'. *Family Law*, 9 (2005), 707–11.

Wikeley, N. 'Child Support Reform – Throwing the Baby out with the Bathwater?' *Child and Family Law Quarterly*, 19(4) (2007), 434.

Wikeley, N. and L. Young. '*Smith* v. *Secretary of State for Work and Pensions*: Child Support, the Self-Employed and the Meaning of "Total Taxable Profits" – Total Confusion Reigns', *Child and Family Law Quarterly*, 17 (2005), 267–92.

Williams, D. F. 'Tax and Corporate Social Responsibility'. *Tax Journal*, 913 (10 December 2007), 10.

Williamson, R. 'Private Lives'. *Tax Journal*, 791 (2005), 17–18.

Williamson, R. 'Winners and Losers among Low-income Taxpayers'. *Tax Journal*, (879) (2007), 19–20.

Women, DFTAO and UN. 'Beijing Declaration and Platform for Action'. United Nations Division for the Advancement of Women (1995).

Woodman, F. 'The Charter and the Taxation of Women'. *Ottawa Law Review*, 22 (1990), 625–90.

Yngvesson, B. 'Inventing Law in Local Settings: Rethinking Popular Legal Culture'. *Yale Law Journal*, 98 (1988), 1689–1709.

Young, C. F. L. '(In) Visible Inequalities: Women, Tax and Poverty'. *Ottawa Law Review*, 27 (1995), 99–128.

Young, C. F. L. *Women, Tax and Social Programs: The Gendered Impact of Funding Social Programs through the Tax System*. Status of Women Canada (2000).

Zelenak, L. 'Feminism and Safe Subjects Like the Tax Code'. *California Review of Law and Women's Studies*, 6 (1996–7), 323–7.

Zey, M. and T. Swenson. 'Corporate Tax Laws, Corporate Restructuring, and Subsidiarization of Corporate Form, 1981–1995'. *Sociological Quarterly*, 39(4) (1998), 555–81.

INDEX

For EU product safety concerns, contact us at Calle de José Abascal, 56–1°, 28003 Madrid, Spain or eugpsr@cambridge.org.

www.ingramcontent.com/pod-product-compliance
Lightning Source LLC
LaVergne TN
LVHW011522200926
848484LV00001B/113